A PRINCE OF MANTUA

Also by MARIA BELLONCI
The Life and Times of Lucrezia Borgia

A PRINCE OF MANTUA

The Life and Times of
Vincenzo Gonzaga

MARIA BELLONCI

TRANSLATED FROM THE ITALIAN
BY STUART HOOD

HARCOURT, BRACE AND COMPANY
NEW YORK

B/GON

78604

CONTENTS

I	FATHER AND SON	1
II	A SENTIMENTAL EDUCATION	17
III	MARGHERITA	34
IV	THÉ AMOROUS TEST	71
V	LEONORA	89
VI	THE YOUNG DUKE	112
VII	AGNESE	130
VIII	QUARREL WITH A STRAW	145
IX	THE CRUSADER	160
X	THE DYNASTIC MARRIAGE	206
XI	ADRIANA	245
XII	THE ALBANIAN INTERLUDE	261
XIII	RANUCCIO'S REVENGE	271
	INDEX	307

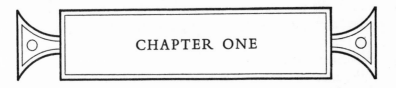

CHAPTER ONE

Father and Son

VINCENZO GONZAGA was born under no mere ducal canopy of satin but beneath the black and gold standard of the Counter-Reformation, swollen by the great north wind of the Council of Trent. It was the 23rd September, 1562. On the 18th of January of that same year his father, Duke Guglielmo Gonzaga, had seen the Council re-assemble for its last laborious session under its magnificent president, Ercole Gonzaga—Isabella d'Este's son—amid all the ecclesiastical splendour of bishops, archbishops and patriarchs, with their golden lappets and mitres.

For his hunchbacked, sickly father, Vincenzo's birth was a sign of divine benevolence. Over the cradle where the beautiful, fair-haired child lay, swaddled from head to foot in cloth of gold and exalted to the majesty, discomfort and splendour of an infant idol, the pious vows of its parents rose to heaven.

Since both as man and prince he was wont to give positive expression to his moral urgings, Duke Guglielmo vowed to build a church. It was to be the Basilica of Santa Barbara. As for the Duchess Leonora of Austria, who was not only daughter of the Emperor Ferdinand I and niece of Charles V but a religious and virtuous wife, her vow was the result of an unconscious rebellion against her husband. For, without reference to him, she made a vow to invite the Jesuits to re-establish themselves in Mantua as teachers. But it took her twenty years of constant petitioning before the Duke would admit the Jesuits and their college to the city. He was too cunning and too jealous of his own supremacy to bring into his own house rivals of such subtlety—at least until such time as he felt mature enough to stand up to them. The first stone of the Basilica was laid in time for the baptism of Vincenzo in February 1563 and the walls began to rise immediately.

It is a stern test to go into Santa Barbara on a wet day and challenge the lowering gloom, which is not fierce and august—as in the Escorial—but at once tired and tortured so that it weighs upon the observer without the power to terrify him. The overwhelming impression is of a criss-cross of broken lines. They are there in the design of the box ceilings and in the recess of the apse. It is a design which comes and goes with the insistence of a puzzle whose solution is not so much logical as mechanical. Its doors, staircases and chapels form the setting for a court, for a procession; but the rest is coldly conceived and has a depressed, uneasy air which recalls the spiritual condition of its architect, Giambattista Bertani. For he was accused of heresy and forced to recant in public on the heretics' bench in San Domenico, in 1567, when his church was already in use. But at least he was luckier than the canon, Antonio Ceruti, who was condemned to life imprisonment at the same time for having said that the soul's life ends with the body's.

A year like 1567 would have been a heavy burden for any prince and should have crushed a man like Guglielmo Gonzaga, who each morning had to accept the humiliation of his own physical deformity and of his ruined health, which constantly threatened to betray him. Instead he made of it one of his years of iron endurance—of triumph in this sense, that every scar he got from it was a sign of a battle won. To set his scars off against his victories was to be his way of having faith in his own existence.

But if under the rule of the Gonzagas Mantua knew no civil strife and if its boundaries were safe—eminently so since the Spanish power, now (alas) established in the peninsula, had accepted and sanctioned them—Monferrato, the other half of their peaceful domain, was far from quiet. This rich and beautiful territory, which had been brought to Federico Gonzaga by Margherita Paleologa as dowry, was to become, in the early seventeenth century, the pretext for quarrels which would involve all Europe and in the end bring destruction on Mantua. To the absolutism of the Gonzagas it had never consented, for absolutism was repugnant to its traditions of autonomy and self-government —traditions which its former overlords, the Paleologi, had always respected. So the inhabitants of Monferrato were in a ferment and Guglielmo's great enemy, Emanuele Filiberto of Savoy, was aiding them secretly with arms, protection and advice. For him Monferrato—like the Marquisate of Saluzzo—was a wedge driven into the side of the renascent state of Savoy.

From 1565 onwards, the citizens' anger had found expression in more than symbolical form; they had constructed a fortress at the gates of Casale. Guglielmo, who saw behind such an overt act of revolt the well-timed and precisely directed energy of Emanuele Filiberto, hurried to Casale to attempt to reach an agreement with his subjects. But he was undone by the harshness of his own nature. While talking peace, he deprived the citizens of the right to maintain a militia, provoked a rising and then gave orders to fire on the crowd. This was tantamount to inciting the more hotheaded of them to flee, which they did—carrying with them the parchments which bore witness to the ancient privileges of the city. Needless to say, Emanuele Filiberto took into his pay all those exiles who wished to enter his service and could in the same way have taken all Monferrato. Meanwhile the leader of the revolt, Oliviero Capello, who was inflamed with the spirit of the communes, imagined he might achieve great things by going to Rome to brave the stern presence of Pius V; for the Pope was at variance with the Gonzagas over certain questions of ecclesiastical jurisdiction and Capello hoped to bring him round to his own way of thinking.

But the attempt was to come to nothing. The strength of Guglielmo Gonzaga's position will become more apparent if we point out that Monferrato was in the imperial gift, that the Duke of Mantua was brother-in-law to the Emperor Maximilian II and that the territory belonged to him by right of inheritance, sanctioned by Charles V. *By right*—these were the words to which Guglielmo continually turned for support with all the blind tenacity of a merciless man. And this—if it does not justify

3

it—at least explains the rebels' case. To discover the grounds of their case, to understand and heal it, would have required powers of comprehension, and an act of grace, both of which were completely foreign to the Duke's nature. The more certain he felt in his own mind the more was he strengthened in his resolution; so he continued to treat Casale as if it were conquered territory. The atmosphere was so charged on all sides that when, on the 23rd October, 1567, the Duke, who had come to Casale with a large following, betook himself to the cathedral for the consecration of a bishop, the melodramatic warning of a mysterious friar denouncing a conspiracy due to break out at the sound of the Sanctus bell barely saved him from death at the hands of the plotters.

Obviously once Guglielmo had decided to play the injured prince he would not easily relinquish the part. Oliviero Capello was put to death at Chiesi. Townspeople were imprisoned and not only the guilty but the innocent, too, were persecuted; there was imprisonment, torture and death for all. Forced to breathe an air so redolent of massacre, the populace seemed to be in its death throes; but it was in vain that the whole of Casale submitted to make a solemn vow of loyalty to the Gonzagas in order that the penalties might be commuted and the sentences lightened. Flaminio, the last descendant of the Paleologi, was taken prisoner and carried off to the rocky fastness of Goito on the Mincio. In this green expanse, this voluptuous Arcadia, which should bring us closer to the sweets of life, Flaminio was to be done to death by poison after three years of imprisonment.

Political assassination did not trouble Guglielmo's conscience; nor had it ever done so. Pride in his rank was so strong in him that he felt able to break all rules. God, he felt, would doubtless take into account the motives of a man who was also a great king and a great prince—motives which had led him to trespass every tenet of the Church. Although he was first at matins and vespers, although he could follow the longest services with devotion, listening with intense spiritual attention and enjoyment to every step in the liturgy, Guglielmo was nevertheless capable of show-

4

ing his freedom from all ties the moment his authority was im-
pugned. There had been an example of this in his quarrel with the
friars of the Inquisition led by the hot-headed Dominican,
Camillo Camprezzi.

Immediately after the Council of Trent and particularly after
the 1st April, 1566, when Pius V issued the energetic bull,
Cum primum apostolatum, in support of the Inquisition, even in
Mantua townspeople of all sorts were imprisoned and accused of
heresy—especially the Lutheran and Calvinist brands. One word
was enough to bring down upon them the harsh light of accusation. The fiery inquisitor shook out his black and white soutane
and began to make arrests with all the ardour of a Neapolitan
cleric placed in the seat of judgment. He arrested them in their
houses, in their shops, in their palaces, in monasteries and even at
court, without warning the Duke, who either refused to hand
over the prisoners or else set them at liberty. The inquisitor protested and complained to his brotherhood. 'It is with God he is
dealing and not with that poor brother, friar Camillo,' he said.
The townsfolk attacked the friars and on Christmas night, 1567,
killed three of them. The Pope complained that the Duke was
hostile to his beloved Inquisition, and terror and indignation
raged in the city.

But what had seemed to be a ruler's solicitude for his subjects,
and should therefore have won for Guglielmo the gratitude of a
people conscious of his protection, was clearly only proud defence
of his prerogative. So much became obvious the moment Rome
meddled in political questions. At this time Flaminio Paleologo,
who was considered to be the claimant to Monferrato and had
been illegally taken prisoner by Gonzaga, was still alive. Pius V
began to ask for his release. To avoid having to release him, the
Duke came to an agreement with the Inquisitor; but the Pope
caught both their heads in one noose by forcing them to cede
half the goods confiscated from the heretics and half the fines
imposed on them.

This was the moment when the struggle shifted from external
events to become an internal conflict between Duke Guglielmo's

two dominant passions—avarice and love of power. In the end the latter won, but it was not a decisive victory; for when the Duke—with Paleologo out of the way—began to protest once more against the Sacred Office and called the Grand Inquisitor a 'private slanderer', the sentences still did not stop. The death sentences were few but the more subtle moral and physical tortures inflicted by the Inquisitor became more frequent—the shameful processions of heretics with paper mitres on their heads and bright friar's gowns, confiscations, fines, arrests and long, wasting terms of imprisonment. And the Duke, for his part, did not come far short of the Inquisitor in harshness. It went hard with the excommunicates, with those who did not go to confession, and especially hard with those who lived in concubinage. The ability to make a law which would in some measure forbid love had been a reward for the Duke's neurotic continence; for since the year 1567 he and his wife, having had three children already, had made a vow of spiritual love. A pious example, their biographers were to say. A model, perhaps, but not a sacrifice, since for Duke Guglielmo love, even in its most legitimate form, had been one of the greatest trials of his life.

As he knelt motionless on his cushion with its satin tassels, his prehensile fingers joined in prayer and his lids lowered over eyes too bright for his hunchback's body, Guglielmo could feel from the physical immobility of his pose how his thin blood traced the accursed curve of his back—that outline which revealed in him, for the last time in the dynasty, the hereditary blight of the Gonzagas. By virtue of its cruel burden, which was always unforgettable and unforgotten, he had acquired fierce patience. He was thus able to exhaust internally his rebellious desires—to exhaust them so that they left no trace except a restlessness which drove him from villa to villa until the necessity of exercising his sovereign powers halted him. The signing of decrees and letters, the dictation of letters, the imposition of his will on others—these were things which sent a fresh current of youthful vigour to his heart.

It is an old story. He had had to call upon all his resources when he was eleven years old and, on the death of his elder brother, Francesco, had seen the right to the ducal coronet pass to himself. His younger brother, Ludovico Gonzaga, who had come easily by his gifts—pre-eminence in intelligence and courage, together with that effortless participation in the life of others which seems to be the outward sign of a secret pact with mankind and is the privilege of a few fortunate individuals—had seemed to everyone to be the natural heir to the dukedom. Had seemed so not only to the populace—we can in any case pardon their enthusiasm for outward appearances—but also to his mother and even to his uncle and guardian, the just, scrupulous and faultless prince, Cardinal Ercole d'Este.

After all these years, Guglielmo's mind retained only the merest memory of dismay at the thought of that morning at the riding-school when Ludovico's horse had reared up and he had fallen off—but without hurting himself. When Guglielmo said a few words to congratulate him on his good fortune Ludovico had replied with flaming eyes: 'You are the lucky one to have been born before me.'

No, he had not renounced the ducal coronet in favour of Ludovico. Let him, if he liked, go off to France to rule the great territories left him by his maternal grandmother, Anne of Alençon, who—like everyone else—adored him. Now, like the great lord he was—being Duke of Nevers—he was busily advising the king of France to treat the Duke of Mantua with alternating favour and hostility. As for Guglielmo, when his uncle offered him all the honour and glory of ecclesiastical life as something more adapted to his deformed appearance, he replied with a phrase which was perhaps over-clever for a boy of twelve—that one does not govern with the body but with the spirit. His spirit had been great enough to prove it and he had ruled well. Not only had he bloodily compelled Monferrato to make peace but he had overhauled the administration of the state, revised the public appointments, scrupulously regulated its revenue and encouraged trade. What did it matter if the saying went round that the Duke put candle-ends on one side because they would

7

do to go through the house with? The gold was piling up in the ducal coffers, although at times it was spent with a magnificent gesture for the good of the townspeople, in time of plague or famine. The coins from the Gonzaga were considered the most beautiful and most perfect of the century. In Mantua, in Guglielmo's day, peace, prosperity and—the Inquisition apart—justice were no mere words. Yet for the people acceptance of the present Duke's rule was a thing of the past and their affection was entirely turned towards the young prince and heir, Vincenzo.

When the Duke passed, everyone uncovered. They no longer stared at his hump, for even it had become popular and was, indeed, indispensable to a complete picture of their lord; but in their homage there was a sense of reluctant and dusty duty. The young prince passed by with his dynamic head, his arresting manner of dressing and his lofty, negligent gait. His smile was still too young to reveal its true significance—was it trusting or merely rash?—but the vulgar extravagances of this youth, so nobly planted on his sturdy but graceful limbs, together with the vivid life which seemed to overflow from him, called forth abundant affection on all sides.

All this Vincenzo had achieved without the slightest effort. By a scurvy trick of fate what might, with ill-timed irony, have been called 'the penalty of being born', was a penalty indeed—but for his father. When he took the crown for himself, young Guglielmo had been worried at the secret disapproval on everybody's face and had known with what pleasure they prated, in court and out of it, of his ineptitude in the art of love. But it was not true; on the contrary, his desire for women had been fierce and lubricious, a hunchback's desire without tenderness. Once he had become aware of this fact he had been able to disassociate it from his real self by dint of reasoning and spiritual examination.

Disdaining to explain himself, and calm with a hard-won calm which, had it been broken, would have found vent in a storm of cries, Guglielmo had chosen for himself one of the throng of ugly imperial daughters the Emperor Ferdinand I bestowed on the princes of Italy with little or no dowry. For her—or rather for both of them—Guglielmo had arranged the most sumptuous nuptial celebrations in the hope that the pomp might compensate for the coldness and uncertain quality of the good wishes offered to himself and his bride. Besides, he had been unwilling to forego the excitement of the balls and tourneys and the nocturnal festivities in the courtyard of the Riding School, ablaze with two thousand torches, flares and candelabras, and surrounded with allusive allegories on the theme of Loyal Love.

Leonora of Austria moved among them clad in gold and pearls, riding on a white steed or in a carriage drawn by pure white horses. She laid claim to no great beauty but showed herself every inch a princess with her air of natural majesty and her guarded gestures. In her very lack of high intelligence there was something withdrawn and aristocratic which won her respect and even veneration. Having been brought up in the Catholic faith on which the Hapsburgs insisted, she had not wished to take a husband, had refused the King of Denmark because he was a Protestant and accepted the Duke of Mantua only at her father's insistence. The fact that the bridegroom was a hunchback came near to pleasing her as an additional mortification. Her quality of obedience—although it derived more from motives of religion than from her real nature—confirmed Duke Guglielmo in his sense of supremacy, to which this daughter and sister of emperors would always bow. His wife's meekness had freed him from the burden of physical inferiority and left him with nerves relaxed. This slackening of tension had made it possible for him to have his revenge on those who had doubted his capacity as a prince and as a man. Out of this laborious effort three children had been born—Margherita, a tawny creature with dimples, who concealed under her soft charms something of her father's iron capabilities, Anna Caterina, sentimental and religious, and Vincenzo, the only son.

Vincenzo had naturally not kept a tally of the hours he had had to spend on his knees thanking God that he was his father's son, but during the long meditative silences, full of the scent of incense, his blood came to maturity. It surged in waves driven by the age-old sensuality of the Gonzagas and by his own capricious nature which, for a whim, at the least suggestion of constraint or sacrifice, was capable of finding an outlet in brutality. Apart from this he was benevolent and even good. His heart and mind were cast in shadow by the *chiaroscuro* he had inherited from his Hapsburg mother. From the same source he took the excessive fairness of his colouring, which, had it not been accompanied by symmetry of limb so pronounced that his very gait, his very movements were visible tokens of his rank, might have detracted from the physical beauty of his type. The passage of the years would make him grow fat and turn his hair grey but they would draw out of him the most genuine qualities of the Gonzagas. In moments of extremity there would arise in him that tempered melancholy which had shaped the lives of his forebears with lofty elegance.

In church, during ceremonial processions, at vespers, at prayers, on horseback, on feast-days, at parades or formal receptions in the staterooms or the palace, Duke Guglielmo had had time to moralise first over the child and then over the young man who stood at his side, a constant proof to God and to the people of a victory won. His own son, moreover, and at his beck and call. But when the child ran off into manhood with precocious steps and grew tall and handsome and straight, Guglielmo began to have to lie to himself.

It was clear that Vincenzo felt a gulf between himself and his father. Although the Duke might obtain from his son respect, devotion and admiration of his wisdom, as soon as the boy began to give expression to his own inclinations and his own tastes, Guglielmo realized what sort of store Vincenzo set by his father's world. A thoroughbred horse moved Vincenzo to enthusiasm. Even as he talked of it he felt the wind rushing through his hair; but for his father, understandably enough, it was an agonizing sacrifice to appear on horseback. Guglielmo was deeply religious and so after a fashion—a highly elaborate one—was Vincenzo.

He liked the beauty of the church services, the altars with their silver statues, the great storied pictures; but instead of choosing churchmen for his friends and secretaries, as his father did, and delighting in their powers of theological and spiritual reasoning, Vincenzo picked as his companions the most degenerate of youths, abnormal libertines. His dress was of extreme elegance. He always wore jewels and velvets and rich brocades. Across his breast he carried silken sashes stiff with symbolical embroidery, and at his wrists, cuffs sewn by his mistresses. His plumed caps were stuck with gold pins. He drank great goblets of Greek wine and ate heartily; he danced and leapt into the saddle and jousted and enjoyed women, with whom he was proving tender, fervent and very fickle. Even in the company of men his amorous adventures did not bear repeating; yet his father was determined to hear them all.

Guglielmo's complaints were put on record. He almost seemed to take pleasure in writing to his minister, Teodoro Sangiorgio, saying: 'God grant, my dear Count, that I may be able so to bring up my son that I shall not have to blush for him if I send him from home.' What he did not guess was that one of the trials sent to test the patience of a good father may be the shame of having to blush for his children. (It is the most rewarding of these trials and the sentiment which survives it is indeed a refinement of love.) At the age of sixteen Vincenzo had gone to the Tyrol to stay with his Hapsburg cousins and, being full of high spirits, at one memorable supper had become so roused that he had replied to the court jesters by flinging spoonfuls of soup in their faces. The scandal of this childish offence had been greatly exaggerated at Mantua—exaggerated on lines suggested by the Duke. Sorrow spread over his face, in which any expression seemed always on the verge of becoming caricature. Yet even the Duke had to admit that his wife managed her sufferings better. From out of her deep silence she could unbend towards her son with a note of sustained dignity, pleading with him without spitefulness and offering indulgent counsel. Even when Vincenzo answered her with a bad grace, he tempered his frank reactions with a kind of angry respect which was still love. The truth was that, in spite of their diversity in dress, inclinations and character, mother and son found common ground where they could commune while the father remained apart. And he knew it.

With mounting disapproval Guglielmo nursed his subtle and secret dialectic and led it to a practical solution—not so much a punishment as a precaution, he thought, but one which was unfortunately closely bound up with his gravest moral defect, avarice. To keep this young man down, he said to himself, to make him mend his ways, let us leave the witless fool with little money in his pockets. He left him with very little indeed and practically drove him, in his constant need, into the hands of the usurers, of his friends and relations, of anyone who would help him. As the young man said himself, it 'filled him with bile'.

This was how matters stood in 1580. Vincenzo was about to enter on his nineteenth year, 'an age,' he claimed, 'which usually brought freedom and unlimited credit to others.' But he was to feel the clutch of his father's avarice twist him like a vice. It upset him to such a degree that even the certain knowledge of his rights as heir apparent was tinged with fear. It required the promptings of his boon-companions to restore his high spirits. Then followed coarse buffoonery and brawls. He had already twice shaken off his father's authority by leaving without warning the places assigned for his residence and setting out on unexpected journeys through his territories, from castle to castle. His father had to send his tutors—Aurelio Pomponazzi, grandson of the famous philosopher, and Marcello Donati—after him to bring him back and make him once more conform to law and order.

These two men, who had been attached to the Duke's court first as tutors and then as secretaries, had a difficult part to play— one which put to the test not only their skill in manœuvre but the fundamental rectitude of Duke Guglielmo, who had chosen them for this post without limiting their freedom of judgment. Pomponazzi had rather a weak character and was sometimes affectionate towards his pupil, sometimes intolerant. He admired his intelligence and the pomp which surrounded him—admired too that power of rising above himself which made of Vincenzo's youth a shining thing. Marcello Donati, botanist, humanist, man of letters and doctor—he had even tried to cure that incurable madman, the poet Tasso—was more cunning and used scientific logic to cast light on his psychological intuitions.

All in all, he had a very firm grip on his pupil, but, instead of taking advantage of his knowledge of Vincenzo, he kept it to himself. It was something he concealed and did not even share with his master, the Duke. Pomponazzi might be intimidated by the Duke's authority and become greatly upset; not so Donati, who stood—respectfully—on his dignity, prepared to act or prepared to do nothing when he felt it would be injudicious to give one of his rare guiding touches. When he became involved in intricate questions he was capable of solving them with precision and acumen and with a determination which bordered on cruelty. As a man must who wishes to be on friendly terms with everyone, he did not take sides. Although, if forced to choose, he would perhaps have favoured the son's abundant vitality rather than the father's avarice, his advice was such that all knew they could bow to it—Duke Guglielmo in the certainty that Donati would never deviate by a hair's-breadth from his moral standards or the best interests of the dynasty; Vincenzo with the feeling that due consideration had been given to his innermost feelings and even to his libertinism. In short, Donati's humanity and discretion had reached the summit of perfection—that of respecting others whoever they might be.

In 1580, Vincenzo had inaugurated his year of rebellion by going off to Ferrara at the invitation of his sister, young Margherita Gonzaga, who had become the third wife of Duke Alfonso d'Este, now almost an old man. He had enjoyed the Carnival and returned to Ferrara in the spring, shrugging off the exhortations to good behaviour his mother enclosed in a heartfelt letter, in which she begged that he would behave himself and not gamble or jest, as they did at Ferrara, nor do anything unbecoming in a prince. Leonora of Austria was quite right to admonish her son thus but Vincenzo felt he had right on his side, too. He went to Ferrara for the express purpose of freeing himself from the malignant humours which were suffocating him at Mantua. We can imagine how Ferrara, which never let slip an opportunity for festivities, welcomed Vincenzo. If there were no Carnivals to offer him, it was now mid-Lent, and after mid-Lent there were hunting and fishing expeditions, weddings, baptisms and receptions. The inhabitants of Ferrara had been forced by the state of affairs in Italy—now unhappily under foreign rule—to accept an inglorious peace interrupted by warlike adventures which the bravest of its citizens sought out in other countries, in France, Flanders and Germany. It was therefore becoming a pressing and almost unbearable need to find pretexts for festivities. One can easily imagine—although much rein must be given to the imagination—what was likely to be the outcome: strange assemblies, amorous expeditions, noblemen dressed as friars and ladies as cavaliers. And more besides. Duke Alfonso II and the Duchess Margherita kept themselves apart as much as possible from this overflow of animal spirits and led a life morally above reproach. Yet, because they stood for the principles of unbounded courtliness, because they smiled on certain customs and were indulgent to certain pleasures, they offered to others the opportunity, if not the pretext, for wild excesses. In their immediate entourage there was no longer to be found that constructive mode of life which had marked the time of the Duke's great ancestors. There was instead a life of sensual pleasure, exposed to the temptations which arise from the most refined extravagances of the passions, and darkened by the ominous shadows of the Inquisitor and the Court confessors, who had entrapped and destroyed the tortured soul of Torquato Tasso.

All these years Tasso was still imprisoned in Sant' Anna, kept there by Duke Alfonso d'Este from motives not of pity but of prudence. Vincenzo Gonzaga, who was already acquainted with the poet, had gone down into his prison to comfort him and promise him whatever help his regard and protection could procure. Fair-haired and animated, with an engaging presence, he must have seemed to Tasso a model of bodily well-being such as a man like himself could not hope to emulate. The fact that Tasso wrote for Vincenzo is not in itself strong proof that he felt close to him, for the poet is by nature condemned to solitary confinement; but that he should have called him 'beautiful', a rare adjective to apply to a man, may express the admiration of a sick man confronted by a person who glories in his splendid sensuality. To Vincenzo he dedicated madrigals for the ladies of his choice, songs and sonnets.

Such was the normal relationship between courtier and prince. As for Vincenzo, it might have been thought that there was no connection between the way he must perpetually engage in the mêlée of daily life and Tasso's troubled internal monologue. And perhaps those who thought so were right. Yet the young Gonzaga was well acquainted with the *Jerusalem Delivered* and liked it. We can go further and say that he had been nourished on the poem and had seen in it a story which would become the textbook of his life. This web of adventure and passion, shot with the gold of a religion æsthetically experienced, which ennobles and sustains the poetic narrative in its subtlest windings, was the vivid tapestry through which there moved the images of his dreams. Tasso had felt Vincenzo's response and could therefore call him 'a young man heroically inclined'—born, that is, to imitate the behaviour of the Crusader heroes. But to be Tancred and meet Clarinda, to be Rinaldo provided he would unfailingly find Armida and her golden tresses, which are loosened to the cadence of the verse with a liquid sense of amorous surrender—such were the preconditions for Vincenzo's heroic dreams.

While in Mantua the Duchess Leonora sought to persuade fallen but penitent women to join a closed order and, when they agreed, embraced them one by one, exulting and saying 'Be glad, for to-day is a day of rejoicing in Heaven', her son in Ferrara found unheard-of and thrilling opportunities for sin. There was no lack either of courtesans or of ladies of the court. There were eager girls ready to do his will in the wildest of orgies. These

15

were readily forgotten; but the ladies and maidens, 'amorous and eager,' of the court at Ferrara, whom he met in his sister's salons and who were nourished on chivalry and sentiment, were more to his taste.

'Seventy gentlewomen, including widows, old maids and the rest', said a Florentine, mixing them in spiteful juxtaposition in his phrase. But amongst them were some of the most vivid beauties of Italy, the last generation of those Cinquecento women who had the courage to assert their right to a personality of their own and freely chose glory and mortification.

At this time Lucrezia d'Este, Duchess of Urbino and sister of Duke Alfonso, was beginning to decline—that Lucrezia who bore the name of her grandmother, Lucrezia Borgia, and who once, in her beauty, had merely had to turn her tiny head on her sinuous body in order to diffuse an air of proud vitality which stirred the imagination of men. But there were others who shone around the gold and white, the modelled beauty of the seventeen-year-old Duchess Margherita. There was Marfisa d'Este, fair-haired, full of caprices and full-blooded gaiety. There were the musicians— Lucrezia Bendidio, beloved by Tasso and herself passionately in love with the Cardinal Luigi d'Este, Laura Peperara, sweet, reserved and slender, Livia d'Arco from Mantua and Anna Guarini, destined to die because she had sinned too much in love's cause. Among the other ladies of the court there stood out the rather affected group of the Scandiane—the wife and sisters of Count Giulio Thiene of Vincenza, all very beautiful and insatiable in the pursuit of pleasure. But over them all Barbara Sanseverino Sanvitale, Countess of Sala, held sway, and her ascendancy was recognized by men and women alike.

CHAPTER TWO

A Sentimental Education

THE Countess of Sala—that was a name which rang like a trumpet-call through Lombardy and indeed throughout all Italy in these last years of the sixteenth century. At the sound the curtain rose on a beauty at once commanding and quick-witted, such as Correggio drew—a beauty which is not wholly expressed in the delicacy of the lineaments but seems to declare, even while concealing it, a more intimate secret, the blood's intelligence and the heart's. She was a very great lady and she had the pride, the spirit and the tenacity of the Sanseverinos. A notable woman, she had all the feminine qualities and raised them to their highest pitch: beauty, quickness of wit, tenderness, the ability to enter a man's life with a message of joy and bring him back to that sensation of fullness which he is prone to forget in his too sterile watch on the course of events and ideas.

Such a woman fills the life of those who happen to be near her. She imposes a style and lends colour to an epoch. But if she is left to her own judgment and relies, with her usual impetuosity, energy and abandon, on her instincts, she fails to see how dangerous it is openly to vaunt her pride in her womanhood. She thinks she can engage in equal contest with all comers and is ready to do so without reservation. It follows that should she encounter an evil enemy she will be forced into a losing fight and plunge to her ruin.

In 1580, Barbara was almost thirty but her beauty was that of a woman of twenty—indeed even more glorious. At this time she was married to the Count Sanvitale, a man much older than

herself, but she was living under the protection of the Duke of
Parma, Ottavio Farnese. The old Duke was a protector indeed.
For her sake he had forgotten his quarrel with her father and
invested her personally with the fief of Colorno, wrested long
years before from the Sanseverinos. Then he confirmed the
investiture in the name of her son, Girolamo, which was no small
sacrifice for the Farnese, for it meant the loss of the delectable
lands of Colorno, the Duchy of Parma's watch-tower over
Lombardy.

Through the spacious villa of Colorno Barbara now moved,
trailing her brocade with the grace of a woman who can bring
into the life of the senses the life of thought and the arts, passing
among her famous pictures—Raphael's portrait of Pope Leo X
and his Madonna della Culla, Correggio's Marriage of Saint
Catherine and paintings by Parmigianino, Dürer and Pordenone.
At Colorno, where the roses in the gardens have a startling
intensity and an incredibly beautiful mingling of colours, the
Academy of the Amorevoli used to meet. Among them were the
Duke of Parma himself, Tasso, Guarini and Nunzio Manfredi.
There were literary debates, discussions on love and readings of
verse, of tragedy and comedy. Barbara fed on this literary nectar
as if it were her natural food, which gave strength to her judg-
ments and liveliness to her repartee. From Colorno a troop of
women and maidens, all imbued with the perilous aroma which
was the very spirit of the Countess, went on a triumphal progress
through country houses and castles, to the courts of Parma and
Ferrara and the petty courts of Guastalla and Bozzolo. They even
reached the great papal court of Rome, where an enamoured
archbishop celebrated her in verse.

Because her praises were sung so often by so many poets and
by Tasso in particular, poetry was for Barbara a matter of little
import among the many others which made up her days. She
knew to what a degree Laura is the invention of the poet, and
so rated her life as a woman higher than her literary immortality.
Her own life she developed on different levels, some public and
worldly, some veiled in silken silence. Her greatest secret was

her relation with the house of Farnese. Did the old Duke love her, that he protected her so much? Was he then the rival of his son, Alessandro, who was to be the great general and governor of Flanders—a man so much in love with Barbara that when she appeared it was the signal for his appearance too? How she played her hand so that everything appeared to be mere coincidence was another of her secrets. What is certain is this—that in 1580, when Alessandro Farnese had already left for Flanders, she had, while enjoying great favour both in Parma and in Ferrara, where Alfonso II adored and worshipped her, brought to his knees the young prince of Mantua. For one like her it was too easy a task. There was a meeting but, contrary to all that has been said, there was no understanding between them.

Between the Countess of Sala and Vincenzo that spark which would seemingly have kindled so opportunely and which we would all have expected, did not fall. Perhaps it was her wish, since her affections were engaged elsewhere. So Vincenzo, who was both attracted and absorbed by the personality of this forceful woman, pursued a tortuous path in loving her. On the one hand, he felt the stimulus of her presence; on the other, he became languid with a page's uneasy dependence on his chatelaine, turning himself all at once from a young man into a child. He called her 'mother' and the name permitted every kind of wooing— even ardent addresses. It lent tenderness to their relationship and an ambiguous flavour of forbidden things. We cannot establish how far licence came short of sinful indulgence. Probably, in deference to Barbara's wishes, it never reached that point, for it was she who called the tune. Indeed it was she—for she was shrewd enough to be able to distribute possible conquests to other women if it suited her—who deflected the ardours of the young prince towards a lady of the Court of Colorno.

Hippolita is unknown to history, or almost so. She seems to have been a woman of the Torelli family and was married in Reggio, to a nobleman of that town. There she lived a life of which we know nothing. She was a beautiful woman; like all true lovers she lived in the shadow of jealousy and distrust, but she was sweet and attractive in her happiness. She was one of those women who can keep perpetual holiday with the man they love and promise a truce with life's harshness.

Vincenzo responded to this love with all the headlong abandon of the sensual lover. Once she had taken the intrigue in hand, the Countess of Sala took a dominant part in it and played a game which passed the comprehension of the prince of Mantua. She had understood the young man's struggle against his father and in her impetuous generosity had at once taken the rebel's part against the restrictions imposed by the Duke, which to her seemed tyrannical. She took the liberty of following her impulse and encouraged Vincenzo in his loves, so that he might play the man more effectively and feel himself free from paternal authority. To match herself against the hunchbacked Duke, who despised women, was a perpetual and exciting challenge to her lively feminine anarchism. She went even further. By lending importance to Vincenzo's rebellion instead of treating it as a boyish escapade, she promised herself the exquisite pleasure of finding in the Duke of Mantua—as the man developed out of the boy—the man she had herself shaped, with her stamp upon him.

So Vincenzo was caught in the first maze; but he did not recognize it as such—on the contrary. His defiant bearing at Ferrara in the year 1580 had manifested itself in games of chance, licentious balls, jousts and quarrels with gentlemen whom he even called out to secret duels. This was already the uncertain progress of a man who did not see his path clear before him. What he missed was not so much a strong hand as a father's experience to initiate him into life—the experience of Duke Guglielmo, who rarely came to town but trailed his painful worries from one splendid country house to another and imagined he could bring his son to heel by pulling the reins ever more tightly. In September the Duke had made the gesture of appearing to accede to his son's request for money and, knowing full well that he was burdened with huge debts, had sent him a handful of gold—about two hundred crowns. Vincenzo refused them point blank and sent an angry reply to the treasurer. Then he disbanded his court and, throwing himself on horseback, rode towards Viadana on the Mantuan border. There he left his following except for a few noblemen, who were his most intimate friends, crossed the border and made for Colorno.

The Countess of Sala was prompt to celebrate his arrival. She welcomed him, fully conscious of the radiance of the look she bent upon him, openly approving his act of rebellion. Her influence, her approval, her assurance—all these we find in the letter the prince wrote from Colorno to his secretary, Pomponazzi, for him to pass on to the Duke. He justified his flight and spoke plainly of the many wrongs done to him by his father. He protested that he was a most humble son and only too ready to prove his obedience; but, he declared, he would not thwart his own inclinations for anyone. Moreover, he believed he was right in thinking that his father hated him and thought him quite useless; it was for this reason he had decided to leave and was ready to seek even more distant lands. He had transferred his residence to Viadana, whither he intended to return whenever it so pleased him; meanwhile he was at Colorno, staying there in the house of Her Ladyship, the Countess of Sala, 'whom I love,' he declared, 'with such sincere affection that, were she my sister, I could not love her more!'

Such a flamboyant declaration of alliance was bound to please the Countess, who doubtless read and perhaps directly inspired the letter. This was the very kind of adulation to make her feel her power in the surest and most telling way. Vincenzo had his reward. It is almost certain—we find allusions in letters of this date, allusions which can be easily interpreted—that the Countess Torelli, the lady Vincenzo loved, was at this time at Colorno along with some close friends. It was a very select company, brought together by the Countess of Sala in a perfect blend of character and intellect. She managed them all in her inimitable, sparkling manner, which vanquished even the most rebellious.

In September, the flat open country between Parma and Lodi is subject to the strict laws of agriculture, but occasionally it is tempted and indeed almost tortured by the delicate pungency of the air. The guests at Colorno were immersed in the ripe odours of autumn, the sun's last appeal to the earth's innermost humours. They passed from rich days of abundance to long, cool, exciting nights played out on a gamut of evocative notes. They allowed themselves to be whirled into such a soft spiral of pleasures that they felt themselves to be gently damned. We may take the word of one of Vincenzo's gentlemen for it—Scipione Guerrieri, who sent a servant back to court post-haste to heap the prince's rich clothes and jewels in their valises and wrote that, at Colorno, there was no truce to the festivities day or night and that they were all worn out.

The holiday at Colorno did not last more than a week. While Vincenzo stole these truant hours his court at Viadana grew tired of waiting for him. They lacked money, credit and everything else. The butcher had stopped serving them and they had no more clean linen. All were complaining, nobles and servants alike. Duke Guglielmo might have enjoyed looking down in detachment on the distress which had fallen like a just punishment on his son, but his disciplined good sense, which was his greatest virtue, told him when it was time to intervene. The Duchess Leonora was charged with the task of reclaiming the rebel.

Leonora had already received from her son a wordy letter and from Pomponazzi, acting as his ambassador, a visit to tell her the rest. The Duchess was familiar with the schemes of her brother-in-law, Ludovico Gonzaga of Nevers; from France he was closely following the fortunes of the state of Mantua, which he considered had been usurped from him. Like her husband she was afraid—but even more so than he—that the prince of Mantua would give ear to the alluring promises of his uncle, who was inviting him to come to France to fight the Huguenots and extolling to him both the French court and the Crusade. Vincenzo's departure would at once have aroused the obscure annoyance of Philip II of Spain. Besides, the pious woman wept in a passion of contrition over the sins committed at Colorno. We can imagine, therefore, with what speed, once her husband had consented, she made her servants ride to recall her son.

Vincenzo responded at once to his mother's appeal and left both Colorno and its troop of accomplices. Having arrived at the villa where his mother was staying he made a scene. With great wisdom his mother allowed him to give vent to his feelings. She listened to his protests and made him sleep on them. Next day she contrived to extract some promises of obedience and some surly words of submission to his father's will. But almost a month passed before Vincenzo could bring himself to write a letter of apology to his father. That was perhaps a trifling thing to do but it meant much to Vincenzo, who had intended to have things out to the bitter end and now capitulated without receiving any guarantee in return except the hope of paternal benevolence. His father paid his most urgent debts and relaxed his grip—but no further than was absolutely necessary. The breathing-space he allowed his son merely aggravated the punishment.

Vincenzo felt instinctively that the Duke, while concealing the fact with great intelligence, was abusing his paternal authority. He had realized, particularly when prompted by the Countess of Sala, that he himself held formidable weapons—such as the threat of taking service at a foreign court. But when he had marshalled his arguments, instead of husbanding them and exploiting them singly, he rolled them into one, got them thoroughly confused and ended by firing them off in a fit of rage which was no less fleeting because it was long and violent. He was then naturally left defenceless while his father's position was both intact and strongly defended; so he learnt all the bitterness, sorrow and anger of a man who feels he is denied all help by his most natural ally.

The Duchess Leonora wished to see father and son united, but she realized more and more clearly each day that the quarrel between them, instead of being dammed up, was spreading. No matter how the Duke might reason with himself, as soon as Vincenzo entered the room where his father awaited him, Guglielmo felt the barbs enter his heart. Gouty and stout, he crouched in the depths of a great armchair between the fire and the chimney and everything in his son roused him to wild envy:

the scarf and cuffs embroidered by the love-sick Hippolita, the insolent attitude of his tall shoulders from which two slender lines descended and narrowed into the slimness of his waist, the gaiety of the colours he wore and of his glance, now purposely chastened in a temporary expression of respect, his every movement, his every word. It was an envy which the Duke could have overcome only if he had been forced to respect his son. But he had no regard for his heir. He felt his son's intelligence as something alien to himself and perhaps did not even consider it intelligence. He blamed him for not being able to control his outbursts and for wasting himself in the heat of his passions. He scorned him so that Vincenzo was perhaps right in suspecting himself to be an object of hatred. But he, in his turn, did not understand that it was not so much hatred as that feeling of irritation fathers feel towards their sons when they feel excluded from their lives.

Peace between Guglielmo and Vincenzo was reached on a political and dynastic basis. It was essential that rumours of discords in the Gonzaga family should not get about at a time when despatches were piling up in the ducal cabinet on that most important of Mantuan affairs, the marriage of the young prince. Once his son had been reduced to a mere political pawn, the Duke showed how quickly his mind could work. He collected information and calculated where his interests lay. He instituted inquiries and drew up pacts and conventions, using quibbles and sophistries to his own advantage. Admittedly the bride must be a *point d'appui* for Vincenzo, but the Duke gave more weight to her family's support, to the alliance of great names, to the nature of the privileges acquired and to economic expediency, than to a harmonious union between husband and wife. All these things had to be weighed up and we must admit that the Duke of Mantua had a sure touch in his conduct of affairs.

Some time before, there had been talk of one of Vincenzo's cousins, Leonora dei Medici, the daughter of Francesco, Grand Duke of Tuscany, and of Giovanna of Austria, sister of the Duchess of Mantua. She had been put forward by Archduke Ferdinand of Austria, who was asking for his own son the hand of Leonora's younger sister, Anna. Ever since Cosimo I had obtained for himself the title of Grand Duke and with it precedence over all other Italian dynasties, who considered themselves of nobler and more ancient lineage, Guglielmo had been very jealous of the good fortune of the Medicis; but he allowed his consent to be won. He abandoned the idea, however, the moment Alfonso d'Este coaxed into being a quadruple alliance between the princes of Northern Italy and brought Guglielmo into it by the force and confidence of his arguments. It was not a military league, for that was unthinkable at a time when foreign powers were in overwhelming preponderance; it was to be a prudent and harmonious system of mutual protection aimed at preserving, as best they could, their prerogatives or —if you like—their liberties. The league was really directed at the growing power of the Medicis, and united the Estes, the Farneses, the Gonzagas and the House of Savoy. To cement the alliance, Alfonso d'Este of Ferrara would marry Margherita Gonzaga and Vincenzo of Mantua would have as bride Margherita Farnese of Parma.

The matrimonial alliance would mean much to the Farneses and Gonzagas. Above all it meant they would have a truce, which had not happened since 1549 when Ferrante Gonzaga, with the connivance of Charles V, had plotted the assassination of Pier Luigi Farnese. On that occasion Ferrante had been acting in full agreement with and, indeed, under the direction of the great cardinal, Ercole Gonzaga, who was a bitter enemy of the Farnese Pope, Paolo III. But the Farneses had paid him back later by shutting the door to the Papacy against him irrevocably. So strong were the motives for hate between the two families, so carefully were they handed down from father to son, that death, rather than healing them, seemed to make them more pronounced. The hand of the fourteen-year-old Margherita was finally to wipe them out. The child would bring to Mantua a huge dowry of three hundred thousand crowns and the splendour of her descent from Maria of Portugal and the great general, Alessandro Farnese.

It would be impossible to exaggerate Guglielmo's delight at so treating those excessively fortunate princes, the Medicis. He broke off the negotiations which had already been started between his son and Leonora. When his brother-in-law, the Archduke, remonstrated with him, he pretended to search for excuses, feigned clumsiness and finally threw caution to the winds. He felt respect and affection for the Medicis, he said, but how could one be expected to tolerate the Grand Duke's marriage to the Venetian lady who had for so many years been his concubine? The little princesses actually went out with her and appeared in the same carriage—yet they were the daughters of Giovanna of Austria and granddaughters of the emperor. How could the Archduke bear such a slight to his sister's memory?

The Venetian lady was Bianca Cappello, who since 1579 had been Grand Duchess of Tuscany. Both she and her husband felt the sharp merciless stabs which the hunchback of Mantua relentlessly inflicted upon them. They kept silence, for they were both very subtle. They would find the memory fresh when their moment came.

Vincenzo was relying on his marriage. He knew that with a wife he would have a properly maintained court, and adequate prerogatives, that his independence would be recognized and that not even his father would be able to deprive him of his rights. His wife's relations, being persons of high rank, would presumably take his side. Under pressure from them Guglielmo would perhaps be induced to open that private study where the affairs of state were conducted in the utmost secrecy and summon his son to collaborate in a government which, if limited in scope, was none the less royal. What Vincenzo felt in his heart was not the desire to rule, which in young men—particularly if they are immature—often swells to vast proportions, but the ability to rule. It sprang up within him from all that was purest in his Gonzaga stock. Once his wife had arrived, family affairs would be put into some kind of order.

'Family affairs' was the very phrase which the young prince used to describe his marriage when he announced it to his mistress, Hippolita Torelli, in a most affectionate letter, adding at once that 'neither wife nor anything else will make me uproot my heart from the spot where I have laid it'. Naturally he did not thereby mean any offence to his wife either as future duchess or as a woman. He had already learnt to distinguish between marriage and love, as do all men who have a highly developed social instinct but are at the same time beset by insatiable and capricious appetites. As far as affection went, there was enough and to spare for everyone in his warm heart—for his wife, for his mistresses and for his children, legitimate and illegitimate. He did not even consider it a problem that, as he said himself in the exaggerated manner of the sixteenth century, his passion for Hippolita should become a 'blaze of love' at the very moment towards the end of 1580 when his betrothal to Margherita Farnese was being concluded. He was delighted with his betrothed and assured her he would not have wished for anyone else. Meanwhile he knew utter abandon with Hippolita and wrote letters which lacked any semblance of control. It is almost as if he could not contain the words. Thus he begins one letter: 'I have so much to write to you and to shout that I do not know where to begin.'

The story of Vincenzo's love, as detailed in his most private letters we owe to the cunning of a secretary who seems to have been and, indeed, was Marcello Donati. We must stress the part the secretary played because, although it was the custom in courts to keep copies of the letters of princes, it did not usually extend to love letters. In fact files of love letters are rare in the archives; although Vincenzo had occasion to write them all his life, this is the only collection known to be from his pen. What calculations, what suspicion induced Donati to trace such exclamations and invocations we do not know. Did he fear that traps were being laid for the young prince and therefore wish to have the full story to hand so as to be able to take action if the necessity arose? Was he obeying the orders of Duke Guglielmo, who would thereby have passed from a policy of watchfulness to one of shady indiscretion? Or was he merely carrying out the tasks of his office and exceeding them with a storyteller's zeal, a storyteller's curious interest in human documents? The fact remains that the cunning humanist doctor copied in his own hand not only Vincenzo's letters to Hippolita but all the others addressed by him to other persons on the same theme—there are few on any other topic—and thus gave us an ordered account of the intrigue in a little notebook. Then he became tired or was summoned to go on some political mission or became distracted by other tasks and left the end of the story untold on blank pages.

That is not important. We have only to open the first pages to breathe the air of romance. When the scene opens Hippolita's portrait has just arrived and we hear Vincenzo improvising passionately: 'The portrait of your ladyship is as dear to me as you can possibly imagine, since I take delight in nothing save in thinking of you, for all my desires have their end in you, my life, and, since I cannot look upon that sun which alone seems beautiful to my eyes, I shall at least find some delight in admiring your dear likeness. So I beg you, lady of my soul, rest assured that my love is not of the kind which fades from one moment to another but will last as long as I live.'

He passes easily from the formal *lei* of the courtier to the informal *voi*. The latter is the form which is repeated in the subsequent letters in which his protestations become louder and more passionate.

'Morning and evening and all day long I speak to myself but you never answer me, my dearest life; perhaps you do it to cause my afflicted heart still greater pain but you do wrong, for my heart is so sore beset at not seeing her who keeps it alive that I think, if you do not come to succour it, it will faint and perhaps my soul will leave my body to enjoy the sweet sight of that beauty which is etched in the very centre of my being . . . there is no one in the world who can love more than I love you, and I adore you because in you alone lies all my hope and whatever good I have in this world . . . Light of my eyes, if I did not hope to see you in a short time, I think that excess of sorrow would cause me to die . . . I have no other desire in this world but to serve you with my blood and I beg you to keep some memory of this service of mine and be sure that nothing in the world can make me ever leave it; but I shall always stand firm like an unshaken rock, buffeted by the waves—the more they beat on it, the more stoutly it withstands them . . . Keep alive your enchained slave who kisses your hands a thousand times . . . Soul of this too, too worn life . . . my dearest life, support of this poor soul, lady of this heart of mine, my queen, my protectress, my sweet darling.'

This is the exaggerated rhetoric of lovers but it has a flavour of its own. We can mark how the argument is urged on at a pace which corresponds to the impulses of the blood and note how, at the same time, it follows the hyperbolical, high-flown tempo of *commedia dell'arte*. It was a language to which Vincenzo was accustomed and one which he delighted to hear. By this time he was already assembling troupes of actors in Mantua. He made them speak their lines. He lent his protection to actresses. He passed judgment on comedies and tragedies. It is significant that when his theme is love he employs for his own needs the accents which had moved him. Here, for the first time, we can discern the sign under which Vincenzo's affairs were to run their course as they evolved towards the splendid theatrical climaxes of his maturity; for he was to escape from his lot only by turning his life into allegory.

Hippolita is sometimes called Andromeda—perhaps because of her dark colouring, perhaps because of some book he had read or some play he had seen. That he should belong to her under the name of Perseus satisfied Vincenzo's passion for disguises; but if the young man insisted on signing himself thus it was merely to indulge his whim, for the veil of false names was too thin to avail against indiscretion. Hippolita belonged to the aristocratic society of Parma and Reggio—elegant sixteenth-century Reggio. Since she was hedged in by an an exacting social round and was watched and spied upon, she was difficult of access. Accomplices had to be enlisted; aid had to be sought, devious means tried out and trust placed in the Countess of Sala. In whom could they trust if not in her? Barbara, like the great lady she was, pretended not to lend herself to the part of intermediary and delegated the office to two of her confidantes, Signora Anna and Signora Lavinia, who, under the invisible direction of the Countess, took charge of the notes, the letters, the gifts, passed them secretly to Hippolita, received the replies and despatched winged couriers to Mantua with the speed and quick-moving intrigue proper to sixteenth-century comedy. Nor was there any lack of repartee, which might be struck off by tiny things—as when Vincenzo wrote: 'I seem to remember that you wrote telling me to give Scipione a couple of slaps or maybe a good beating, so I gave him both to make sure.' And there were quips and jokes, as when the prince sent a basket of fish to Colorno, dedicating it to the whole troop of ladies but especially to 'poor little Isabella' because 'she says she is pregnant— in the hope that she may not bear a son with a fish for a nose.'

'Little Isabella' was a dwarf—perhaps, since brother and sister continually exchanged dwarfs, actors and singers, she was the one who had lived at the court of the Duchess of Ferrara and to whom Tasso dedicated so many madrigals. This dwarf, whose temperament must have been of the most piquant, so pleased Vincenzo that he made her one of his confidantes. Therefore when his twenty years cried out so that he felt lost, unable to bear or understand Hippolita's womanish whims, out of the dwarfs' apartments, all decorated with stucco on the smallest scale, there slipped this tiny ambassadress habited in her veil, her gloves and her silk skirt. She listened to all his protestations and instructions and left Mantua, bouncing about in a carriage much too big for her. She touched at Colorno and returned with messages—loving ones from Hippolita, messages full of news from Lavinia, captious messages from the Countess of Sala. And so she was to be seen trotting along in the wake of the prince, laden with gewgaws, or skipping round him as he gazed on the likeness of his lady, echoing his lover's sighs with gentle buffoonery, which, far from offending Vincenzo, merely strengthened his love.

From November onwards the exchange of letters, messages and gifts grew apace. Hippolita sent typical woman's gifts—bands or cuffs embroidered in her own colours or with her own device. Vincenzo swore to wear these precious objects 'as long as my bones shall hold together', said they would follow him to the tomb and sent in return long-haired dogs, lengths of satin or fine silk, elaborate jewels or baskets of fish. The latter, which were apparently much sought after, demanded the speediest possible delivery. The baskets first reached Colorno, where Lavinia and Anna were waiting to receive them (there was always a share for them and for the Countess of Sala) and from there were sent on immediately to Reggio, as if they had come from the ladies.

Hippolita was clearly in love, for she was far from happy. She made nervous plans to stay at Parma and for the prince to stay at Reggio. She trembled if he hurt his hand while jousting. She called him cruel if he took too long to write to her. She became terrified at the thought of the talk their loves would cause among their enemies, of whom one of the bitterest was the Bishop of Osimo, a close friend of the Farneses. Above all she was unsure of him. She felt that she was not received into that sphere which faithful love builds round a woman, and her heart was filled with anguish. As for Vincenzo, his hyperboles no longer sufficed her now that it was a question not of declamation but of consolation. The words of suffering addressed to him—words like 'unhappy soul, miserable life, desolate heart'—fell away from him unavailing. Perhaps Hippolita was discovering that he was one of those men whose communion with women is only physical. Perhaps she felt the irremediable pain of the discovery and, hard upon it, like a lightning flash, the desire to delude herself. There was no way out—she had to betray herself, prostrate herself to his every whim and seek love's fullness in the bodily presence of her lover. She left home, reached Colorno, and was received tenderly by the Countess of Sala. Her whole being invited him. In Vincenzo's mind the thought of joining her jumped with his desires and made him chafe at the bit, but he could not move at this particular time without giving his father good reason for leaving Mantua. He begged in vain to go to Parma for Christmas or the New Year. Perhaps the Farneses said No on purpose, which they did through the Bishop of Osimo and with Duke Guglielmo's approval. Even if Vincenzo went to Ferrara he could not reach Colorno. Christmas came and with it, instead of the prince, Count Claudio Gonzaga of Novellara with a message for the Countess of Sala and one for Signora Torelli. But this was no longer sufficient for Hippolita, who felt that her arguments no longer carried weight with Vincenzo. Already she was feeling the solitude and tortures of those in love. Then she turned upon herself and did not write, but allowed Vincenzo to storm and rave and plead with her like a man out of his senses.

Little Isabella, the dwarf, ran off to Colorno to explain everything. She spoke to the Countess of Sala, to Signora Lavinia and to Hippolita herself. Signora Lavinia undertook the task of calming Hippolita's rage and succeeded in placating her. Hippolita, alas, asked for nothing better and perhaps did not even weep as she capitulated. The news of her surrender arrived back in Mantua and reached Vincenzo as he was arming for the lists in the presence of a certain Father Tullio, who was very prone to indulgence. The young man's joy embraced the messenger, Father Tullio and his bewitching 'mother' in Colorno. He was at a loss how to express his gratitude. He felt his muscles swell and shouted: 'I shall perform miracles in the lists.' For Barbara he chose a jewel; to Hippolita he offered his life. He demanded a piece of paper. 'From the half-dead state in which I was,' he wrote and the pen danced in his hand, 'I have returned to life only to serve my dear and sweet Andromeda, whom I love more than all the world.'

Perhaps Vincenzo contrived to see Hippolita in January and February 1581. It is certain that, at the end of February, when he was setting out for his marriage at Parma, he visited Colorno and passed a week there. This visit on the eve of his marriage scandalized both Parma and Mantua. But the Countess of Sala insisted that it was a mark of respect to *her*, to his 'mother', his 'sister' and his friend. She laughed at Duke Guglielmo's fury; he was never to forgive her. Caught in the toils of his own sensuality, Vincenzo delighted to lay at Hippolita's feet the insolence of his gesture. Now she believed him at last, although in February her doubts had returned and she had almost succeeded in gaining control of herself, only to be vanquished anew. The whole company at Colorno was in a state of excitement over the amorous ribaldry of the young prince and perhaps the only one to feel a tremor of fear was Hippolita. She knew she was being given more than was permissible. At the same time she was unwilling to probe too deeply into her own heart, for then she would have had to confess that she was in fact being given too little—a cry, a burst of flame, which soon would be nothing at all.

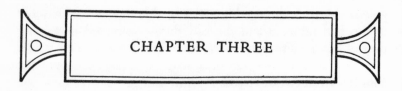

CHAPTER THREE

Margherita

MARGHERITA FARNESE arrived in Parma between the end of January and the beginning of February 1581. She had left her father in Flanders, where he was governor of a territory which Spain insisted on curbing beneath a cruel yoke. He was intent on his work of government and conquest and proving pre-eminent in both, as Philip II had known he would when he appointed him—so much so that he did not wish the Farnese to have full powers. He therefore summoned Alessandro's mother, Margherita of Austria, who was Duchess of Parma and daughter of Charles V, and granted her all the civil powers. Alessandro had rebelled against this division of power and was trying to induce his mother to resign; but the great old lady, who had grown in energy and intellectual stature in the course of her adventurous life, did not help him greatly to that end. In fact, she was to take three years to retire from the position assigned to her by the King of Spain. All this was before the famous siege of Antwerp where Alessandro Farnese was to show, over and above a soldier's skill and power of decision, that mastery of strategy which marks the greatest generals. He had already given more than an inkling of these qualities—had indeed displayed them to the full, along with others subtler still, when he pitted his intelligence and courage against the upright and capable Flemings, who were so obstinate in their desire for independence. True to his Italian upbringing, Alessandro took with him into military life a sense of balance (that sure sign of intellectual refinement), firmness without ferocity and the Italians' quick, enlightened mode of thought whereby they understand, through their own humanity, the humanity of others. Incredibly, he succeeded in governing in the name of the hated King of Spain without being himself hated.

His wife, Maria of Portugal, had died leaving him three children, Margherita, Ranuccio and Odoardo. The princess had been beautiful but she had been famous, above all, for her virtue. A significant anecdote is told of her. On her arrival in Italy someone at the court gave her Petrarch's Canzoniere, that bible of Italian Renaissance courts, to read. No sooner had she glanced at it than the Princess hurled it from her in a rage at the courtier who had dared to offer her such an immoral book.

Her indignation probably concealed a heart so prone to love that it felt its scorching power to be a sin. Undoubtedly Maria of Portugal was a bitter woman and a distrustful one, accustomed to turn over in her mind the doubts and torments engendered by a jealous discontent which was not without foundation; for her husband was both passionate and practised in the art of love and only too ready to burn for other women. He had, it seemed, a discerning preference for the women of Piacenza but he enjoyed others, too, with gusto. Nor had he any intention of limiting his choice, as he had proved at the time of his unbridled infatuation for the Countess of Sala. Unfortunately for himself, the heir to the dukedom, Ranuccio, was to take after his mother—but Margherita did not, for she was devoted to Petrarch and Ariosto and poets in general, even if it was usually without much discernment. Since she loved to find music in poetry and poetry in music, Margherita mixed words and music in accordance with an alchemy of her own, which had the power to make her rediscover herself in a new, exalted guise. Song, for instance, she found to be a more natural mode of expression than speech. Besides music and poetry, Margherita liked dancing, riding, plays, suppers à la belle étoile, races in the garden, the company of her pages and ladies and all the amusements of the Court which, with childhood's playful, magic fantasy, she wove into a beautiful story. All the tenderness of childhood was in her limpid sweetness,

which was free of any pride—a rare thing in a princess of that
time and rarer still in a Farnese.

Margherita had the slimness of fourteen years when she came
south for her marriage with Vincenzo Gonzaga. She had come
from Namur, travelling happily with her ladies-in-waiting, and
giving the name of adventure to every incident on the way,
delighting in the snow, the mist, the frozen rivers and the crystalline landscapes lying in the depth of winter. At Parma they had
prepared endless festivities for the marriage. There had come to
join the Farneses the lords of the principal fiefs of the dukedom—
the Pallavicinis, the Scottis and the Sanseverinos. From Milan,
Ferrara, Brescia, Piacenza, Reggio, Mantua and Cremona, nobles
were invited with their ladies, headed—needless to say—by the
Countess of Sala, who moved about among them in a great dress
of brocade with her laughing and beguiling grace. Naturally
Margherita, being so prone to joy, allowed herself to be conquered by this cunning weaver of intrigues, who had been so
close a friend of her father, and found it necessary to have her
preside at festivities and dinner parties. Certainly when she was
there everything took fire and a thing could even happen which
no one had thought possible—in the sad eyes of the old Duke of
Parma, whose smiles could be counted on the fingers of one hand,
there appeared, if not a dazzling light, at least a pale glow of consent.

The marriage took place on the 2nd March, 1581. Barbara
saw her most spoiled 'son' arrive for the nuptials fresh from the
embraces of Hippolita—she had meanwhile probably returned to
Reggio—with the air of a man good-naturedly fulfilling his
duty; but she quickly became aware that a new note had crept
in. No sooner had Vincenzo set eyes on his bride than he realized
that she, too, was one of those beings who think of the world as
a mere point of departure for their fantasies. He welcomed her
eagerly and the memory was not obscured but rather enhanced
by the discovery of Margherita, of Margherita's eyes, brimming
with love, of her vivacity, at once childlike and womanly. For the
attribute of libertine given by all the historians to Vincenzo is,
like all generic definitions, a rather clumsy way of defining a

character. His great tenderness, his lack of fierceness, cynicism or contempt for women, his readiness to serve, love and rely on them for the sweetness of his days—all these reveal not the haughty punctilio of a Don Juan but rather a constant readiness to give of himself. His desire, generous at first, would in the end, through following too many varied impulses, be led astray, shattered and lost. But what a risk it was for any woman to encounter the like of Vincenzo Gonzaga, who could ensnare with the mere joy of his ardour and make her feel a vile creature if she did not respond to him. To Vincenzo it came naturally to fuse past and present loves or to mingle present loves with each other, so that they all combined to produce a pitch of physical pleasure; nor did it point to moral disorder but rather to moral deficiency. He was intent on external lures and did not refer them to a profound inner self or examine them to see how they would stand up to the times when his ardour was appeased. He simply accepted them out of an abundant but ill-regulated vitality; no sooner were they his than he had already passed on to something else. Even if melancholy and grief were at work within him he did not notice it. Often he felt himself reborn, as he did now with Margherita in these lengthening winter days, while the veils of the spring mist dissolved over Parma and no one guessed at the approaching drama.

Four days after the marriage ceremony the bride and bridegroom were at Borgo San Donnino with their own private suite, for they had left their guests to enjoy the festivities at Parma. Their flight, which might have been thought a kind of nuptial rape, instead concealed a secret so painful that it demanded to be surrounded by silence.

Those who had to be, were admittedly informed. Duke Guglielmo in Mantua was struck by the full gravity of the situation and knew he had good reason to be alarmed. He dislodged Marcello Donati from his study crammed with books and codices, and sent him hotfoot to his son.

Quietly solicitous, Donati arrived at Borgo San Donnino and had a talk with the prince. He found him moved and overwhelmed and realized at once that this was no trifling matter. Between husband and wife there was an obstacle. Perhaps it was a case of witchcraft; certainly it was a terrible thing to be condemned to. The story Vincenzo told his secretary is a document we wish we could report, so pitiful and moving is it, but that is impossible. Suffice it to say that the young man went the length of admitting that on the wedding night the fault might have been his, overwhelmed as he was to find in his arms a creature so fragile and shy. But on the following nights he could swear it had not been so. To bear witness to this there were the ladies of the court who had rebuked Margherita severely for her faint woman's heart. What was all this trembling? they had asked her with hard eyes. The child had promised to be brave and had welcomed her husband with a heroic smile, but afterwards screams and weeping, as if someone were being tortured, had been heard by the women in the neighbouring rooms and had made their flesh creep.

Donati thought it over for a long time and then concocted a mild version of the affair for the Duke, stating with a euphemistic periphrasis, that Margherita was too young—'May has not yet flowered for her.' But a few days later, when he had examined her, he sent the medical diagnosis. It would be difficult for her ever to be a wife and certain that she could never present the Gonzagas with an heir except at the risk of her own life and the child's.

The Duke of Parma was also informed. He felt a shiver of distaste at the news. When the matter was whispered in the greatest secrecy to the Bishop of Osimo, who had been the prime mover of the marriage and a man who had sternly rebuked Vincenzo for the follies he was committing with Hippolita, the Bishop, with a quick gesture, declared that he was 'stupefied, beyond himself and in despair'. In fact he was hardly in a fit state to sit in council with the Duke and the Jesuit court confessor. All three were brought round to Donati's view that it would be best to have the opinion of the most famous physician and surgeon of the day,

Acquapendente. The latter was summoned to Parma, to which the bride and bridegroom also returned. The doctor's reply seemed to be favourable and the festivities went on more gaily than ever, brightened by the rippling laugh of the Countess of Sala. Cesare Cavriani, Duke Guglielmo's most conscientious informer, who was attached as gentleman-in-waiting to Margherita's person, sent accounts of balls and festivities and the court gossip, announcing—amid all these trifles—that Acquapendente had found the bride better than he had expected. Vincenzo sent the same news with his own hand and added particulars. So Acquapendente finished his task and departed in the greatest secrecy.

As for Margherita, she kept her own secret, which tormented and humiliated and frightened her. She was terrified to feel its burden upon her. She did not even choose to play a heroic part but almost asked for pardon as she distracted herself with the improvised effusions of her fourteen years, toyed with a monkey, tried a dance step or sang to the sound of the lute. Under Acquapendente's scalpel she must have brutally realized what it meant to be deficient in the physical attributes of a woman; but why nature had betrayed her or how far-reaching that betrayal was, she could not and would not realize. She loved Vincenzo and instinctively felt safe within his encircling protection. She caught herself in tears at the sweet sound of the name of husband. When she did not see him, a tremor of anxiety possessed her—he had disappeared, he was gone, he was lost; then she suffered the world's hostility and her own. Let him but reappear, and under the quick glance of his blue eyes, all promises became accepted truths.

Absorbed with what went on within her, Margherita paid little heed to anything else, to the astonishment of the gentlemen of Mantua, who wrote to Duke Guglielmo about it. The Farneses were paying a great dowry for her of three hundred thousand gold crowns, to which they would add jewels and rich garments; but since the old Duke Ottavio was very loth to hand over ready money to his granddaughter she cheerfully did without it. Her orders and commands showed a child's lack of perception rather than any consciousness of her rank, but she was always courteous and restrained. They had made her a few fine dresses and made her still more beautiful ones when, after two months of marriage and delays whose bitter significance she alone knew, Duke Guglielmo decided to summon her as a bride to Mantua.

The moment the day for her departure had been fixed, everyone saw that Margherita's nature had undergone a change. Now she gave orders indeed and tried on the rich ceremonial dresses. One was of cloth of gold on a grey ground, covered with gold and silver embroidery; the other, a robe of immense splendour with skirt, overdress, the great high collar and the hat with its curling brim all of white satin. This sea of shining white was contained by sinuous dykes of gold and silver braid, and deigned to moderate its gleaming splendour only with the discreet iridescence of an embroidery of pearls. The tuft of white plumes in the hat atoned for the baroque effect of the apparition by adding a touch of theatricality, at once lofty and airy, which called for the balanced rhythms of a Monteverdi ballet.

For Margherita music, as we have pointed out already, was not so much a diversion or a stimulus as a pre-requisite for self-expression. At her court, as her gentleman-in-waiting, Cesare Cavriani, announced in a letter to the Duke of Mantua, the musicians were always on duty with harps, lutes and flutes for chamber music, fifes and tambours for excursions by carriage or on horseback. The whole troop of them was coming to Mantua with an entire programme to get through in the course of the journey for the company was travelling by barge along canals and rivers.

Singing and playing as if it were the finale of an opera, they left Parma towards the end of April. Beguiled by the music, the journey was pleasant. When, on the last day of the month, the little princess made her entry into her new home, she might have seemed overcome by the superabundance of white in her ceremonial dress had hope and a vibrant, ingenuous vitality not sustained her and lent radiance to the pallor of her face. From Ferrara there had come the Duke, Alfonso d'Este, with his

Duchess, Margherita Gonzaga, Vincenzo's beloved sister—his accomplice, companion and champion in all things, whose hair was more red than fair and who was not so much high-spirited as fiery-tempered. They had brought with them their exquisite court with its gay and polished ladies, its delicate singers and its mannered gentlemen. The beauties of Mantua, Monferrato, Parma and Ferrara passed in the carriages, displaying faces framed in the petals of their white flower-like collars edged with point lace in the Spanish fashion. They cheered the bride, who grew bravely pale beneath the weight of her braided and bejewelled gowns. They listened to the ladies singing. They jousted, wearing the ladies' colours. They danced with the ladies themselves. The very air was full of dalliance. Only the marriage chamber, once its door was closed, remained a place of mortification.

Now that there was someone in this world more humiliated than himself, it seemed to Duke Guglielmo that he could carry his hump more lightly. Once he even tried to dance a galliard, but the attempt was not very successful. Perhaps it made him aware of his appearance, which he saw mirrored in a woman's glance, where pity and scorn fought for mastery. His genial mood was spoilt. One evening, while the ladies were making music, Guglielmo could no longer contain his impatience at the sight of all the company intent on the singing, on the sound of the viols and lutes—could no longer bear to see how their enjoyment was rounded off by their admiration for the beautiful faces of the singers, their shapely hands and young thoughtful heads. Then he turned to the Duke Alfonso d'Este and exclaimed loudly: 'A fine thing women are! Truly I would rather be an ass than a woman.' Shrugging his shoulders, he rose. The music died away, shattered. Then he caused the guests to pass into the salon which served as theatre and gave orders for a comedy to be staged with musical interludes written by himself. In Harlequin and the other comic characters he saw not goodnatured caricature but mockery of humanity. To be able to have a hand in it himself, relieved his feelings and tempered the bitterness of his suffering.

But when the festivities had come to an end and, with them,

the grounds of his anger, Guglielmo discovered that his daughter-in-law intrigued him. Not as an object of pity but as a pheno-menon he wished to understand—so different, so remote from himself, yet so alike; for it was her lot, too, to be betrayed by nature itself. He would see how she bore her physical disability. Disarmed, docile and—as often as she could be—gay, Margherita looked into his eyes without irony or repulsion, seeing in him only the father of the man she loved. When the Duke let her hear his own musical compositions, whether songs or sacred music, she listened attentively, as became a pupil. To be able to transfix her with a piercing glance, as she trustingly abandoned herself to him, must have given Guglielmo intoxicating spasms, whose cruel origin was not unknown to him. He tried to recover himself and show a fatherly benevolence devoid of any warmth, forcing him-self to hold off the cloud of sorrow which—as he now knew—he would undoubtedly call down upon Margherita. In the end he felt a kind of compassion for this creature who gave herself to him without reserve. But he had only to think of the obstacles to the continuation of the dynasty, or how an accident to Vin-cenzo could make Ludovico Gonzaga and his children descend out of France to lord it over Mantua, for him to feel his hand raised inexorably to strike.

As for the Duchess Leonora, she did not love her daughter-in-law—Christian benevolence apart—for she was still enamoured of her son's first betrothed, that Leonora de Medici who was the daughter of her sister, Giovanna of Austria, and who bore her own name. Although they were hushed and veiled, the rumours circulating about the Farnese girl's conjugal misfortunes reached the Duchess and caused her much pain. She was able to accept them only after long debate. The young woman's fanciful nature, her continual habit of expressing herself in music, of feeling life as a perpetual joyous summons, ended by alienating her from Leonora. All the more so since Leonora foresaw how well the girl's character might agree with that of her son and, so she thought, lead him still further astray.

When he began to think over what was happening to him,

Vincenzo felt himself caught by a torturing form ot tenderness. His defence was to put all thought from him till the morrow. He asked his father to wait until the adolescent girl had become mature and went off to seek distraction. Once he went to Colorno and more than once to Ferrara. Then he returned and found Margherita again, noticing how she would discreetly try to seem used to it all, impervious to emotion. The danger that he might be too greatly moved aroused something approaching resentment in the young man, who shook it off by a superficial gesture—by giving her gifts as men often do when they pity women but refuse to share their suffering From Vincenzo Margherita received jewels, flowers, necklaces, purses of gold, and meantime she underwent treatment from the doctors, putting her trust in their skill, for she refused to accept disappointment.

For husband and wife there now came a time of bitterness and pain which lasted almost a year. Duke Guglielmo watched with a coldly determined eye. 1581 ended and 1582 began; with it there came the invitation from Ferrara to celebrate Carnival. Vincenzo and Margherita went off together and arrived when the great court was already plunged into the excitement of the festivities. They had barely time to don their masks before they were whirled into the round of amusements.

That year Carnival at Ferrara, which was always lively, had a giddy tempo. Gaiety was pursued with fanaticism and no one had time to eat or drink at the usual hours. The little rest they contrived to get had to be snatched when the occasion offered, with their masks always ready to hand. Some of the maskers returned at dawn and some, when it was hardly day, were already setting out in carriages or on foot, all bent on adventure, men and women alike. There was jousting and running at the ring. Comedies were staged. There were concerts. They sped through the streets on sleighs. Masks, masks, masks! shouted the drunken crowd.

How much these days of misrule pleased Vincenzo can be imagined—all the more since, according to informers, he had met one of his old 'special loves' at Ferrara. Perhaps Hippolita.

At first Margherita had seemed to wilt under the fatigue and even more so under the cruel sentence which shut her off from participating in these great carnal festivities; but in the end she too found a way of her own to amuse herself. *She* danced too and was present at the gay series of musical ballets devised at the court by her sister-in-law, the Duchess, all lace and feathers, embroidery, satin and gauze. But childish pleasures took her out of herself more effectively. She ran through the streets with a few others, slender and vigorous, with a mask on her face, and knocked one by one at all the doors in an entire district; then she ran off and went through the streets, eating as she went things she had bought in the market. She dressed like the Ferrarese, adorned herself like them and adopted the customs of Ferrara. When she returned to Mantua she would introduce Ferrarese fashions with an enthusiasm which was moving in its allusiveness.

That year it seemed there was love enough for everyone. In Mantua even Duke Guglielmo managed to forget his misogyny and his hunchback and fell in love with an actress, in whose honour, overcoming his horror of gallantry, he appeared in various new garbs—in shades of pink and crimson and wearing 'very becoming little caps', laden with plumes and feathers. The actress would have been unworthy of herself had she not been equal to such an extravagant moment in her career. So Guglielmo deigned to delude himself and seemed to be almost setting up as a rival to his son. Thus once, when he learned that Vincenzo was giving a great dinner to the noble ladies of the city, he insisted on inviting them all to a magnificent luncheon on that same day.

Carnival came to an end. It was spring and a year had passed since Margherita had entered the Gonzaga household. In a discreet letter Duke Guglielmo informed Duke Ottavio Farnese that he would have to send Margherita back to him. In Parma they felt all the shame and offensiveness of her return. But Cardinal Alessandro Farnese begged and entreated them to keep the matter secret and await the arrival of the Bishop of Osimo, who was already on his way to Mantua. Events took place exactly according to plan. Vincenzo left after a most affectionate leave-taking in which he said they would meet again soon; the Duke and Duchess left, too. When she had been abandoned to her solitude, Margherita was told she must go to Parma to undertake treatment for her barrenness. In time, when she was cured, she would come back.

A presentiment of tears hung over the young princess's court. One evening—it was the 26th May—after a pilgrimage to a sanctuary, Margherita, who was completely exhausted by the tenderness of prayer, gathered her ladies and gentlemen-in-waiting round her in one of the rose-filled gardens of the ducal palace, amidst the statues and fountains. She spoke of herself in a little, broken voice and predicted her death before six months were past. Her request to be remembered in their prayers made them all weep. When Cesare Cavriani, her gentleman-in-waiting, arrived in the midst of it all and tried to turn things into a jest, Margherita was offended as all women are when the right to suffer is denied them. Then she reiterated her prophecy and assured him that she did not speak out of superstitious vanity but out of a foreknowledge of what would happen. She put into her words her certainty of an impending doom, and it is of no importance that the prophecy in no way matched events. Speaking to Cavriani, she went to the extreme of saying that either she would be cured or she would die.

Although they were supposed to know nothing of the true reasons for Margherita's return to Parma, the ladies and damsels of her court allowed themselves to be discovered bewailing in the princess's misfortune their own ill-luck at being born women. Cavriani attempted to stem the flood of lamentations, but he was not always successful.

Ranuccio Farnese came to fetch his sister. He was two years her junior; he was agile, with long shapely legs beneath his doublet and hose; his face was rounded off by the soft line of his chin and one would never have guessed that he was to become a man of morbid fantasies and of a cruelty based on sophistical reasoning. At this time he was passing from adolescence into youth. The world was beginning to reveal itself to him as a confederation bound together to work him harm—and he meant thereby not only the world of people and events but the world of spirits and ideas too. The one exception was his sister, who was an inventor of fantasies, who could calm his every fear with a mere glance of her laughing black eyes. Ranuccio knew that for her he had remained the boy she had used to rouse with her innocent rompings and laugh out of his revulsion from life. The more he departed from the reality of the image, the more he loved his lost innocence mirrored in the radiance of his sister. In the very midst of his adolescence he was to suffer the sad story of the Gonzaga marriage, Margherita's humiliation—for even she was a victim of the curse of existence—and the bitter offence to the Farneses. Never again would he think of Vincenzo Gonzaga without his blood curdling with loathing. He would dog Vincenzo's steps in the future with cunning and determination, would enmesh him for thirty years in a ferment of madness until at last he embroiled him in his darkest hallucinations—conspiracy, betrayal and death.

Margherita, out of the depths of her despair, saw her brother come to meet her and welcomed him with rising spirits. The ancient spirit of family loyalty, which is charitable even when it deceives us, made her feel that his presence was the first sign of further help to come. A tremor of vitality put new life into her. Then, bidding them prepare her coffers and taking only a few belongings —for she promised herself a speedy return—she set off towards Revere to bid farewell to her father-in-law, the Duke.

The pensive company set out early in June. They followed the course of the Po and saw the great theatrical pile of Revere rise in the distance, flaming above the plain. She halted at the castle and was received by Duke Guglielmo. His face was composed in the set, tranquil expression of a man who has passed judgment after weighing it with scrupulous care. Certainly when he spoke of his daughter-in-law's early return his words—based firmly on the premise that she would be cured—did not ring false. Comforted by an upsurge of hope which first took her breath away and then restored it again, Margherita returned to Parma on the 6th of June. The few shabby rooms reserved for her in the palace seemed to augur that she would live here for a short time only, camped out with her court. There were no women in the Farnese family except her aunt, Vittoria Farnese, Dowager Duchess of Urbino, one of the celebrated women of the sixteenth century—intelligent but too old now and too set in her wisdom to unbend and share in such a distressing story. If asked, Vittoria would have advised the cloister under her breath and did indeed advise it. Her words were eagerly echoed by the old Duke Ottavio who, after a hasty visit to his granddaughter, washed his hands of her and sent her his own Jesuit confessor, Father Piero Angelo, who set about assailing her with questions. But for the sad, pessimistic company of her brother, Ranuccio, Margherita was alone.

Without going into too many painful details, we shall follow the main episodes in the development of this dark drama whose meaning only women—and perhaps a handful of the most understanding of men—can appreciate and interpret as a pitiful allegory of the condition of womankind. First of all we shall observe how Margherita at once inevitably assumed the air of a victim destined to undergo sacrifice. Doctors called to examine her declared that she could be restored to conjugal life. She stated that she was ready to submit to anything which would enable her to return to Mantua and her husband. But the Farneses let the empty days slip past so that, in their cold familiar atmosphere, she felt the messages from Vincenzo and even from her father-in-law all the more warm and affectionate. She failed to see that her husband's tenderness, while human, was increasingly remote; she did not discern in Guglielmo's solicitude his intention of dashing her to the ground. For ambassadors had already left Mantua on their way to Pope Gregory XIII, who was a friend of both the Gonzagas and the Farneses, asking him to judge what ill effects the lack of heirs in the ducal house of Mantua might have on Italy and on the Church.

'Let the Pope consider,' wrote Guglielmo, 'how dangerous it

would be if our line were to die out and the children of our
brother, the Duke of Nevers, were to succeed to those states
which are the twin gateway to Italy, bringing with them—as His
Holiness may readily imagine—a nation infected by the contagion.'
The contagion was the Protestantism of the Huguenots and the
nation was France. From this it is clear that the fear which kept
the Duke from sleeping stemmed from the old antagonism against
his brother and rival, Ludovico. The thought that he had
triumphed over Ludovico as a young man, only to be ousted by
his children, so irked the Duke that his pressure on Margherita
inevitably became relentless.

This the Farneses understood but Margherita did not. She could
not see beyond the polite greetings which arrived from Mantua
and insisted on seeing the doctors, thought her father-in-law right
when he insisted on hastening the treatment, and grew impatient
and rebelled if Duke Ottavio imposed conditions on the Gonzagas—such as that once a surgical examination had declared the
bride cured she should return to Mantua without running the risk
of being sent home once more. There was one comforting thought
in which Margherita secretly took refuge and so renewed her
courage, the thought of her father, who both loved and understood her. Some time back a messenger had left Parma for
Flanders and Margherita had put her hopes on his journey,
following his road from country to country in her mind, completely confident that she would have a reply which would in
truth be a message of hope.

The courier, Pedro de Castro, was announced in November
1582. The moment Margherita was told of his arrival she summoned her favourite companion, Countess Langosco, and gaily
arranged a setting. For herself a suitably stiff and imposing chair
fit for a princess; for her friend, a seat behind the arras so that she
could hear the secret conversation unseen. Each of them went
to her place, laughing and excited. De Castro came, presented his
letters of credence, made his bow and delivered the verdict. All
things considered, Alessandro Farnese counselled his daughter to
retire 'to a convent since it has pleased God to put such im-

pediments in her way that it is of no avail to think any longer of earthly things but only of how to serve His divine majesty; he therefore begs and commands her not to resist his advice.'

Behind the curtain the Countess Langosco felt the last curving trace of her smile die painfully away at the corners of her mouth. At first she heard silence fall, driven home like a stab from a dagger. Then came the sound of Margherita's weeping mingled with protests, denials and cries—her father had given her a husband and she meant to keep him by hook or by crook. She distinguished de Castro's cold admonitions—let her Highness pay heed to what she was about and not run the risk of death through wishing to live too much. Then Margherita's protests came thick and fast, illogical, accusing, threatening—even threatening her father who wished to make her die of despair.

De Castro withdrew and her ladies came forth along with her gentleman-in-waiting, who did not scruple to read her a lecture on etiquette and how little rebellion and shouting became a princess, who should express herself calmly and with dignity. Thus by shifting her attention from its painful focal point, he sought to distract and comfort her.

From that day on it is impossible to keep count of the secret consultations at the palace. Once the word 'convent' had been uttered by Alessandro, all the other Farneses, who had been torturing it over in their minds, voiced it too and sought by every means in their power to force it upon Margherita. Spies came and went between Duke Ottavio's apartments and those of the princess. Some confided in her, some feigned to do so. The corners were full of little groups of courtiers, true men of their time, who when they vowed secrecy did so with a mental reservation. It was impossible to lift a curtain without the risk of finding a spy behind it—perhaps in a cassock. Once Duke Ottavio himself took to eavesdropping in order to learn more closely what his granddaughter thought when she was off her guard. At the court of Parma people did not breathe but suffocate. Margherita replied roundly to her father that she did not intend to obey him, and appealed to her father-in-law, who pretended to support her and carefully preserved in the archives all her letters with their devout protests and thanks. Then she had an idea born of despair. She wrote a letter of supplication to the Pope, telling him of her case, and secretly consigned the letter to Countess Langosco. The Duke of Mantua not only let it be despatched but insisted that it be conveyed to the Vatican by the ducal councillor, Aurelio Zibramonti.

There was a great uproar in Rome. Cardinal Farnese was summoned to report on the affair and asked why the Farneses wished to force the vocation of a soul and why they did not help the princess to assert her rights. The ambassador of Philip II, the Mantuan ambassador and the cardinals who supported each house were summoned together. Vague dangers threatened which the Pope already imagined turning into armed strife. He must prevent the ancient enmity between Farneses and Gonzagas from taking advantage of recent events to flare up and disturb the equilibrium of the Italian states. It was an artificial equilibrium, a drowsy calm, but—in the Pope's opinion—the only chance the peninsula had of enjoying a safe existence. Once it had been put into legal terms and set forth in the pedantic Latin of the Curia, the sad hap of one woman became a difficult case, well adapted to the exercise of subtle minds. Cardinals, bishops, priests and friars, all discussed it, turning over the pages of canon law, and all gave their opinion. Nothing was more calculated than these discussions, confined within the cold realm of the written word, to irritate the sensibilities of the dynastic heads of Parma or Mantua. Already the Dukes were at their desks drawing up instructions for their ambassadors and covertly accusing each other of distrust and disloyalty. At this point Gregory decided to impose his authority. He nominated an arbiter and, so that his decision might be beyond discussion, he chose the greatest figure of his time—the Cardinal Archbishop of Milan, Carlo Borromeo.

The moment San Carlo's great sickle-shaped nose appears in this story we know that Margherita's cause is lost—not so much because of the difference between this young girl, as yet hardly conscious of herself, and the priest wrapped in complete mail, who was considered the strictest man of his day, as because of the extraordinary kinship between the twin forces which make the woman the slave of the priest. For it was thus that Iphigenia was induced to mount the altar of sacrifice and was rapt with sweet fanaticism beneath the murderous gaze of the priest of Diana. The dialogue between a priest and a woman who has to be reduced to reason against her nature is always an unhappy one.

Little did Margherita suspect what the great Lombard saint had in store for her; she awaited him as an ally sent to her by the Pope, the great saviour of the world. Her ignorance would in itself have deserved punishment were it not redeemed by a candour not of this world. We cannot but shudder with compassion when, to celebrate the triumph of her rights, Margherita hastily has a song composed on certain verses by Ariosto:

> Io parlo dei begli occhi e del bel volto
> che m'hanno il cor di mezzo al petto tolto.

'I speak of those fine eyes and handsome face which stole my heart from out of my breast.' A declaration of love offered to her husband, which she sang over and over again, filling with harmony the cold emptiness of her great rooms in the palace. But although she had moved the Vatican to serve her love, and congratulated herself on her achievement, Margherita's boldness stopped there and she did not even dare to ask her grandfather for a suitable dress. Yet now she had grown out of true childhood and her figure had developed, as her gentleman-in-waiting reveals to us by his request to the Gonzagas for a dress for Margherita who, even in his misogynistic eyes, appeared a 'fine girl'. Duke Guglielmo sent two dresses and they were lovely ones. Vincenzo sent a cross of pearls and diamonds, adding to them with a touch of fantasy a little golden whistle.

Meanwhile Carlo Borromeo had left Rome and was coming north through Italy, passing through Loreto, on one of those

designedly uncomfortable journeys which were part of his perpetual penance. Out of obedience he had accepted the papal
behest to act as arbiter between the Gonzagas and the Farneses.
If the question at issue was distasteful to him he nevertheless contrived through his lofty powers of reasoning and his deep sense of
justice to rob it of its murky nature. 'It is not a private matter,' he
said, 'but one affecting the public weal.' Having found the *mot
juste*, the cardinal had taken up the seat of judgment and would
spare himself neither interrogations nor investigations. His purity
of mind was in any case so uncompromising that women were
ashamed of their very existence in his presence. This he knew and
approved—just as one day he commended the gesture of a woman
who, at the mere sight of him in the distance, drew her veil over
her face in dismay.

By about 1583 this splendid general of the Church was enjoying
the years of his maturity. He had triumphed not only over subtle
ecclesiastical pitfalls but over political enmities—his clashes with
the Spanish governor of Milan are famous—and hatred rising in
arms against his unarmed power. By imposing a severe and
salutary reform he had triumphed over clerical corruption, and he
had triumphed over the plague of 1576. In those days the people
of Milan had seen his reassuring figure appear everywhere at
once, and thanks to his fiery energy, provide for their needs as
men and women fell around him and everything else seemed to
fail—including humanity. There was no one, prince or com-
moner, who did not recognize in his majestic bearing an emana-
tion of the majesty of God. In the more practical sphere, there
was no one who would not submit to the judgment of a mind so
supremely fitted to legislate.

Both Guglielmo Gonzaga and Ottavio Farnese had readily
accepted him as arbiter—Borromeo was related to both families;
but the Duke of Mantua, who knew the Cardinal through having
had him in his city several times, either during the period of his
disagreement with the Inquisition or to preside at such ceremonies as the translation of Saint Barbara's jawbone, brought by
river from Venice in a barge, remained on the defensive. In order

to discover the Cardinal's intentions he had already dispatched from Mantua a most able envoy, the governor of his castle, Luigi Olivo, laden with instructions.

On the pretext of paying his respects to the prelate, Olivo went down into the Romagna and, on the firm yet soft line of the canal at Cesenatico, found the Cardinal's small party. He had himself introduced into the saint's presence, contrived to speak to him, and at once turned the conversation into something in the nature of an assault. It was in vain. How could a man like Borromeo, used to discerning the reality beneath appearances, fail to guess that the governor had come to spy out the land? But since he had no personal interests—for he thought entirely in terms of a better world—and no reason to play false, he could afford to conquer without giving battle. He would, he declared, abide by the terms of the Pope's missive—that was to say, separate interviews with husband and wife, consultations with the doctors and, if consultations were favourable, treatment for the princess. Then would come reunion of husband and wife.

Where? How? And why had Parma been chosen for the *rapprochement* instead of Mantua? asked Olivo. Because the princess's honour demanded that matters be clarified in her own home, replied the cardinal. What of the honour of the Gonzagas? insisted Olivo, feigning surprise that Borromeo should concern himself more over the honour of the Farneses than that of his own Duke. At this point the Cardinal was able to make the excellent move of repeating coldly that he would obey only the Pope. When Olivo then asked cautiously about Margherita's taking the veil, he received the reply that it must not be spoken of. It was true that the Duke of Parma had tried to persuade the princess, but since she had no vocation the step must not be forced upon her.

Let the people pray, added the Cardinal with hand uplifted in exhortation, let them pray. But Olivo did not slacken and passed on to a discussion of the young prince and his quarrels with his father. Did the Cardinal intend to speak to the young man, as the Duke wished, and admonish him? Certainly, Borromeo answered

patiently, he would admonish him. Then he followed up his reply
with an unpleasant query: What should he say if the prince were
to complain of his father, who kept him so miserably provided
for and so far beneath what his rank demanded that it encouraged
him to sin? 'For God's sake,' said the governor in terror, 'let your
reverence keep to generalities and simply exhort the young man
to obedience and respect.' In fact, he added, the Cardinal ought
not to ask the Duke that question for it would only confound
everything. Did the Cardinal not know that the vast sum of
money demanded by the prince would be his father's ruin?—and
so on.

It might surprise us that the austere Cardinal should take the
part of the prodigal against that judicious and temperate man, the
Duke, were this not the surest proof of how easily a disinterested
observer could see to what extent Guglielmo Gonzaga had failed
as a father. Perhaps the Cardinal made even the Duke realize something of this when he arrived in Mantua some days later. However that may be, when he reached Parma he was convinced of one
thing—that he would have to base his every gesture on canon law
and papal authority, for should things not go as the Duke of
Mantua wished, the latter would resort to legal quibbles over
points of detail.

That explains why every day of this episode is so carefully
documented for us with so many accounts sent by so many
different envoys. The prince must be interviewed in his own
home and not at Parma, said Guglielmo, who went on to dispute
the section of the papal brief which ordained the visit. They came
to an agreement on the place, choosing the neutral territory of
Ferrara. Patiently Borromeo went to Ferrara. It was January, the
high season of Carnival; they doffed their masks when Duke
Alfonso d'Este saw a grievous sweat on the saint's brow at such
a display of sin. He had his meeting with Vincenzo, who was
fascinated by such an arresting personality, answered his questions
reasonably and listened to his admonitions with affection and
contrition—but without intending to vary his conduct one whit.
Meanwhile, in Parma, the collection of doctors, surgeons, re-

porters and witnesses was swelling in numbers. Master Andrea da Fano came from Rome with the assurance that he could cure the princess. From Mantua there came the ducal councillor, Aurelio Zibramonti, and shortly after him, Marcello Donati. Through Donati, who was at his best in difficult situations, the Duke played his trump card. What this card was we shall at once understand if we remember that this humanist doctor had made the very first diagnosis of Margherita's unsuitability for marriage a year before. More firmly convinced than ever of his diagnosis, which coincided with the interests of the house of Gonzaga, Donati, without appearing to do so, sounded opinion, watched over things and reported back. It was clear that, of all those present, only one could vie with him in acumen and that was Carlo Borromeo.

On his return from Ferrara, the Cardinal began a rigorous fast on bread and water, offering penance to God. Propitiatory processions had been ordered and the people summoned to the churches. Nuns and friars prayed continually in convents and monasteries. For Margherita even this outburst of prayer took on the heady quality of wedding incense. After the cruel probings of the doctors and their no less cruel cross-examinations, she felt in a mood not averse to joy. She called for her musicians, summoned her court together and arranged small festivities, which were unbridled yet innocent, improvising on the carnival *motifs* she had learnt at Ferrara the year before, with her women and her own and Ranuccio's pages. For the most fantastic of her entertainments she decided to re-enact an imperial coronation, tingeing all its Spanish ceremony with caricature. Signora Ginevra Visdomani was the Empress. Margherita acted as majordomo, almost as if she were announcing the numbers of a revue. Prince Ranuccio was the drummer-boy. The doctor was a lady called Bagno. The captain of the guard was the fair Antonia, nicknamed Togna, dressed up as a soldier with pike and cuirass. The chaplain was a page. And so on. Gilt paper, garlands and ornaments transformed the largest room in her suite of apartments and what with frolics, music and dancing, they kept up the merriment for seven hours.

It was the nineteenth of February. At about three in the morning the last torches were extinguished in the great salon. The pages and ladies-in-waiting were all asleep, exhausted by the laughter and the dancing. At dawn that same day Carlo Borromeo raised his resolute prayer to the dull February sky. Let us look back for a moment. He had conducted the affair with exemplary caution and scrupulousness. The repeated interrogations of the protagonists, witnesses and relatives, the doctors' examinations, his consultations with doctors, midwives, surgeons and lawyers, the prayers ordered in the convents and churches day and night, the fasting he had imposed on himself in order to achieve an absolutely clear solution—all this amounted to the martyrdom of a soul which suffered at having to mix in matters so grossly contaminated by human failings. Because she persisted in wishing to become a woman capable of love, because she was willing to face any tribunal and any test, Margherita's love for Vincenzo was completely feminine, warm and unabashed; but it therefore inevitably secretly irritated—if it did not scandalize—a man like Borromeo, who was heroically dedicated to the things and the world of the spirit. His burning sense of charity came to his aid and allowed him to overcome his initial repugnance—but perhaps not always and not altogether. The documents provide us with an episode which it is not easy to relate and extremely difficult to interpret. It concerns an examination carried out by the doctors— perhaps on the Cardinal's advice and certainly with his consent— on four fourteen-year-old girls chosen from an orphanage run by the nuns. The doctors were to ascertain, by direct comparison with living subjects, the precise difference between normal women and the Farnese princess. The account of the examination is followed by the information that the girls whose modesty had been so roughly handled would at least be given a dowry. But the very fact that the Cardinal should have been led on from one scruple to another to permit such a thing can only be a symptom of his horror. It was horror, however, which he overcame by force of reasoning until a human situation was reduced to a coldly formulated problem. And we all know how easy it is to fall into inhumanity through theorizing.

His task of arbitration in Parma was to be one of Carlo Borromeo's more costly penances. For a time he had found himself suspended between the bold surgical views of Master Andrea da Fano and the objections put forward by the others—which, if truth be told, were not always convincing. In the end the Cardinal found a strong argument in the very quarter where the Duke of Mantua had cunningly placed it—in Marcello Donati. The latter swore on the Gospels that, in his opinion, the surgical operation might be fatal to Margherita. As he listened to him, Carlo Borromeo felt the serious-mindedness of the man, his conviction as a scientist, his serene, detached honesty as a scholar. He felt it right, therefore, to oppose an operation which might be tantamount to murder. He felt even more certain in deciding that Margherita was in danger of mortal sin, for, instead of shutting her mind to it as a suicidal act, she implored them to operate. She must come to see her error and renounce her intention.

Once he had found the moral key to this thorny problem of the heart, Carlo Borromeo felt relieved and freed from a burden. Doubtless his prayer contained something approaching thankfulness. Hence, strong in the rightness of his conviction, he no longer suffered or hesitated. Charity invested him magnificently with its majestic executioner's cloak. When, about midday on the 19th of February, he was announced in Margherita's apartments, his authority was wellnigh overpowering. With that voice of his to which a slight hesitation, overcome by his inner strength, gave an irresistible power, he announced to Margherita the end of her romantic dream. The college of doctors had given their verdict against the operation, which would not take place and must no longer be thought of. She could, it was true, try other cures and call in other doctors, but meantime she must be prepared to resign herself to the will of God—whatever that might be. In obedience she would find consolation and her true reason for existence.

The weight of the sentence bowed Margherita down in a state of exhaustion. Now indeed, she felt, no one would help her any more. She knelt down and wept. But, although in her heart she refused to submit to the power of the benediction the Cardinal called down on her head, she could not but be touched by the luminous flow of his argument. When Borromeo had gone she began to feel her conviction that she was right grow weak—yet that was her strongest point. But she did not surrender yet. She wept, she recovered and achieved her finest hour of spiritual independence when her whole being revolted against Borromeo and she said she wished to be damned in both body and soul. Then her spirits fell again and she clung to what the Cardinal had said of other possible cures to which end, being always earnest and meticulous, he was recruiting doctors in Pavia and Milan. Meanwhile she spent her energy to the point of complete exhaustion in balls and masquerades—the burning protest of her sixteen years. Once she prolonged a ball which had begun in the evening until it was time for Mass next day.

But her little victories—such as her refusal to accept the Duke of Parma's confessor, the Jesuit father, Piero Angelo—were offset by the closely co-ordinated manœuvres of her opponents. If she happened to enter the cathedral in time for the sermon, the preacher suddenly began to extemporize on the happiness of those who followed the example of Charles V and abandoned the miseries of this world for the blessed state of the contemplative life. In her apartments she had to submit to the visits of the Duke of Parma, who now assumed the role of head of the family and kept pointing out to her that her acts of rebellion were blemishes for which she must atone. Cruelly he brought it home to her that no one in Mantua loved her or wanted her any more, revealed Guglielmo's request to Rome for a divorce and convinced her that she must consider herself abandoned by her husband. So what was she left with but her own family? But she must return to her family in a penitent and submissive mood, renounce the Gonzagas and promise to withdraw from the world. Then they would all be on her side. She would be allowed legitimate pleasures and amusements. She would once more be paid the honour due to her rank and enjoy once more her father's love to the full.

It was a pitiless game Duke Ottavio played—that of leading her on from one surrender to another by speeches in which the words 'dignity' and 'affection' gleamed like lures. Meantime, since she could expect from the new doctors sent by Borromeo treatment but not a cure, they persuaded her not to allow herself to be tortured by their experiments but to send them packing. She dismissed them in a daze. No sooner were they gone than she burst into tears, for with this final departure she felt any positive hope she might have left fade for ever. Then she asked God why, instead of making her die as a child, when she was happy in her mother's arms, He had preserved her for such torture. She felt the spring to be a last agony and sought to gain time—snatching a walk, a ball, a day of illusion. At last Father Piero Angelo, the confessor she had refused, took upon himself the vindictive task of going to talk to her. The conversation left her raving and wringing her hands. The words 'divorce' and 'nunnery' had been spoken and defined. A definite period of time had been set.

Margherita collapsed completely. She was never seen to laugh again. She became very pale and thin and dressed in black. One by one she put off her jewels, smoothed her hair modestly and no longer went out for pleasure as she had been wont to do with so much zest. She had not lost her habit of translating her feelings into music but her song took on a note of pain and despair, ending in a sob. A prey to suffering, she capitulated like a true woman, accepting the male will where it showed itself strongest—in the man who had decreed her sacrifice. She withdrew her appeal to the Pope for help and wrote to Carlo Borromeo, asking his permission to retire from the world and lead a life of chastity.

Not as a cloistered nun, she explained to her courtiers, but as a nun living apart in her own house, in a princely apartment and attended by pages. She clutched at this last hope of a life which, in appearance at least, would not be one of complete renunciation; but Cardinal Borromeo knew only too well that, by canon law, Vincenzo's marriage could not be considered dissolved until the convent gate was barred behind Margherita and she was truly dead to the world. So he gently advised her to sample this life which

was so repugnant to her and proposed to her, in order that she
might feel sure of herself, to come to Milan and spend some time
with the nuns of San Paolo. She would be quite free, it was
understood, to think things over at her leisure. The offer once
again proves the excellence of the Cardinal's psychology. It was
true that, for Margherita, to leave Parma meant abandoning the
field; but she saw in the journey an opportunity of leaving rooms
in whose every corner there lurked a murdered hope. So she
accepted the invitation with some joy, which found expression
in her lighthearted choice of pages to attend her to Milan. Yet
even now that she had put herself entirely in the Cardinal's hands,
her repugnance to a forced withdrawal from the world and her
attachment to life pulsated so strongly within her that, when on
the 26th May, 1583, her Mantuan courtiers accompanied her to
Lodi to the house of Signora Ersilia Farnese Borromeo, she was
unable to maintain to the end the prudent demeanour that had
been enjoined upon her. All her ladies and gentlemen-in-waiting,
her pages and servants, were around her to bid her farewell as she
climbed into her carriage, assuring her in confused words of farewell of their affection for her. She distinguished the broad accent
of Mantua and from it rapidly called up a presence. She wept
softly, bitterly but without sobs. 'Well done,' said Cavriani with
cruel admiration; with his report he brought to an end his office
as gentleman-in-waiting. Her tears were already a commemoration of something long past.

Vincenzo was well aware of the melancholy and drama of
Margherita's story, but his pity for his wife was tinged with the
irritation men experience when they feel their manhood mortified. We may add that his unreal marriage had brought him none
of the advantages he had expected—neither a more independent
way of life nor help from his new relations, who united in hating
him, nor a larger share in his father's confidence. On the contrary,
his father persisted in keeping him in check. The only weapon
Vincenzo could use against the Duke's determination to restrain

and immure him was rebellion; it was one which was all the more persuasive when used with destructive violence. In the end the inner ferment, which he himself stirred up, shut him off in a kind of feverish delirium and would not allow him to listen to any voice, however winning. Cardinal Borromeo had reason to learn this a few days before leaving Parma when he had to have the young man medically examined once again because of some quibbling doubts on the part of the Farneses.

The second meeting between the prince and the Cardinal took place in Reggio, Hippolita's town. It is unfortunate that we have no detailed record of these days, for Vincenzo was extremely inattentive and impatient with the Cardinal—almost certainly because of Hippolita—and slipped away to a masked ball as soon as he could, leaving Marcello Donati and Zibramonti to look for him and lead him back to the interview.

At this time Vincenzo was very friendly with a certain young nobleman, called Ippolito Lanzoni, who was the most senseless libertine in all Mantua, given to wild impulses and always ready to use his sword and dagger. Vincenzo cultivated this elegant ruffian and was constantly giving him beautiful clothes from his own wardrobe—and not only clothes but jewels as well and buttons set with rubies, diamonds and pearls. The adventures of the two young men do not bear repetition and even Vincenzo must have realized that they passed all bounds, for every so often he promised to break with Lanzoni. But when he was suffocating in his father's vice-like grip, his companion's tonic humour was so essential to him that he ended by recalling him to his side. It now required only the stimulus of hostility on someone's part to make Vincenzo's rebellion crystallize into revolt.

At this point there falls into place one of the most notorious episodes of late sixteenth-century Italy—one which has continued to be discussed from that day to this. But the disputants have never been able to explain it for they have been too much caught up in polemics. For those of us, however, who are following the inner development of Vincenzo's personality it is so clear that we shall not require to waste many words on it.

Round about the year 1580 an archangel, albeit a treacherous
one, had reached Italy from Scotland, taking in Paris on his
flight. Both his parentage and place of birth were known. He
had been born at Elliot, the son of Lord Robert Crichton, and
was himself called James Crichton—a name which, the moment
he crossed the Alps, was Italianized into 'Critonio' with the
addition of the epithet 'admirable'. All the Italian humanists
swore by this wonderfully handsome young man of twenty—this
horseman, gymnast and dancer, whose head was crammed with
Elizabethan poetical conceits, vaporous philosophy and studies of
the occult and of chivalry, whose powers perhaps lay rather in a
mechanical memory than in any lyrical gift, who knew ten
languages and many dialects. They swore by him but they were
surpassed in enthusiasm by the Venetian nobleman, Alvise Cornaro, who gave him not only trust but credit, money and
hospitality—all in a blaze of friendship. Moreover he set himself
to enlist the aid of others since the young Scot, for all his virtues,
had come to Italy in search of a livelihood with neither money,
bag nor baggage. From Venice they succeeded in finding him a
post through the good offices of Annibale Cappello, who commended him to the Duke of Mantua as an ornament for his court.
From a man like Guglielmo one might have expected a refusal;
instead he not only took Crichton into his service but immediately appointed him his privy councillor, allotted him a salary
and set out to make him his favourite. But for that time proved
too short.

Crichton, in whom we may recognize a rare type of adventurer endowed with an icy intellect, arrived in Mantua at the
beginning of 1582—in February. A month sufficed him to explore
the situation and to succeed in acquiring mastery over Duke
Guglielmo, who, listening to him, truly enjoyed himself—perhaps
for the first time in his life. To engage in theological and philosophical debates with the Duke's most polished councillors was
for this youth a mere game to be played on intellectual themes
with fantastic variations which the Ciceronians of the court were
hard put to follow. Not so the Duke, with his extremely subtle

mind, who loved to see his courtiers start when Crichton spoke of that 'demon Socrates' or that 'madman Homer'. With the Duke, Crichton discussed politics, music and architecture, and discoursed on heraldry, overlaying with the arabesques of his imagination the fiddling, boring realities of etiquette—those questions of precedence, coats of arms and titles, which were Guglielmo's mania—and extracting from them, as if by magic, a flavour of intelligence. To all this he added a patient gift of adulation; because of his very coldness he was able to put it into words and launch himself into feats of verbal juggling. We will not stop to speculate on the equivocal element in Crichton or on the echo it found in the deep ambiguities of the Duke's nature. Let us, without dwelling on it, bear in mind, as a signpost to guide us in the darkness of their secret inclinations, the trial which was later rigged to trap a friar from a Mantuan convent who had accused the Duke of dark leanings and worse. Certainly there existed between these two men, otherwise so dissimilar, a bond of understanding which was perhaps not merely recognition of mutual esteem.

The Scot stayed in Mantua during February and March 1582. Then he returned to Venetian territory, asking his protector, Alvise Cornaro, for permission to withdraw to the Villa Codinico to 'look to his soul'. Why he should have found this spiritual exercise difficult in Mantua, packed as it was with monasteries and friars, we do not know. Perhaps those people who in secret smiled sardonically over the reasons for his absence were right. Cornaro, for his part, delighted that his protégé had been accepted by a man as difficult to please as Guglielmo Gonzaga, opened up the villa for him, provided him with court dress and lent him money.

In May, when Crichton returned to Mantua, he found that the air was full of shadows. Only a few days passed and he had to make complaint to the Duke's councillors against a gentleman who let slip no occasion of mocking him and was speaking ill of him to the Duke himself. If we note that the Scot's manner when denouncing his rival was restrained, not to say respectful, this will be another reason—over and above the logic of the case—for identifying him with Vincenzo Gonzaga.

May came to an end and the situation deteriorated. The Scot was enjoying increasing favour. Vincenzo's rancour had contrived to fuse into hatred, for it was continually blown upon by Lanzoni, who was always blustering on the subject and full of hints and threats. But the ducal councillors reassured Crichton as to his rival's intentions and the adventurer, although still on his guard, made an attempt to launch into a lucrative mode of life. He trafficked with certain mysterious phials containing oils and liquors. He opened and held back certain letters given to him for delivery. He incurred debts and swore he would pay them all. And when it was to his advantage—for example, with his friend Cornaro—he abased himself with high-flown expressions of adoration which did not ring true. The Venetian was right when he later declared bitterly: 'In his heart of hearts he did not truly have regard for anyone.'

At the end of June, Duke Guglielmo was at Goito, where he had lately begun to have a great villa built high above the Mincio, full of colour and paintings but 'without wanton pleasures', as he told the decorators, censuring with a frown the amorous pictorial license of the villas of Marmirolo and del Te. The villa at Goito was to have seemly heraldic paintings—among others the famous series of paintings by Tintoretto on the military exploits of the Gonzagas—four storeys and four chapels. That summer work went on apace under Guglielmo's vigilant eye. The ducal councillors, including Crichton, had remained in the city.

On the evening of the 3rd July, Vincenzo Gonzaga and his favourite, Ippolito Lanzoni, left the castle saying that they were going to visit their friend, Valeriano Cattaneo. It was a night of full moon. On these nights some of the bewitched origin of Mantua lurks in the shadows, which are marked off as clearly as if the moonlight had cut them. They are not compact and velvety zones of rest but are black and sink deep into the earth and invite one to listen to summons from afar. Out of the depths there rises a chill foreboding. The two young men were alone and without retinue. Lightly clad, with their caps cocked over their brows, they feigned to be walking idly but there was a well-defined purpose in their steps. That was clear from the little round shield each carried on his left arm—the famous buckler which figures in all seventeenth-century ambushes.

They went down towards the Piazza del Purgo. At the corner they took the road which ran towards San Silvestro. There they saw a man coming towards them by himself, tall of stature and with an easy stride. His face was covered by his cape. It was Crichton. We cannot believe Vincenzo, who was later to declare that he did not recognize him—that indeed he had taken him for one of his gentlemen, Baldassare Langosco. Certainly they expected to meet Crichton—so much so that they had no sooner caught sight of him than they made swiftly towards him and jostled him hard. 'In jest,' Vincenzo said later. He had vented his ill-temper and passed on. But the man they had jostled realized to the full the insult which lay behind the jest. Then he felt all his icy resentment rise to the surface and with it that contempt for others which was the basis of his real nature. Unsheathing his sharp, thin dagger—an arm banned by the law—he turned and, since the prince was already two paces away, plunged it to the hilt into Lanzoni's back.

Lanzoni started, whirled quickly round, raising his buckler to shield his face, and took to his sword. Then he began to sway. Mortally wounded, he leant on the wall while Vincenzo set upon their assailant with his gilded rapier. The other defended himself but was unable to withstand the prince's onslaught and fell pierced through. Then, recognizing Vincenzo—for although he had probably guessed who inspired the provocation he had not imagined that the young Gonzaga had come in person to take part in the brawl—he begged him with his failing breath: 'Your Highness, I did not recognize you, pardon me and grant me my life.'

'I left him,' Vincenzo was to relate, 'and turned to my companion, who could scarcely stand on his feet and, when I tried to support him, fell.' In the Mantua of Guglielmo Gonzaga the shadows were full of monkish magic and Vincenzo had merely to lift his eyes to discover two Capuchins waiting there, deep in meditation. He called to them to commend the soul of the dying man to God, and soon after Ippolito Lanzoni was dead. Meantime, wounded and losing blood—it was thick and dark in the moonlight—Crichton had taken to his heels and disappeared. Too good a swordsman not to know that he had struck a mortal blow, Vincenzo bade them call his pages and gentlemen and made a show of fearing that Lanzoni's assassin might have fled and might reach safety. He did more—he went personally to the captain of the castle, Luigi Olivo, and asked him to post men on the banks of the lake to prevent Crichton from swimming to safety.

'He won't be able to escape now because he is dead,' said the captain of the castle coldly. He had learned that the Scot, after going some way on foot, had had himself carried into a pharmacist's and had there breathed his last like a good Christian; for in his case, too, there had been friars to absolve him. Olivo added the sort of remark a 'humble servant' may allow himself, including a few severe words for the prince; for Vincenzo had felt he must excuse himself, saying that he had not recognized the Scot, whereas the latter had certainly recognized him. There was this amount of truth in it—that he, the only heir of the Gonzagas, had run the risk of falling under Crichton's terrible dagger. And it was also true that a gentleman, Lanzoni, was dead. When Vincenzo recalled his friend he seemed to go out of his way to express his grief in an insincere, contemptuous tone. By piling up empty bombast he tried to keep at bay the very human fear of a man who has seen another die at his side.

From Goito, Guglielmo stormed at his son. He would have him tried, he would have him sentenced in spite of his rank. He called the captain of justice, gave orders for the facts to be reconstructed and sentence to be passed impartially. (The captain said Yes but knew already how he would get out of it.) And he sent off an angry letter to Marcello Donati.

This letter strikes one as a strange document. Certainly the father had reason to be incensed with his son but his anger, instead of progressing from the minor to the major heads of the accusation, mounts with an inhuman logic, at once cerebral and coldly abstract. Among the charges which Guglielmo enumerates are that Vincenzo has stained his hands with blood and that he had committed a crime against one of the ducal councillors. But these are as nothing compared with a further crime, namely, that having given his word of honour no longer to keep company with Lanzoni, he should have taken him as his companion on an adventure which was to become the talk of the whole city. Who, Guglielmo insists, will place trust now on his princely word? Who, indeed, if his father, out of the contempt he feels for his son, is tempted to feel himself involved in the guilt merely because he gave him life?

When the letter arrived from the Duke, Donati was in bed feigning illness. From his bed he replied most skilfully, rising in Vincenzo's defence in the only manner possible—by explaining what sort of a man he was. Undoubtedly the youth had gone too far but did the Duke not feel that it was a barbarous thing to reply to a jostling with a stab? Yet what else could they expect from Vincenzo, abandoned as he was to idleness and bad company? So from being accuser Duke Guglielmo found himself being accused. So clearly did he see that he had been caught out that he proceeded to defend himself to the secretary. Thus Donati became the arbiter of the situation. He directed Vincenzo how to behave. He made him write measured letters in which he recounted the event with decorous grief. He made him consent to the investigations of the captain of justice. The latter's conclusions were that it was a casual brawl and the prince was absolved.

People said that Duke Guglielmo and his councillors had aimed to banish Vincenzo from Mantua for a year and that, hearing of this, the prince had broken into the house of the First Councillor and put him to the sword; for the populace had been thrown into a state of excitement by the flash of daggers and was already spinning events into a tragic romance. Undoubtedly Vincenzo was uneasy. His father's ill-framed accusations, which had not touched him where he was truly at fault but had made of his crime a point of honour, helped to put him on the wrong path. That hint of the equivocal in the dead men—not only in Crichton but in Lanzoni as well—drove him further and further away from any warm expression of remorse. Since he was unable to absorb the facts and make them a part of the stuff of experience he tore them to pieces in his heart in order to forget them. At the end of July he could bear it no longer. We find a last echo in an oblique letter to Zibramonti, the ducal councillor, in which he restated not his affection for his dead comrade but the right to choose the company he liked best. He asked to be allowed to leave the city and that no one should ever again speak of what had happened. So he set out for Ferrara to clear matters up with his sister and from there went on to Colorno, where the consolations of the Countess of Sala awaited him.

He was received with the usual festivities; indeed they were, if anything, more lavish than ever. Although after Vincenzo's marriage both his son and his daughter-in-law, Margherita Farnese, had pressed him to do so, the Duke of Mantua had refused to hear of re-admitting to his favour a woman who had merely to make her appearance to deny the very grounds of his existence. Thus the feud between Guglielmo and the Countess continued. We do not know if Vincenzo's Hippolita was at Colorno at this time but certainly, in one way or another, and particularly by a method of her own, Barbara led the young prince to find himself again. She was one of those women who do not fear bloodstains on a man's hands. Their spirit derives its strength from the conviction that every man is subject either to the brutal reactions of instinct or the arid reactions of logic, and that if he is to attain a harmonious pattern of life he must some-how have a woman's help. At Colorno Vincenzo's crime was dis-entangled, thanks to the interpretation of his own character which the Countess was able to offer the murderer. In conversation with him she recapitulated his story in which he figured as neglected son, mortified husband and man without office. She ran over

events, toning them down, until she had made of them an intelligible succession of human adventures. In the end Vincenzo
seemed to understand himself clearly. His was the story of a man
who reserves all his rights for the future, of a man who has
suffered persecution. Once this definition had been reached the
instincts which had urged him to flee from himself and from
Mantua disappeared, one by one. Her woman's hand, skilled in
compromises, brought him back from moral horror to reconciliation with life and the two dead men were left there in the bewitched moonlight, futile and forgotten.

In September 1583, Margherita Farnese returned to Parma
with such a joyous face that the people said 'she has won'. In
fact she had yielded to the idea of the convent, so one might say
that she had lost everything—that she went about relieved and
smiling in a trance of inner freedom like a person who has been
freed from everything, including hope. But that would be going
too far. To tell the truth Margherita had had a surprise. At the
very moment of capitulation, when she thought she must renounce any fresh burgeoning of feeling, she had realized that
convent life might equal that of the court—that, indeed, being
more mysterious and less cruel, it would offer compensations at
least as great as those she had renounced. All it required was a
little courage, a little imagination, and she would find them.

Perhaps it was her sixteen years which consoled her rather than
the company into which the iron piety of San Carlo Borromeo
had thrust her. Certainly she had responded fittingly to the
invitations which the Milanese nuns had extended to her with so
many sugared refinements. What a miracle it was, for instance, to
see the humiliating cause of her suffering become a sign of election
or to see all these women, some of them with famous, ancient
names, cast themselves at her feet and offer her authority over
them like a sceptre. The daughter of Alessandro Farnese, the
niece of Margaret of Austria, the great-granddaughter of
Charles V, could not refuse command. The woman in her,

however lacking in cunning, guessed instinctively that she could use this privilege to build up a life of her own. She would be able to reduce the whole world, as if it were a spectacle, to the level of those theatrical and choreographic visions which had used to please her so much. She herself would stand apart untouched by the pangs of suffering. We know little of her as a nun, but it is typical of her that, in 1623, forty years after these events, the leading lady of a company of actors called her her protectress and dedicated to her a devout play. Yet something of herself continued to live and act and from that fragile, mortified being an implacable ghost was one day to be conjured up.

CHAPTER FOUR

The Amorous Test

ON the 30th October, 1583, the wife of Vincenzo Gonzaga, having changed her name to that of Sister Maura Lucenia, took the veil and made her vows into the hands of San Carlo Borromeo, who had journeyed down on purpose from Milan to Parma. So she entered the convent of San Paolo where, in the Abbess's room, Correggio had painted the story of Diana with such a swift, smiling sense of youth that mythology itself was created anew. Watched over by her brother Ranuccio's gloomy love, Margherita was to live in the convent more than sixty years and die in 1643, a very old woman, thus outliving all the personages of this story, for by then not only Vincenzo Gonzaga but all his children, too, would be dead and over Mantua, sacked and ravaged by the plague, there would reign the detested line of the French Gonzagas, the descendants of Ludovico, Duke of Nevers.

Thus it would profit Duke Guglielmo nothing that he had outwitted a woman by such astute manœuvres—nor Vincenzo that he had sacrificed not only love but the moral duty of recognizing himself in another's suffering. He was to pay dearly for the fastidious shrug with which, when faced with the stubborn problem, he struck out of his mind even the pity of it. He began to pay at once, for when Margherita had been removed and was securely in their grasp, the Farneses would take her side against the Gonzagas.

We can imagine what was said in Parma between the fourteen-year-old Ranuccio and his Farnese grandfather. Needless to say the blame for Margherita's plight had been cast on her husband's physique. There had been so much gossip so eagerly spread abroad that everyone in Italy was commenting on the case. In fact, too much so. Thus, hardly had the question of a divorce from Margherita Farnese been broached and hardly had Duke Guglielmo in great haste reopened the marriage negotiations with the daughter of Francesco dei Medici, than the Grand Duchess Bianca Cappello remembered the contemptuous things Gonzaga had said of her three years before when he had indicated to Archduke Ferdinand of Austria that she was the reason for his reluctance to become related to the Medicis. Bianca remembered and that meant that Francesco, too, remembered, and although a marriage between Leonora and Vincenzo Gonzaga now seemed an extremely good match, they both contrived to force Mantua into it with a gesture of contempt.

Certainly such contempt seemed justified. While Margherita Farnese was still undecided, still overcome with terror at the thought of the convent, secret correspondence was already passing between Cardinal Cesi, the legate at Bologna, and the Court of Florence. The Cardinal, who was eager to show his zeal for the Medici house, collected evidence of Vincenzo's presumed physical deficiencies and sent them off, embroidered with anecdotes and sources. The Grand Duke and his Duchess read them, commented and meditated on them—Francesco with that way he had of continually turning things to and fro in his mind, spinning them with a silkworm's slow industry, and Bianca with her hasty yet intelligent fashion of interpreting events and reading her own reactions into them, ready and waiting for her hour to come. And it was not only from Florence but from Pratolino and Poggio a Caiano, spots whose mere names awaken in the reader's mind something bright and shimmering behind these old letters so that we feel the Tuscan sky stretch overhead like an airy canopy to shelter our limpid dreams, that the despatches began to come in one after another, full of excitements.

In November 1583, when Margherita was no longer even mentioned, negotiations between the Gonzagas and the Medicis were in the hands of two prelates, Cardinal Cesi, and Zibramonti, that arid man who was Bishop of Alba and councillor to the Duke of Mantua. It was the Cardinal's duty to state—with some attempt on his part to gloss over the words—that there was no way round it. In Florence they wished to be materially certain of the husbandly qualities of the young prince. Zibramonti reported this to Mantua, where the Duke had to submit to discuss the matter and suggest as witnesses the companions Vincenzo normally chose for his escapades.

One of the most constant of these was Don Cesare d'Este. He and his father, Don Alfonso, the son of Laura Dianti and Alfonso I, Duke of Ferrara, were the first to be brought forward by the Medicis. Both men were bound to the Florentine house by bonds of the closest· friendship, which was not without a political basis; for, seeing that the direct line of the Estes was about to die out in the person of his nephew, the Duke of Ferrara, Alfonso hoped the dukedom might fall to his son. He knew that the transfer was strongly opposed by the Papacy, which was unshakeably determined to recover the territory of Ferrara—it was in the gift of the Popes—and equally determined not to recognize the legitimate marriage, now of long standing, between Alfonso I and Laura Dianti. He hoped, however, that if he were linked to the Medicis the power of that family might help him when the moment came for the delicate operation. To this end he was negotiating the marriage of his own son, Don Cesare, with Virginia, one of the Grand Duke's sisters. At the same time, secretly and without arousing the suspicion of the Duke of Ferrara, he maintained close ties with the Medicis' ambassador at Ferrara, with whom he shared all the secrets of the ducal court.

Don Alfonso, a typical incarnation of the sixteenth-century nobleman with grand manners and an astute, sinuous mind, was a man on whom the Grand Duke knew he could count. In case of need he would, to help the Medicis, express pessimistic views on the subject of the Prince of Mantua. So when on the 11th December, 1583, Don Cesare's testimony was despatched from Ferrara—'finding myself unable for the debt upon my conscience to fail to testify such things as I know of His Most Serene Highness, the

Lord Prince of Mantua, I hereby declare and testify, etc., etc.'—
such positive evidence from an individual who had, on more than
one occasion, accompanied the young Gonzaga on amorous
expeditions should have sufficed. Such at least was the opinion
Cardinal Cesi expressed when he transmitted the testimony to the
Medicis along with the statement, which sounded somewhat
incongruous in such a letter, that 'it is clear for all to see that this
marriage is the will of God'. Duke Guglielmo, for his part,
judiciously pointed out to Florence that the accusation came from
a corrupt source—the ducal palace at Parma. They should, he suggested, be chary of giving it credence. The Duke, moreover,
stated that he was ready to sign the marriage contract and added
this clause—that, whatever might happen, he undertook to maintain his daughter-in-law in Mantua and treat her like the great
princess she was.

The Grand Duke Francesco was not one of the great men of
his family. Although his political judgment had consistency and
sureness, for it derived from his father's excellent school, it was
incapable of expansion in time and space and was directed not so
much to new adventures as to safeguarding the gains made by
Cosimo I. He had able ministers to help and the good sense to
let them work in their own way; but the power of the Medicis,
which in these last years of the sixteenth century was still intact
and a great force in the peninsula, had lost momentum. It was
the prisoner of its own formulae and already on the brink of
decadence.

Dark-complexioned, sinewy and taciturn, withdrawn behind a
courtesy which was sober beyond reproach, Francesco might have
given the impression of being a man who transmuted words into
deeds—a sage. But his glance betrayed him. Quick to catch at
images, it discarded them when he had scarcely begun to understand them. The distortion, the error with which he saw himself
surrounded—as if the world were perpetually out of focus—lay,
in fact, in his own mind, which was darkened by hereditary

traits, particularly on the side of his Spanish mother, that unhappy graft on to the Florentine stem. The chronic twists in his temperament were revealed by his strange diet of sweetmeats, stuffed with juniper, pepper and spices, and his leanings towards alchemy and magic, which he shared with other princes of the time, but which he alternately praised and condemned, even mocking them in cold-blooded jests when the humour took him. He would suddenly shut himself off and take refuge in deep hermetic silences from which he was capable of re-emerging by unexpected paths—through a love of the land, for instance, tender and wise to a degree. No one knew better than he how to cultivate dwarf shrubs and little trees bearing sweet lemons or rosebushes which his own hand tended or transplanted. He loved his family and his daughters in particular, but the various disconnected phases of his existence merged and became an active life only when he allowed himself to be caught in the irresistible net of Bianca Cappello's Venetian smiles.

When he looked into her eyes, he lost himself in their magic blue where, after so many years, he still seemed to see a dancing gleam of amorous folly. So he declared Don Cesare's testimony to be insufficient to guarantee fullness of life for his daughter in the future. He wished, he went on to explain, to take certain precautions, because the friendship between the Gonzagas and the Medicis must not be disturbed—that would be too painful to him. In fact, however, the insult to the Gonzagas was an offering to Bianca to cancel out the offence she had endured at the hands of Mantua years before. Duke Guglielmo and his son swallowed it, since swallow it they must. In order to make them feel his wife's power to the full, Francesco further directed that the marriage negotiations be carried out directly between the Mantuan court and Bianca. She would dictate the settlements and sign them. In the bonds dated the 6th January, 1584, and signed by her we find the bitter condition that the marriage between Leonora and Vincenzo would take place only when he had put himself to the proof.

At last the scandalous word had been uttered. Bandied from

court to court, it drew to Mantua and Florence the attention of all Italy, not to say of all Europe. After all, said the Grand Duke—and he felt he was making things very simple—it merely required 'the choice of a young woman' whom the Prince would visit one evening. Don Alfonso d'Este was ready to arrange the meeting and make all the necessary dispositions. The Grand Duke would bestow an ample dowry on the girl and the meeting would take place in Ferrara with all possible secrecy.

But it was Carnival and speech was very free behind the masks. The network of talk and intrigue was spun in the morning in the vegetable market, where masked ladies and gentlemen met in accordance with an old Ferrarese carnival custom to buy provision for their festivities; it was developed during the day and later still, in the evening, at balls and dinners, the various stages of the affair followed each other like parts of a long novel.

The name of the girl selected was going the rounds. It seemed that she was one of the daughters of Pirro Ligorio, the architect with the imagination worthy of Ariosto, who had given the name of Cardinal Ippolito d'Este to the famous villa at Tivoli. He had given freely of himself with the daring imagination of a builder and the painstaking skill of an antiquarian. The end of it all had been that his widow, a woman of good reputation, and her virtuous daughters, were reduced to living on charity scarcely four months after his death. So poor and miserable were they, these women, that for them the shameful role would have meant great good fortune. Apparently they refused, for soon after there is no more mention of them but only of a little plaster saint of a girl whose habit it was to kneel all day with her rosary in her hand and whose virtue was guaranteed a hundred times over. She had been brought out of a convent and put in a country house by Don Alfonso d'Este along with various matrons and attendants. There she awaited her fate.

The vision of this innocent young creature made the hot blood of the men of Ferrara turn cold beneath their masks. Meanwhile, on the 3rd January, Vincenzo arrived in Ferrara. He ran through the streets in masquerade and basked in the feminine warmth of his sister's court. His mere presence was the signal for balls and junketings. In the evening he danced and gambled and even lost heavily—four thousand gold crowns in one throw. But this was of no importance to him compared with what he felt he had won through his marriage into the Medici family. He talked unceasingly of his nuptials and invited to them all the gentlemen of his court and all his friends. Meanwhile the Florentine ambassador, always on the alert, tightened his lips and murmured, 'Has he forgotten the conditions?' The 16th January came and from then on things went badly. On the 20th everything was ready—four waiting-women, four matrons, the girl and the guards—but no agreement could be reached on the question because Vincenzo did not feel disposed to abide by the limit of three hours laid down by the Grand Duke. Don Alfonso d'Este feigned deep sorrow but was unable to alter by a jot the rules he had received from Florence. When reporting his conversation with Vincenzo to the Florentine ambassador he made a great parade of impartiality, but frowned at the same time with a perplexed and thoughtful air. The ambassador made things worse by reporting all this in his despatches, thus provoking a reaction from Francesco dei Medici, who could not get over his astonishment and indeed almost took it as an affront that a young man of twenty did not accept any condition and any time limit without more ado. Things dragged on so long that a quarrel broke out. Waiting-women, matrons, and guards were all dismissed. The plaster saint was put back in her convent and disappears from our story. The prince, too, went off and shut himself up in a monastery. In Ferrara, where the Countess of Sala had just arrived with two exquisitely beautiful companions, the Duchess Margherita confided between one ball and another that her brother had gone to live with the friars to have them deal with his ill-humour. She turned the whole thing into a joke, insisting on trying to make it appear as if the joke were on the side of the Gonzagas. But she did not altogether succeed in averting the hail of malicious gossip.

How Marfisa d'Este, the fairest and sharpest-tongued lady of the court, thought up a malicious little story about truffles and

who should eat them, how very amusing but hardly seemly jokes
went the rounds about affairs in Mantua and how all this talk
made the Carnival more brilliant and more luxurious at Vincenzo's expense—all this the Florentine ambassador relates, adding
a measure of spice of his own making. In Mantua all this gossip
was resented as a perpetual insult. Duke Guglielmo, realizing that
he must be the petitioner, sent envoys to Florence as fast as their
horses could carry them to ask for audience with Bianca Cappello.
She was most affable, fair-haired and in high spirits, and she
allowed herself the satisfaction of charming them; but in the end
she said that, without proof, nothing could be settled. On the
other hand, since there had been all this gossip and since it was
quite obvious that third parties had been embroidering things
further, the whole affair would be settled within the family circle.
The Grand Duke would pick the girl in Florence and they would
arrange the meeting in a safe spot, such as Venice. The men in
charge of the mission would be Marcello Donati, Vincenzo's
secretary, and Belisario Vinta from Volterra, one of the Grand
Duke's leading ministers.

Meeting him thus without previous knowledge of him, one
might be tempted to look on Belisario Vinta with a certain suspicion. The *désinvolture* with which he assumes the direction of
the intrigue strikes one as too facile, too smooth, his nature as
being too dry and ironical not to suggest the word cynicism.
Yet this man, who was one of the most powerful figures in the
Florence of the Grand Dukes and constantly in office as minister
and chancellor, while he had a mind as subtle as a razor, combined
with it an almost tangible sense of Tuscan realism, which always
came to his aid when the moment arrived to translate his abstract
schemes into human terms. It must be added that he reduced all
his powers to a common denominator—the political advantage of
his prince and his state.

Just as for an artist any object may become the centre of a
whole universe, so for Belisario Vinta any political situation,

however trivial, was a problem to be stated, thought over and solved. He concentrated as hard and applied himself with as much effort to the results of an embassy to the court of Catherine dei Medici in France as to the despatch of certain types of grain from Sicily. As soon as Francesco dei Medici had appointed him for the task, he applied himself to presiding over the troublesome affair of the Gonzaga marriage.

'I feel sorry for him, seeing him involved in an intrigue so contrary to his nature,' wrote his friend and rival at court, the minister Antonio Serguidi. But Belisario, who had stifled any personal feeling of impatience and was already quite at his ease, sceptical and patient, had gone round all the charitable institutions in Florence and been disgusted to find only 'mangy, ill-favoured girls'. At last, in the foundling hospital, he discovered two pretty ones. 'To tell the truth,' he remarked, 'they are more remarkable for their florid bodies than their angelic faces. But,' he adds, and here we can catch the hiss of his voice, 'they are just what we need for our purpose.'

About this time Marcello Donati, who had been invited to inspect the girl, arrived from Mantua. In court circles there was great distrust of the Mantuan secretary—indeed, Francesco dei Medici, warned by someone whom Marcello's intelligent ways had made suspicious, sent a despatch to Vinta from Leghorn, warning him about this man who seemed to be 'very close and difficult'. We can imagine how Vinta's intellectual curiosity was whetted at the thought of encountering a difficult opponent. For him, the time of waiting was almost like a long ambush.

Marcello Donati arrived on the 6th March, a day of deep mourning at court. His private coach met the funeral in the street —the funeral of Princess Anna dei Medici, who had died in her first youth, much lamented by her sisters, Leonora and Maria, but less so by her father, who had not stirred from Leghorn, perhaps because he was impatient to see her end. Marcello, who was not so sceptical as to overlook the human awkwardness of such a melancholy coincidence, took note of it and dedicated to it a

philosophical sigh. Then he began his conversations with Vinta.
Each delighted to recognize in the other a man of the same race,
a man of intellect and loyalty—except where interests of state were
concerned.

'Your Highness need not fear,' Vinta reported at once to the
Grand Duke, 'this Donati is a man with his wits about him,
practical and eloquent but in no way false—besides, we shall be
on our guard.' But there was no need. Vinta tried to launch into
an extremely clever speech on the beauty and virtues of Leonora,
which were such that there was no protecting her from fine offers of
marriage. 'And what of us at Mantua?' said Donati, running over
the names of all the princesses his Lord could have married. But
after all these panegyrics, which both parties recited in a detached
manner, the Mantuan invited the Florentine minister to listen to
a statement, based on the simple truth, which would clear up the
whole matter. This wedding must take place, he said, and the fact
that it was upsetting so many people—Spain, France, Ferrara and
Parma—was another reason for bringing it to a quick conclusion.
Certainly the Spaniards were not overpleased at the alliance
between the Gonzagas and the Medicis because they would like
to see the princes of Italy disunited, weak and vassals of Spain; on
the other hand, the French were putting pressure on Vincenzo
and trying to lure him with the promise of high honours—they
were offering him the daughter of the Duke of Lorraine, a relative
of the King, because they wished to have, in the Duke of Mantua,
a partisan of France; and Vincenzo, who did not give much
thought to the interests of the state, would not be above satisfying
these whims. The Duke of Ferrara had no great love for his
brother-in-law and would willingly style himself his lord and
master. The Farneses, as everyone knew, could not be on friendly
terms with him because of what had happened over Margherita,
etc., etc. 'I say all this,' Donati went on, 'to show that one must
not give heed to gossip from outside and, since we lack neither
the means nor the intelligence, let us try to clear things up as far
as possible between us.'

The directness of the speech pleased Vinta, who willingly

adopted the same language. So the two ministers, while pursuing the interests of their respective masters, reached full agreement. But when the Mantuan asked to be allowed even a glimpse of the princess, because he had been charged by Vincenzo to make a detailed report on her beauty, Vinta was quick to reply Yes, of course, but unfortunately the princess was on the point of leaving for Leghorn, where her father had summoned her in an attempt to distract her from her grief over the death of her sister, Anna. They could see her without being seen, Donati suggested, while she was getting into her carriage. Vinta made a show of agreeing and meantime gave orders to the princess's majordomo to bring forward her departure. They should leave Florence before dawn. The reason he gave to the Grand Duke was that the princess, being so grief-stricken, would have seemed too pale and thin in the eyes of so keen a judge.

Meanwhile the girl who had been chosen for the test was being decked out. She was a girl of twenty-one, tall, of medium build, with a good figure and a face—it was no common one—which her coiffure and her elegant dress made even more refined. She was modest and bashful but of a lively disposition, a bastard of the Albizzi family. Her name was Giulia. They gave her a dress of coloured silk with embroidered cuffs and collar. She combed and smoothed her hair and presented herself to Donati, who, after looking her over and murmuring that he could have wished her to be better looking, declared that she would do. The appointment was fixed. While the secretary returned to Mantua, the Florentine party prepared to leave the city.

Duke Guglielmo followed events step by step from Mantua but, learning that he was being criticized by the Papal court for planning to make a mortal sin precede the sacrament, he thought it better, after managing the affair in its initial stages, to wash his hands of all moral responsibility. Saying that the matter was too delicate for his conscience, he thrust all decisions upon his son and with a steady, icy gaze, in the depths of which there was a glow-

worm spark of envy, he watched Vincenzo throw himself headlong into the affair.

Vincenzo, for his part, continued to lay bare his character. He
had no suspicion of his father's malignity but discussed and
accepted the conditions, not in the least cast down and confident
of excellent results. To him the Medicis' request, which, in the
opinion of the French ambassador, was an insult, was merely a
challenge. The fact that he accepted it not only on the physical
but on the moral plane, without feeling anything akin to shame,
is an indication of how unguardedly he lived; he was thus prevented from bringing to fruition the good and intelligent impulses which even Belisario Vinta recognized in him.

Gaily Vincenzo set off for Venice with a fine company of
gentlemen assembled under the discriminating gaze of his secretary, Donati. He was accompanied by a prudent relative, Carlo
Gonzaga, who in this story plays the part of the wise man and
sometimes of the tragic chorus. They left on a small but well-
built barge and were sailing down the Po towards Commacchio
when they encountered two mills, torn from the bank by the
force of the flood-waters, adrift on the river. 'A horrible encounter,' says Donati, who felt himself more than ever a reasonable creature when confronted with irrational nature. The
collision was severe. Cries of 'Jesus, save us' arose. The prince was
already preparing to dive overboard when the barge contrived to
slip between the mills and resume its quiet voyage.

On the morning of 5th April they arrived in Venice and took
up lodgings on the Grand Canal. Immediately the city wafted
from balcony to balcony murmurs, whispers and secret hints.
Vittorio Cappello, the brother of the Grand Duchess Bianca,
visited the prince to spy out the land, nor can it be denied that
he contrived to learn a certain amount. The ambassador of the
King of France did the same and he, too, managed to pick up
something from the hints and reticences of Vincenzo, who, in
order to enter into the spirit of the adventure, did not stint
piquant foods, oysters and special warm Lenten fare.

The Florentine party arrived on the 9th. Unlike the prince,

Giulia no longer ate or slept, for she was deep in the task of listening to and absorbing the instructions which Belisario Vinta imparted to her with precision and crude detachment. The minister, while protesting the difficulty of his task, watched the progressive effect of his instruction on his pupil. Already her timidity had become expectation; her virginal fear, curiosity. In the course of the journey, Giulia's glance had lost the clear light of innocence.

What a farce this journey had been! They had set out as private persons with Vinta masquerading as an ordinary citizen, without the decorations and badges of his office; but in the inns their hosts bowed low with a 'Cavaliere! Cavaliere!' for they recognized by his face the powerful minister of Florence. Naturally the sight of him in this odd company, with the pretty girl and the equivocal matron for escort, was a source of excitement to them all. How could he dispel the air of secret adventure which the company had about it? He had invented a story worthy of a Renaissance comedy, making it as pathetic and romantic as possible. This young girl, he told the innkeepers in feigned confidence, was the daughter of a friend of his, a German captain, and she had been born in Italy twenty years before. He even gave the captain's name—Freuchberger—and said he was anxiously waiting in Germany for this daughter he had never seen. At each stage in the journey the story became more elaborate. When they reached Venice it was so rounded and came so trippingly off the tongue that it was a pity to have to discard it.

Venice served well for this, as it does for all amorous intrigues. Truly there is no city in the world better fitted for these secret expeditions, declared Vinta, unbending with the ladies in the house by the Grand Canal which belonged to an agent of the Grand Duke. Then something unexpected occurred. The Florentine agent was at death's door and died that evening. Still almost warm, he was carried out of his house to the nearby church and the rooms were put in order, the setting prepared for the encounter. Belisario Vinta devoted excessive attention—indeed it went beyond the natural scruples of his office—to testing

the locks and shaking the doors to ensure that there was no deception. Perhaps the mood of caricature, of comedy, which he had
assumed on leaving Florence, still lingered on. He kept pondering
over a certain little terrace which he thought looked accessible,
measured the distance from the ground, and finally posted one of
his men in the neighbouring lane with the task of keeping watch
on the terrace, the windows, the doors, the roof and the whole
house.

The 11th April came. In the evening Vincenzo, given over to
a gay mood, disembarked at the house where the Florentines were
staying along with one of his gentlemen and Donati. In a mood of
confidence he undressed for the night, talking gaily and moving
about with all the lithe assurance of his fine young body. He
laughed and shut the door. Without, the Tuscan minister stood on
guard. He and Donati counted the hours.

Three hours. No sound broke the thick curtain of silence, and
minister and secretary were already consulting whether they ought
not to go and 'see how things were' when suddenly the door
opened and the young prince appeared, bent double and crying
out with pain. He wanted to go home, he cried out in a piercing
voice, he wanted to go home. He had been taken with his usual
colic, he added with difficulty while they brought him hot
flannels and Vinta congratulated himself on not having sent in
the supper which stood ready—there was no knowing what hints
might not have been made about poison. The prince had eaten
too much—in particular, too many oysters and too much carp—
and now he thought only of bed where he could suffer alone and
in peace. They set off. The gondola had scarcely swung round
from the side canal into the Grand Canal when Vinta went into
the room. The report was negative.

The days which followed were days of delirium for those
around Vincenzo Gonzaga. The prince was still suffering from
stomach-ache but even more from humiliation and depression.
His attendants moved around him with long gloomy faces.
Marcello Donati felt a wave of nausea and muttered for a moment
that it was quite clear even to him that God's will was manifestly

against the deed. Carlo Gonzaga was downright terrified. What was needed here, he insisted, was an exorcism carried out by a friar of great holiness and strong powers over the evil one. Had the malevolent presence not been demonstrated by various ill-omens? The good gentleman enumerated them. First of all, on his arrival at Florence, Donati had met a funeral, the funeral of Princess Anna, Leonora's sister. Secondly, on his arrival in Venice, Vinta had found a dead man in the house. Thirdly, on his way to Venice, the prince had run the risk of drowning in the Po. And other minor omens were not lacking. One had to have lost the light of one's eyes not to recognize the cloven hoof.

Whether he caught a whiff of sulphur or not, Vincenzo had lost his head. He was already giving up his Medici bride, and wrote to one of the Mantuan ministers to tell his father the whole story and make him decide whether he should or should not go on with this damnable test. Would it not be better to open marriage negotiations with the French ambassador for the daughter of the Duke of Lorraine? This was Duke Guglielmo's chance and he took it with both hands. A chance to lash out at his son and strike at his sexual vanity—he himself, after all, had been neglected by nature, was unhappy, blighted, hunchbacked. His reply was cold in the extreme. The Duke was determined not to meddle in the affair. He advised his son, however, to make a clear distinction between an odd bout of colic and his own powers. If the illness were an excuse, let him avoid it in future. As for the link with France, here Guglielmo rose up as a man of logic and as a politician. It seemed to him, he said sternly, that he was already involved in too much embarrassment with Parma and Florence without embarking on more with the King of France—so let Vincenzo renounce the thought of any pointless negotiations.

Even before this biting dispatch arrived, Marcello Donati had got back not only his patience but his energy and coolness of judgment. There was no other way out—the prince must be persuaded to return to the Florentine's lodging. Marcello felt his own responsibility in the matter. Indeed, to spur himself on, he indulged in an outburst of personal vanity. Had he not in Florence himself guaranteed the physical powers of his pupil? He remembered the exact words. And it was with words that he now put new life into the prince, urging him on to bawdy conversation, full of broad hints and encouragement to play the libertine. And meantime, while feeding him on light nourishing foods, he even agreed to the idea of the exorcizing priest. Why not? he explained coldly. If nothing else it would serve to reassure the young man and entertain him. His deliberate task of cultivating the prince's humours succeeded. On a carefully chosen evening, Vincenzo entered the lists. A quarter of an hour later, Vinta was called to bear witness to the evidence and was able to tell of a victorious encounter.

What was described as the greatest scandal of the sixteenth century was now over. The honour, not only of the Gonzagas, but of Lombardy, seemed to be restored in the eyes of all Italy as Marcello Donati said, bestowing on himself the title of 'most excellent bawd'. Given this result it can easily be imagined whether there was room for thought for the tiny, painful drama of Giulia weeping over herself under the gaze of the Florentine minister, Belisario Vinta, who almost forgot himself in invective against the way women's minds worked. For even he was incapable of seeing in those tears the disillusion of a woman revealed to herself. Everybody else was in high spirits. Carlo Gonzaga, delighted to see the wiles of the devil circumvented, even felt that his old complaint of gravel was cured from sheer pleasure. Marcello Donati presented the Florentines with confirmation of his pledges. Belisario Vinta heaved a sigh at having brought the affair to a conclusion favourable to the interests of his lord and master. The waiting-woman, like the old complacent creature she was, knew she had earned a substantial present. Even Giulia smiled in the end. They told her she would have a handsome dowry and a husband and it was certain that henceforth she would no longer lead a life of poverty. As for her future as a woman, she, too, would begin to lie and she had an opportunity to experiment successfully one evening when the prince visited her and fêted her greatly.

At Florence the Duke and Grand Duchess snatched Vinta's report from each other. 'Your despatch has restored our spirits, for the first you sent robbed us of all hope,' wrote Serguidi to Vinta, adding with the suspicion of a smile, 'Your excellency has done a deed which will truly put your name in the histories.' It is incredible how amused they had been in the Palazzo Vecchio over the story of the deed. With her vivid, sensual realism Bianca Cappello reconstructed the scenes described by the minister, and as she spoke, felt once more the keen urgings of the Venetian spring. Francesco dei Medici felt that his vanity was satisfied now that he had succeeded in imposing on a race as proud as the Gonzagas something so extraordinary—something 'truly unworthy, not only of princes, but even of commoners', and in the nature of his satisfaction he revealed his tortuous character and that unbridled secret brutality which even Bianca Cappello's blandishments had not succeeded in dispelling. So the marriage was decided on. And while the banns were being proclaimed in Mantua and a thanksgiving mass was being held in Sant'Andrea —Belisario Vinta was there, the pampered darling of the court— news of her forthcoming marriage was at last announced to Leonora in Florence and, without loss of time, they began fitting the gold and silver brocades.

Although he was somewhat affected by the ups and downs of the 'Congress of Venice' as the wits called the incident, Vincenzo was determined not to show the humiliation which lay behind his victory and he went about Mantua like a dandy, leaving it to Duke Guglielmo to see to the marriage agreements. The latter, casting an eye once more over the documents already signed, found a clause that needed changing. The contract said that, should the bride die, the dowry was to be returned to the Medicis in its entirety. Why in its entirety, asked the Duke, and suggested that the article be modified as follows—that, in the event of Leonora's death, half the dowry would go back to the Medicis and half would be retained by the Gonzagas.

Belisario Vinta bridled. That on the eve of the wedding, anyone could go back on agreements sealed and delivered seemed to him an insult. Cunning as he was, he understood immediately that the Duke wished to gain some practical advantage at least from his compliance. 'Your Excellency,' he said, 'will not want it to be said that you wish to be paid for the test.' He kept complaining to Vincenzo about it. The latter could not refrain from a smile, for he caught a whiff of his father's avarice and took upon himself to settle the affair, pretending to take an interest in it out of respect for his father but resolving firmly not to take it any further. Meantime, he put up the portrait of Leonora at his bed's head and prepared to set out for Florence to meet his betrothed.

CHAPTER FIVE

Leonora

WHEN Vincenzo arrived with his fiery retinue of young gentle-men who had hung their saddles about with horse pistols and jangled their gilded, damascened, bejewelled weapons, everyone fell in love with him—the populace who saw the very picture of a future husband in this showy Lombard, clad in white and gold and crimson, with the fair down which rose from his chin to his cheeks like gold, his vivid glance, his frank manners and the mad way he rode; Bianca Cappello, who recognized the generosity of his temperament and was delighted to find herself deciding the nuptials of the son and daughter of two Austrian princesses who had hated her so much and doubly scorned her, as daughters and sisters of emperors and as ladies of virtue; Francesco dei Medici, who was surprised at the prince's free and gay manner; the court, enlivened by the presence of the Man-tuans, who brought a wave of pleasant frivolity into the intelli-gent, but over-tense and sometimes arid life of Florence; and finally the bride, borne along by the current of sympathy to feel love for her betrothed, who was also her cousin. Their first meet-ing was stiff and almost awkward but a day had scarcely passed before Vincenzo was kissing her in public and—so an ambassador wrote—tumbling with her.

Once more this history is lit by love at first sight. The Mantuan chronicler was to be proved right when he said that no woman was able to resist the affectionate fascination which Vincenzo was able to exert if she pleased him. Now it was Leonora's turn to be ensnared.

The daughter of Francesco dei Medici was neither an easy conquest nor a woman whom one could easily classify. To Marcello Donati, who judged her complexion and the robustness which fitted her to be a wife and future mother with a doctor's eyes—doing so in that humiliating way doctors have, which is almost enough to persuade any buxom woman, were they not all so patiently faithful to nature, to take to a life of asceticism and renunciation—she seemed extremely beautiful. Yet Leonora was not beautiful by classical canons. Well-built and tall, she had in her features a certain lack of harmony which accentuated the long line of the jaw, ending in an almost pointed chin—a sign this of mental acuteness. From her mother she had the overfull lips of the Hapsburgs. Her serious air, which was later to acquire an expression of intensity, was relieved and heightened by a flawless complexion and by gestures and movements of a delicate yet spontaneous grace. Through the extreme elegance of her appearance, Leonora declared her inner quality—analytical, ironical intelligence, working on a basis of melancholy which might have cast a shadow over her had she not defended herself against its attacks, rallying bravely in a manner typical of Florentine women in general and women of the Medici family in particular.

Although quick to criticize and not in the least carried away by the surprise and intoxication poured out for her from Hymen's cornucopia, Leonora had allowed herself to be swept off her feet by her betrothed. Against her will, we may say, since although she had suffered with her mother, Giovanna of Austria, when she was sick with jealousy over her husband's betrayals, and had deduced from that experience her own wise and pessimistic moral views on conjugal relations, she now found nothing in reality to coincide with her theories. She almost felt as if the happiness of loving and being loved was a betrayal so that it was well-nigh painful to accept the gift.

But these days were the spring of 1584—days in which to let oneself grow as if in a warm garden. And to the impulse of her blood, there corresponded the gay whirl of the court: her father in black, her stately stepmother, fair-haired and dressed in blue, her uncle the Cardinal a blaze of purple, her youthful aunt, Virginia, all white and pink, her ten-year-old sister, Maria, who some years hence was to marry Henry IV and become Queen of France, with her rosy cheeks. There were colours everywhere against a background of brocades, of cloth of gold, of velvets and satins, among the gleam of jewels and the cascades of pearls. Ambassadors came, ladies, damsels and gentlemen. Companies were formed for a masquerade, a concert or a ball. And during one of these balls, Leonora might chance to hear amidst the confused chatter to which she listened out of a habit of attention, one of the long subdued arguments which went to and fro between Mantua and Florence over the question of titles.

Dead history for us, the question of titles was a cruel torture for the nerves of the Italian princes—a sure sign of the sickness of an age which relied upon external appearances and put into them all its ambitions and passions, all the angry, wearing labour of the ambassadors at the Imperial and Papal courts, all the comings and goings between the petty Italian courts over a trivial right of precedence. Ever since Cosimo I had acquired, together with the title of Grand Duke, primacy over the reigning dukes of Savoy, Mantua, Ferrara, Parma and Urbino, the ill-feeling against the Medicis had swelled into hate. The whole thing was complicated by the mutual ill-feeling between the various courts, which quarrelled among themselves and split hairs over the appellations to be given or not given according to their various alliances or family-trees. Guglielmo Gonzaga was one of those who suffered most from the greed for titles to the point of being positively ill with jealousy because his wife, being the daughter of the emperor, had the right—denied to him—to be called Most Serene Highness. He had petitioned the Emperor Rudolf so passionately that he had won the right to the same title and he succeeded in being addressed by it in his own court and even by some of the princes—but not by the Medicis, not even now that there was the wedding, although Leonora had been given permission to call her father-in-law whatever he liked. Things came to this point of pedantic subtlety; Belisario Vinta received detailed instructions from the Grand Duke, ordering him to call the Gonzaga, both father and son, Highness, but not to give them the title in writing. In order to obey, Belisario had to fall back on the stratagem of writing to the Duke in the third person or addressing himself to his secretary. He himself, the Grand Duke explained to Marcello Donati during a ball, would willingly have met Duke Guglielmo's wishes, but then he would have had to grant the same title to the Dukes of Ferrara and of Urbino. What then? Were they to be all Highnesses? All Most Serene? Donati agreed that they could not all be, but that was the very reason why Gonzaga should. Alive to every problem, he was not embarrassed by certain statements which he breathed in like the surrounding air. On the contrary, he used them as themes for a series of logical variations. That within himself he judged them more severely is probable but not certain. In him, as in so many others, criticism of and respect for the passions of his times could exist side by side.

More yielding than her husband, Bianca Cappello had quietly come to terms with Donati. She was pleased that he was a doctor because she could tell him all her physical woes, which were already undermining her constitution and causing her to overflow in a corpulence which would soon be described as beyond all measure. They laughed and talked together, alternating the mocking manners of Venice and of Lombardy but always without losing any whit of control or of their natural refinement. Donati confided in her ear that apparently there was to be living evidence of the Venetian episode. Giulia, the Florentine girl, believed herself to be pregnant. What better omen was there for the marriage of Leonora and Vincenzo?

Although it boded so well for the betrothed, Giulia's destiny seemed to lie under the shadow of a moral condemnation, but why she should have to atone, being the most innocent, is an enigma which it is not our task to resolve. When Vincenzo's child was born, it was sent to Mantua where, however, it does not turn up among Vincenzo's many natural children. They then made her marry with a handsome dowry, three thousand golden crowns, a musician at the court of the Medicis. He is referred to as Giulio the Roman. In him we may perhaps recognize, with an exclamation of surprise, a name famous in musical history—that of Giulio Caccini, a gifted artist and one of the men who renewed the art and practice of music. Caccini was, however, morally so brutish that he was able to play the part of Iago in one of the most terrible dramas of the house of the Medici—the assassination of Leonora of Toledo, wife of that gloomy prince, Don Piero, younger brother of the Grand Duke. It seems it was the musician who passed to Don Piero a love letter written to the Spanish princess by her lover, Bernardino Antinori, and so both were killed when scarcely out of their teens. The denunciation had not, however, brought Caccini luck, for thereafter the court barely tolerated him and if he married Giulia, he must have stooped to it merely to return to the Grand Duke's good graces. What sort of life he made her lead is a conjugal secret and remains hidden from us. But after having given her husband several children, among whom was Ceccina, who was to be famous as a singer and composer, Giulia died young before the turn of the century, perhaps worn down day by day by the tyranny, vanity and even the contempt of her husband. For her the memory of the event in Venice had time to become a secret legend.

But at the time of which we are speaking, Bianca Cappello and Donati smiled together over the 'event in Venice'. Then, without appearing to do so, Bianca went on to other things. Was it true that the Gonzagas had such wonderful pearls and as many of them as people said? Of course they had, Donati answered jovially, although not as many as the House of the Medicis—besides, the Duchess wore them all. (This was not true—the old Duchess dressed most modestly and wore jewels only on state occasions.) And would they present the princess with dresses? Marcello felt he must reply yes, certainly, and at once the Grand Duchess, precise and practical, asked how they had managed to make them without her measurements. Donati invented a dressmakers' conspiracy. They must have got them secretly, he assured her and realized why he was being cross-examined. The Medicis were afraid that Margherita Farnese's gowns would be passed on to Leonora.

Margherita's phantom hovered timidly over the wedding and almost everyone handled it roughly. We do not know whether Leonora saw it or what she thought of it. What is certain is that Cardinal Ferdinando, the brother of Francesco dei Medici and Bianca Cappello's implacable enemy, inquired which cardinals and how many had accompanied Margherita on her entry into Mantua and displayed great jealousy of the honours done to the Farnese princess. And that Vincenzo thought of his first wife with a certain melancholy, which he insisted on believing to be distaste, is evident from one thing—he would not hear of Leonora's entering Mantua on the 30th April, the date of Margherita's entry the year before.

The Grand Duke was never done apologizing for the ceremonies which had been prepared at Florence. Poor things, he said, improvised festivities lacking in invention, since there had not been time for anything. But meantime there was a game of football played by princes and nobility in gold livery which was both animated and elegant, thanks to careful stage management which included even scornful jests. There was a battle with quarterstaves for the populace—a sport in which the artisans of the various corporations gave vent to the riotous instincts of Sanfrediano by throwing stones at helmets and armour of pasteboard and wadding with such conviction that many of them went home having lost the use of a limb or an eye or with their teeth broken. 'A mad affair,' Donati sagely comments. There was a superb corrida. Every evening there was dancing in the Palazzo Vecchio; by day there were concerts of chamber music in the new style, the last fruit of humanism, which was to renew the language of music and, liberating it from contrapuntal virtuosity, bring it closer to the expression of feelings and sentiments and so lead to the Olympic heights of Claudio Monteverdi and seventeenth-century Italy's great musical achievements.

On the evening of the 22nd April under a clear starlit sky, there went through Florence a great masquerade preceded by a triumphal car of men and boys singing madrigals; both words and music were by Giambattista Strozzi the younger. The procession was made up of eight allegorical groups which surrounded eight buffaloes, each saddled and mounted by an expert jockey. Then one saw the marriage deities putting Melancholy to flight, the Amazons fighting Licentiousness, the vices of Circe conquered by Chastity. One masquerade was composed of dark Abyssinians, another represented the six ages of man; yet another brought back to earth the heroes of the twin houses of the Gonzagas and the Medicis. But the most extravagant of them all was that presented by the Grand Duke Francesco, which by its mere title 'The Spiritual Humours of our Brain' proclaimed itself a product of its age and of its author. It was an elegant extravagance, this festival with the buffaloes, and very rare because it was so costly and difficult. By torchlight, amid singing and music, the masquerade arrived in the square of Santa Croce where the young men threw to the ladies, crowded in the wooden stands around the square, eggs filled with perfumed water and the buffaloes raced for the palio, exposed there on the steps of the church. The Grand Duke's buffalo won.

Everything in Florence pleased Vincenzo. Even the spiritual humours which filled the head of the Grand Duke and which frequently coincided with his own sudden caprices. One morning father and son-in-law found themselves of one mind and, while in Santa Maria del Fiore the solemn ceremony of the presentation of the golden rose, the Pope's gift to Leonora, went on, they stayed outside in the square, shooting with their arquebuses at the jackdaws nesting in Giotto's *campanile*. They were entirely of one mind over the mad boar and deer hunts in the Medicis' well-stocked hunting grounds. So the hunting expeditions, like all the other festivities, were repeated several times in order to await a favourable day for the departure of the bridal pair, which had been postponed by the Grand Duke's astrologer, who seemed uneasy as to which conjunction of stars would most favour their future. The wedding-guests let themselves be guided by him.

At this time Bianca Cappello had devoted herself entirely to the practices of magic. She believed in it and was indeed determined to do so in order to be able to hope. She knew that only one thing could have availed her against the savage enmity of her brother-in-law, Cardinal Ferdinando—namely, the birth of a son to ensure direct succession from Francesco dei Medici. She had not yet lost hope, but it must have been weakening if she required such desperate aid as that of the astrologers. Bianca's astrologer had become her adviser, and all that was lacking was for certain of his prophecies on the health of the Grand Duke to come true for every word of his to acquire the dignity of an oracle.

At last the astrologer gave the word and the company of young Mantuans set off with their pistols hanging from their saddles as usual and the usual din, fit to daze peace-loving people. Two days later there followed the bride and her escort—a more decorous company, but gay and happy, with ladies and damsels, cavaliers and pages. Great strong-boxes enclosed her trousseau and the first instalment of the dowry, a hundred thousand crowns in pieces of silver, on which Francesco dei Medici had calculated the Duke of Mantua could earn colossal interest.

Albizzi, Strozzi, Pitti, Salviati, Capponi, Neri, Acciaiuoli, Guicciardini, Bondelmonti, Bardi, Ricasoli, Panciatichi, Tornabuoni, Ruccellai—going through the list of the company, one seems to read the whole history of Florence in the names. Dressed to a nicety with well-plumed caps, the colours of their dress matching and their accoutrements chosen with almost excessive taste, the Florentines stood there very much on the alert, quick to perceive shortcomings, eyeing each other and eyeing the Mantuans—all of them, from the high-born gentlemen to the soldiers of the escort. The company was led by the Grand Duke's two brothers, Cardinal Ferdinando and the eighteen-year-old Giovanni, a bastard by birth, ready for any adventure, handsome, insolent and daring; he was yet to show that he alone had inherited the military gifts of Giovanni delle Bande Nere.

On the 28th April, the bride arrived at San Benedetto in Polirone, a magnificent monastery which still contained the tomb of that great manipulator of kingdoms and consciences, the

Countess Matilda. It had required a Papal brief to allow the gentlewomen to lodge with the friars who, unused to so much female company, went to and fro uneasily through the guests' quarters with a swish of gowns, hastily organizing their pictur-esque but most disorganized attendance.

But a pitch of truly nuptial excitement was reached the next day at the Palazzo del Te where Leonora halted before entering the city and was received by the most exalted members of the ducal house. Grand Duke Guglielmo himself had come by carriage to embrace the bride and left again, taking with him Cardinal Ferdinando who, for some subtle reason of etiquette, had not wished to take part in the entrance to the city.·

The squarely-built Palazzo del Te, in which Giulio Romano seems to have attempted to catch in an architectural design the secret of the people of the plain, who are in constant communica-tion with the earth, is seen from afar off as a low building, almost flat in comparison with the lofty lines which surround it. But as you approach it it acquires depth and then the moment you enter its walls rise up in a whole fantastic landscape. The abundant, perfumed, muscular gaiety of the sixteenth century breaks out from this palace, which was created in a happy moment for the loves of Frederico Gonzaga and Isabella Boschetti. Naturally, there is nothing which strikes one like the Mantegna in the bridal chamber in the castle at Mantua, but over the architecture, which is patterned in accordance with geometric but humanist canons, there is laid the eloquence of a painter's and pargeter's art ex-pressed in the gay company of amorous nudes in the chamber of Psyche, in the delicate virtuosity of the decorations and the theatrical horror of the chamber of the giants. Here Leonora was certainly brought—it is the wonder of the place—and was made to hear, perhaps by Vincenzo himself, how the voice of someone speaking very quietly and standing in a corner of the room reaches the opposite corner, rising again from underground with a muted vibration. And indeed for a brief moment, something of us has descended to the nether regions and returns to us crying for help.

But for Leonora that day, the fears and enchantments of certain forms of natural magic were a remote concept. The reality was the charming half-opened coach surrounded by young merchants of the city clad in white and gold; it was her bridal dress in white silk, sewn with pearls and set off by the famous collar of pearls, diamonds and rubies which her father-in-law had set on her neck as he embraced her and which Vinta, with a hint of belittlement, describes as 'showy'; it was the procession, the cheering people; it was the tears of joy of her Austrian mother-in-law as she welcomed her at the door of the church of Santa Barbara; it was the glance from Vincenzo's blue eyes, as he came up to her and summoned her—how could she resist?—to the pomp and splendour of the altar.

The marriage ceremony took place and the Te Deum was sung. Then Leonora entered the Ducal Palace, went through a whole landscape of pictures and tapestry and cloth of gold, crossed the great Sala di Manto and finally was led to her own rooms where her mother-in-law came to see her once more, being still unable to believe in so great a consolation. The Duke was enjoying the company of the intelligent Cardinal Ferdinando. The Florentine's natural distrust had been overcome by lavish Lombard hospitality, and leisurely hours of waiting stretched out toward the night. The sun set. We can imagine how Mantuans and Florentines, relatives and friends, strained their ears towards the bridal chamber. In the morning the princess's gentlemen-in-waiting, assailed by questions, seemed satisfied and so was Belisario Vinta, who noted that, by the bridegroom's eyes, he could tell how little he had slept. Vincenzo sent Bianca Cappello his report on the night and she sent back her congratulations. The cardinal took up his pen to ratify the whole affair.

Thus the official festivities began. The prisons were thrown open, quintains set up; there were jousts and comedies. Ten days had not passed before Vincenzo, in a burst of enthusiasm, which one might have been pardoned for thinking came close to lack of perception, confided to Vinta that relations between himself and his father were now genuinely on a footing of love, trust and satisfaction. Thus he succeeded in deluding himself, but not the cold perspicacity of the Florentine minister, who continued to consider relations between father and son a running sore.

Vincenzo had high hopes. He was happy and he was in love with his wife. Perhaps it was at this time that he had prepared for her that apartment in the Nova Domus which one approaches by a sunny gallery painted in bright colours on a joyful yellow background. A flight of thirteen small steps seems to lead one up to rooms floating in space and wide open to the bright green of the garden by the lakeside. Can it have been true that Leonora immediately felt at home with the lake—or did she not imagine she was in love with it because Vincenzo had first opened her eyes to its delights? She was head over heels in love with her husband and was unable to explain it to herself, even if she used her most subtle powers of comment. She gave herself over to it and although she was used to the open seas of Leghorn, she delighted to go fishing on boats and barges on the lake with music and song, with time stretching out limitless before her and the whole of her being lit with the sun. By water once more, husband and wife ventured in June as far as Venice, where Leonora at last understood the meaning of the fable of the town, which had sometimes seemed to her too highly coloured in the accounts of Bianca Cappello. 'A miraculous city,' she murmured, and was uneasy to feel her senses reel.

On their way back they passed through Ferrara and here the festivities took on a note which she could more readily recognize, although their rhythm was quieter. To live through these days she no longer required the outburst of nervous energy which, in Venice, had worn her face until the skin gleamed tightly on a voluptuous mask; nor did she feel descend upon her terror and astonishment at no longer recognizing at night the regular succession of the hours, which seemed to have been upset by some mysterious tempest. It was with reluctance that Leonora had surrendered to this obscure enchantment, being too intelligent and too rational to derive great pleasure from it. She did not feel slighted—as she perhaps wished to feel—nor did she rebuke her husband for treating her more like a mistress than a wife, although she felt such treatment to be unfitting and almost unseemly, not so much because Vincenzo's revelations were too much for her as because of her certainty that the future could not raise such a relationship to a higher plane. In the end she accepted in the present the future she already foresaw. This was her great discovery, whose intelligence lies in a word which many might consider dead and dull. Patience. Not the colourless passivity of a person who has renounced life, but the bright constancy of a human being who is prepared to pay dearly for the hard privilege of feeling herself alive.

At this point there comes one of the decisive moments in the formation of Vincenzo Gonzaga's character. His father's wrong in refusing to believe in him promptly was to weigh on his son all his life. Each of them had nominated a representative to agree upon the young people's court, which was to constitute a gathering-point for youth in the ducal palace. But this arrangement was so repugnant to Guglielmo, who felt his avarice touched and his absolutism eclipsed, that negotiations did not succeed in getting under way. Vincenzo remained in a subordinate position, always without money and forced to turn to his father-in-law, who sent it to him condescendingly and with caution. It was money again that he asked for from his brother-in-law, Alfonso d'Este, making his debts rise to six thousand gold crowns. He even felt himself restricted in family comings and goings, for when he was invited to the famous Medicean hunting parties at Poggio a Caiano, Duke Guglielmo was adamant in refusing permission for the journey on the grounds that something might happen to upset a hypothetical pregnancy on the part of Leonora. Vincenzo had to beseech Bianca Cappello to dispatch a letter to Mantua to the Grand Duke, asking him to send her daughter and son-in-law 'certainly and without fail'.

It sounds incredible, but we inevitably discover that the son unfailingly replied to each of his father's restrictions with an outburst of ferocity. We have seen the case of Crichton in its day. In this year of grace, 1585, a mysterious murder took place at Poggio a Caiano. A gentleman of the Grand Duke's, Beccaria by name, fell dead in the damp, shady wood. The arquebus of one of the group of Mantuans was smoking—did it belong to the Cavaliere Verri or to his gentleman, Gianantonio Fallaguerra, or to Vincenzo himself? People feigned to believe that Fallaguerra was guilty and Francesco dei Medici asked for him to be surrendered by the Duke of Mantua so that he could be punished. Then he wisely ordered him to be set free. Having been suppressed, the unpleasant story began to go to and fro between Mantua and Florence by devious ways. The truth was that Vincenzo had killed once more—that he felt no remorse but merely impatience. Once more what he did is explained but not justified by his desperate sense of constraint.

Even Duke Guglielmo began to understand something of the situation for, between 1584 and 1587, he frequently promised to summon his son to take part in the government—even if he subsequently broke his word and left his son disappointed and hurt. Nor can it be said that he did not try to come to terms with himself. Once he went so far as to nominate Vincenzo master of the horse; then taking advantage of the fact that Vincenzo and his wife were in Florence, he had sixty brood mares removed and sold to a common horse-broker. On his return, Vincenzo was distressed and demonstrated how rash the sale had been and how much money they had lost by it. Thereupon Guglielmo played the hypocrite and said he had needed the money, which was absurd even to those who did not know the contents of the locked chests in the vaults of the Treasury. On another occasion, spurred on by the exhortations of the Grand Duke of Tuscany, he summoned Vincenzo to the Council of State; but it was sufficient for him to see how the deference and attention of the Councillors was addressed towards this young man in whom they already saw the future head of the state, for him to be out of his wits from jealousy.

Guglielmo was ill. Feeling the pulse of his physical life wane, he attempted to take refuge in that life he had constructed for himself, free from the miseries of the body. There were his dominions, so well balanced in their various departments, obedient to a rule which from the centre stretched to their furthest limits. There was this state, which he kept bringing to perfection by a touch here and there—devoting to it increasing attention and enlightenment, sometimes dealing with the reform of the senate to ensure that it deliberated calmly and justly, sometimes dealing with commerce to see that they exported the magnificent grain, the rich salami and fat milk products in exchange for goods of equal worth and quality, sometimes seeing to the exact stamping of excellent coins, dealing sometimes with the Ospedale Maggiore, which was reformed from top to bottom, while he himself even coped with the foster-mothers for the foundlings. Yet it seemed to Guglielmo that this state, which he protected from future harm, for instance by acquiring and paying for out of his own pocket lands offered for sale by private persons in order to prevent them from being acquired by congregations of priests or friars, whose influence might thus increase unduly—it seemed to him that this state was fated to crumble away as soon as he left it in the hands of Vincenzo.

It was a sad state of restlessness. One moment of happiness and almost of love came to Guglielmo in 1586 when a grandson was born to him—Francesco, the heir to the dukedom, a plump child, pale and handsome. Then the envoys whom he sent from court to court to announce that the dynasty showed promise of stretching out into an unlimited future left with a flourish of trumpets, and gifts showered upon Leonora and Vincenzo. But when, some time later, Vincenzo wished to visit the castle of Solferino, the gift of his father, he was forbidden to stay there. Once more the pressure was being applied, as we can see from a letter by Vincenzo, who writes that he wishes to set out for some place where what he had would have been won by himself and where he could live and die like a soldier.

This heroic tone was not merely a case of words bursting out in a flash of rebellion, but hinted at a reply to the offer made to

him by the King of France. For some years now, Henry III—
undoubtedly on the suggestion of Ludovico of Nevers—had been
trying to lure the heir of the Gonzagas to his court. That was why
at one point he had offered him a French wife, the daughter of
the Duke of Lorraine. What a victory for Ludovico, to overthrow
his brother, Guglielmo, by making his son rebel against him!
And politically what a gain for the King of France at a time when
Italy was entirely subject to Spanish influence, to win over such a
person as the future lord of Mantua, lord and master of the twin
gateways to Italy—the territories of Monferrato and Mantua—a
prince who could counterbalance Spanish predominance and
the influence of the house of Austria on Italian and European
affairs.

At this time Ludovico of Nevers, the exile from Mantua, was
fighting against the Huguenots as one of the French King's commanders in the field and distinguishing himself by deeds of valour,
which reached their epitome and peak in the great victory won
on the Loire in 1586 against the German allies of Henry IV,
King of Navarre. The story of his triumphs reached Mantua and
excited Vincenzo greatly, for he recognized his true lineage in a
man of arms so different from his own deformed father. It seemed
a logical consequence of his inclinations but was in fact merely a
whim that Vincenzo's second son, Ferdinando Teodoro, born in
1587, had as god-parents the King and Queen of France. This
compromised him more than he imagined, although he knew
only too well that to show himself a partisan of France might
mean awakening the suspicions of Philip II and, even more
quickly, those of the Spanish governor of Milan. What the
French offered was undoubtedly very fine—a great army, a
picturesque and heroic cause, so that one felt like a crusader, a
paladin of the faith. And what a different life from his present one,
harassed by the economic and psychological caprices of his father,
which even Pope Sixtus V had recently denounced in a stiff,
ironical letter. More than once Vincenzo would have accepted but
for the advice of the faithful Donati, who asked him to take his
time. Then there were the tears of Leonora, the mother, and the

harangues of Leonora, the wife, as she pointed to the little children with that gesture which warm-hearted men cannot but obey.

Francesco dei Medici intervened in the matter. He was more than surprised, he was scandalized that Guglielmo should goad his son instead of worshipping him, as he himself would have done, for he was consumed with desire for fatherhood. The lack of a son to the Grand Duke and Bianca Cappello was becoming a tragedy in the Medici household. (Clearly the famous Antonio around whose birth there is so much mystery did not count.) The fact that Bianca had had an illicit maternity had even struck the Grand Duke as reason for rejoicing and he had announced to his daughter in words gross to the point of brutality his hopes of giving his wife a son, now that she had renewed her youth.

When it seemed as if Bianca was showing signs of pregnancy, guards were set on her apartment to make it impossible to bring into the Palazzo Vecchio newborn children to be palmed off on the Grand Duke as his legitimate offspring. The humiliating and diabolical suggestion had come from Bianca's two brothers-in-law, Cardinal Ferdinando and Don Piero, who both hated her. We can imagine how, tortured by his paternal passion, the Grand Duke sought to soften Guglielmo Gonzaga's bitterness and to restrain the revolts of his son-in-law—two men who did not know their good fortune. But no one could have made the peace between them last if, in February 1587, Guglielmo had not suddenly fallen ill. Vincenzo saw that this was the time for him to stay.

But man is strong. When he recovered, Guglielmo once more began to temporize, to set checks, to constrain, to diminish Vincenzo's importance. Vincenzo, who had stooped so far as to ask for pardon, began to give heed once more to his own wildest humours and became entangled in foolish adventures in which he found, on the one hand, a kind of desperate vainglory and, on the other, compensation for his inactivity and lack of freedom. It is said that at this time, having already been unfaithful to his wife— a natural daughter, who was later to become a nun, was born to him in 1586—he was in love with a woman of plebeian origin who lived in the house of a certain Fabio Asinello to whom she was related, being either his daughter or sister, and that he had as rival, not a gentleman but a humble organist from the Basilica of Santa Barbara, Ruggero de Trofeis. It was a pleasure to Vincenzo to wax angry against this man, so insignificant in comparison to himself, for thus he could give vent illegally to the bitterness which boiled within him. So on the evening of the 10th May, 1587, when the prince looked in at the great hall of the archers and called one of the young men of the guard, Antonio Bardellini —a tall young man with long legs in the yellow stockings of his livery—and ordered him in a low voice to prepare, along with his companion, Alessandro Lomasso, to come out with him, it was clear that they would not be wearing their swords for nothing.

The three walked towards San Sebastiano, the archers on either side, the prince in the middle, all in black—black his suit of satin, black his short cloak and black the felt hat set rakishly on his fair tufted hair. The night was quiet and dark with a mere suggestion of freshness from the lake. Vincenzo carried a little lantern in his hand. They were near San Sebastiano and turned into a street then called Contrada Nuova where a woman was talking to someone in the street from an open window on the ground floor of a house. When he saw the man, Vincenzo turned to the archers and indicated him briefly, 'That is Ruggero.'

The three of them passed in a compact, threatening group, their six legs moving with the same sweeping rhythm under the shifting yellow eye of the lantern. Ruggero saw them draw near and realized their intention but was unperturbed. In fact, as they passed, he went on speaking with the person at the window—the woman who had perhaps been there had withdrawn, leaving, in her place, a man, probably the owner of the house, who commented in Bergamasque dialect, which in these days was the language of buffoons, on the silly way people went about with lanterns. He outfaced them to the point of laughing at them and his laughter was long and loud. Meantime the group of three men had stopped a little way off. Vincenzo had passed the lantern to Lomasso with a brief command and the archer went quietly over towards the organist. When he was near him he intimated with heavy courtesy that he must please be so good as to stand aside and remove himself. He could return later, if such was his wish. Suddenly Ruggero crossed the street and put himself on guard with his back to the wall. The archer followed him, repeating in an arrogant crescendo would he please go, as a favour, out of courtesy. 'Oh, why should I, why?' asked the victim. The prince himself came up and, already inflamed by the altercation, said, 'Will you go?' 'I don't want to,' said the other, in dialect. 'I'll make you,' said the prince, and drawing his sword, laid about him so violently with the flat of it that he struck one of his archers on the arm. At this signal all the swords leapt out. A companion of de Trofeis appeared out of the shadows, exchanged a couple of blows and fled, followed for several yards by Lomasso. The fray spread. One of the archers flung himself on the organist and struck him several times until he saw him fall. 'And I stabbed him again when he was on the ground,' he confessed under examination, 'out of some inhuman vanity.' Vincenzo ordered the sword to be taken from the fallen man; then, when he saw him raise himself up, all bloody, he asked him whether he knew who it was. That Ruggero was one of those who, even at the point of death, cannot govern their daring wit, is proved by his answer, 'Sir, I know who you are and wish I might know you in Eternity,' meaning that they would meet in another world. Vincenzo understood and raised his sword. 'You will be in Eternity,' he said, 'insolent dog!'

'I meant eternally,' the wounded man explained, summoning what little strength remained to him. They made him tell the name of the comrade who had come to his aid and set off all three to look for him. Ruggero, streaming with blood, went to be dressed by a barber. He meant to survive, if he could.

A report was made to the captain of the castle. There were investigations, a harsh summons from the Captain of Justice, arrests. Ruggero, who was covered with wounds, was grievously ill but struggling to recover. Being interrogated, he at first made no mention of the prince's name but spoke only of the archers:

but since everyone in the city knew how things had gone, in the end he gave a complete account. When the news reached Goito, Duke Guglielmo, enraged by his own illness and his son's senseless rebellions, gave orders for the arrest of the archers, their interrogation and trial; whereupon Vincenzo, having returned an uncivil answer, that same evening once more took up the lantern which had figured in the brawl and brought his two accomplices out from an inner room where he had kept them shut away and led them down to the lake by a secret postern. He called two boatmen, had the archers taken to one of his own craft and sent them off on their way to Savernolo. Thence they would pass on over to Bologna, to Count Camillo Malvezzi, who would shelter them in one of his keeps as secretly as possible to prevent Duke Guglielmo from having them arrested by the Cardinal Legate.

All these conspiratorial precautions were necessary because with the passage of the days Guglielmo's anger increased as his ministers' reports on popular reactions reached him. Undoubtedly the affair was more serious than that with Crichton. For one thing it was Vincenzo's second public affray, not counting all the other incidents, especially at Carnival time. It thus pointed not to a chance, isolated gesture but to a tendency which had never before revealed itself in an occupant of the Gonzaga throne, among whom there had been libertines and hotheads but never tyrants. Quarrels among gentlemen and, in particular, with a foreigner the Mantuans not only tolerated but actually enjoyed as if they were a play. But if the prince laid hands on one so much below him, he laid hands on the people. All felt themselves threatened by tyranny, a monster which had up to now never appeared on the banks of the Mincio. In their uncertainty the Mantuans asked themselves whether they ought not to recognize as *pater patriae* the hunchback who was slowly sinking at Goito, and whether they had to fear in the splendid young prince the terrible madness of a future Caligula.

But Vincenzo, too, felt these things. To see his own person under a cloud in the minds of his subjects was a severe lesson indeed for him—the first he ever understood to the full. The documents are lacking which might tell us how this intuition developed into the workings of conscience. But the gesture for which historians later rebuked him—of having the two archers brought to him at Mantua to be handed over to justice—shows that he had understood that he could not, for a mere whim, change the law at his discretion. He would save them later, and in fact the two archers must shortly have been included in an amnesty, for we do not find their names included among those condemned or imprisoned in these years. But meantime there would be a trial and the rule of law would have been obeyed—if only formally. No documents have survived to tell us how Ruggero was after the judge's examination at his bedside; but apparently he showed the toughness of his plebeian stock by surviving his numerous wounds.

Meanwhile, at court, there was a feeling that Guglielmo was nearing his last journey and inevitably the influence and importance of Vincenzo increased. Ministers came to ask his opinion, to submit questions to him, to read his despatches. If he went to Innsbruck to his sister, Anna Caterina, Archduchess of Hapsburg, he was no longer left to his own devices but news was regularly sent to him of what was happening in the state. Naturally these changes took place gradually and were not always noticed by the young man; but, without his knowing it, his patience and his interest in his future subjects were encouraged and grew. He held long conversations with the ministers and took pleasure in gaining skill in the art of government, which was part of his nature, and he was more equably affable when he unbent towards the members of his court. And most affable and generous he showed himself to be—it is a gesture which has always stood him in good stead in later days, even with his most severe critics—by unbending to a man of genius who in that same year wrote, 'I am in Mantua, lodged with His Serene Highness the Prince and served by his servants as I myself would have wished to be served and in other things cherished at His Highness' pleasure.' That man was Tasso.

Vincenzo had succeeded in liberating the poet from the Hospital of Sant' Anna at Ferrara after seven years of painful durance. Over and over again he had requested the poet's release of his brother-in-law without achieving his aim. But, in the end, Alfonso d'Este gave in to him, warning him, however, that Tasso (that poor man, the Duke called him) had to be kept continually under surveillance to ensure that he did not take to flight—that *idée fixe* of the insane who can nowhere find a balance between the intense internal vision and the outward reality of things. Vincenzo promised to have a watch kept on him but from a distance, thus leaving him the illusion of freedom, and brought him to Mantua on his barge on the 14th July, 1586.

So, under surveillance, discreet though it was, the poet began to live again, revelling in the discovery of Mantua, its wine, its bread and its countryside. But, alas, here as elsewhere, he had to repay the hospitality offered him in poetry, which is too valuable a currency. This is a matter for regret, for Tasso's mental state, in relation to life at the court, was so hallucinatory that he barely noticed his own sacrifice. Perhaps he did not even feel it as such but as a way of increasing his prestige—thus far have we come from Ariosto who would have preferred a turnip from his own garden to the partridges on the Duke's table. To Tasso it seemed his duty to thank Vincenzo in verse—his duty, too, to compose posies of madrigals dedicated to the ladies whom Vincenzo favoured. Since they found favour with his prince the women of Mantua found favour with the poet, too, who confessed in a letter to be strongly tempted to fall in love and indeed to have almost chosen his lady. Perhaps some flirtatious girl flattered him to add piquancy to her own amorous caprice. For the ladies of the last years of the sixteenth century to have a madrigal or sonnet by Tasso meant that they belonged to a privileged caste, which was courtly, humanist and poetical. The great drama of the poet's life touched their hearts—but with that feminine pity which is at once pleasantly soothing and entirely superficial. And can we blame the ladies who halted for a moment to distil the obvious grace of his poetry and were enchanted by the liquid mingling of harmony and words—can we blame them if they were unable to discern on what an obscure and desperate framework these delicate fruits were trained?

'These leisure hours by the banks of the Mincio, where I flourish in sweet study and read and write and sing, were procured me by my lord, who lists my song and whom I adore and revere next to God.'

So Tasso spoke of Vincenzo. Now his friends could hope for the poet, if not absolute peace, at least a period of quiet. But already, out of his disordered melancholy, he was eyeing his lord's doings askance and weighing them with his own bewitched measure. Naturally the Prince, having lodged him in the palace and set him in a privileged position in the courtly hierarchy, did not concern himself with him daily. But for Tasso the least sign of diminished interest was a sign of downfall and disgrace. He took it to heart and spoke of ice that had to be broken and of immured solitude. At the announcement of a journey by the prince, he became quite lost. 'What shall I do here when the light of my eyes has gone?' About this time, he was awaiting from the Ferrarese printing-press *Floridante*, a romance of chivalry, by his father Bernardo, corrected and finished by himself. It was dedicated to Duke Guglielmo, under whom Bernardo had served. Tasso promised himself great honours from the Duke and from his son for this poetic offering but Guglielmo was never to see *Floridante*.

August came and at the beginning of the month a hectic fever struck the Duke in his lair in the coolness of his villa at Goito. The days passed and the fever grew as did the determination of the sick man to bear it. He recognized the signs of approaching crisis and knew that he must accept it if he were to deserve the symptoms of recovery; so he lay quietly in the big bed under the baldaquin and suffered and waited. But at the end, a crisis of horror was reserved for him.

It was brought on by his strength of mind and his courage. It was true that in the course of his grave conversation with his gentlemen he had more than once said that he would consider a true friend whoever, when the hour of his death came, would tell him of it. He had been sincere then, as we are all sincere when the word 'death' gives us a stronger, more vivid sense of our present vitality; but when Count Cattaneo, out of an elevated and in-human sense of duty, came to the sick man's bed and told him that for him it was over, even Guglielmo, for all his great strength, rebelled. For a time repugnance at his fate laid hold on him and racked him. He refused to accept the duty so suddenly put before him of bringing an exemplary life to an exemplary close. Perhaps he was tempted to storm, to cry out, to rebel because of all that he had accepted in life. Certainly the courtiers saw him struggle with himself to the point of extreme physical exhaustion and only then did the spirit triumph.

Then they were able to call the confessors, the friars and the councillors to a kind of solemn conclave which might bear witness to the lofty calm of his last hours. He was able to look at his praying wife, for here everything was as it should be, as it always had been, as was natural, and then at his son on whom his glance fell with an anxious query which found both consolation and pain in the thought of their far-off meeting in the same plight. Hence-forth everything was foreseeable and foreseen. The prayers ran in his veins and lulled his vital spirits. There were two or three flashes of lucidity, twitchings of the mind. On the 14th August, 1587, Guglielmo Gonzaga died.

CHAPTER SIX

The Young Duke

THERE is a sickening giddiness in liberty—a bitter sense of bewilderment when we realize, at the very moment when our bonds are loosed, how tightly we had been bound. It is a bitter chastisement, too, to be punished by the very thing that sets us free—by death; this was the punishment which now fell upon Vincenzo and bowed him down in reverence and respect for his father's memory. Vincenzo felt an access of affection for the miserable body of the Duke, laid out under the baldaquin of cramoisie. With it there went overwhelming grief and that suspicion which lays hold on sons when their fathers' defences collapse before their eyes—the suspicion that they have never penetrated to what was best in them. So their secret is lost to us for ever.

In Vincenzo this suspicion became a moral burden, a sense of oppression. He emerged from the misty depths of this melancholy fit, not through meditation, which might have transmuted his feelings into thought, but by means of a symbolical gesture. He ordered a coin to commemorate his accession and chose an old dye of the Gonzagas—a crucible encircled with tongues of fire to quicken the pure gold. And from his heart there slipped, consolingly, the motto: 'Probasti, Domine.'

In what respect he, who was a Duke at twenty-five, who was handsome, rich, dearly loved and ready for any adventures—and he had no intention of avoiding them—felt himself tried by God, perhaps even he himself did not know. But if in part his choice is explained by his love of high-sounding phrases, he indubitably felt in a vague way the drama of his own limitations, which he felt all the more keenly now because of the liberty which had come his way. He had been constrained for so many years to accept a position of dependence; now, for the first time, he realized how greatly it had cribbed and confined him. There was a danger that he would have to suffer in the process of freeing himself. He had desired independence greatly; now it was his fate to feel overcome by it—as if through some languid malaise he had lost the power of muscles and nerves.

However, the young Duke's moment of bewilderment was of short duration. Just as his choice of the coin shows him in a more thoughtful mood, so the list of dazzling projects which made his coronation stand out among all the great festivals of the Gonzagas reminds us that he was quick to recover from it. But in this case recovery did not mean that he had got his bearings. Suddenly finding himself free, Vincenzo obviously exploited his liberty impatiently and hungrily, with brutal decision and without moral scruples, not realizing that, if he were not careful, the gates of the labyrinth would open to receive him and he would never be able to escape.

Vincenzo considered the coronation celebrations to be the opening scene of his life as Duke and therefore naturally and auspiciously triumphant. He gave orders for the invitations to his chancellery, and saw the roll of reigning princes stretch out under his secretary's pen—the House of Savoy, the Estes, the Medicis, the rulers of Venice, the Emperor Rudolf and Archduke Frederick of Hapsburg, all summoned by him, and it seemed like the prelude to the fanfares of the silver trumpets. Instead it proved to be the starting point for a maze of intrigues, points of honour and ill-temper. Tight-lipped envoys made their appearance from Ferrara and Venice—what else should bring them but the thorny question of precedence? It was not the Venetians who took alarm—they knew that, by ancient right, they had precedence in any court—but the Estes, the house of Savoy and the Medicis, who even on their deathbeds would never come to an agreement on this incurable point of difference. Worst of all was Francesco dei Medici,

who first sent his most elegant condolences—as did Bianca
Cappello—and then despatched a special messenger to his
daughter.

Leonora had been ill for some time—'murdered', she said, by
a low fever (perhaps malaria), which kept recurring. She listened
to her father's emissary and then informed her husband that the
Medicis insisted absolutely that first place after the Venetians be
reserved for them—before Ferrara and naturally before Savoy.
Vincenzo, who had perhaps compromised himself somewhat with
his sister and his Este brother-in-law, answered vaguely. Leonora
insisted, stating the question in such precise terms that there was
no eluding it. Then, like any man when he cannot break down his
wife's logic, Vincenzo lost his temper and said the Grand Duke
was trying to meddle in his affairs. We can almost hear him add
the phrase which no man, in cottage or palace, has managed to
avoid during his married life—that he was head of the house and
so on. At one point the buzz of voices became so insistent that
Vincenzo said it was not to be borne and, mounting his horse,
left Leonora in bed, left his mother too, handed his worries over
to his secretaries and went off to a villa. 'At least he might take his
wife with him,' Francesco dei Medici muttered in Florence,
shrugging his shoulders in his ill-humour, for he knew—or
thought he knew—to what extent the September moon led his
son-in-law into voluptuous excesses.

The 22nd September, 1587, dawned with a clear sky. The rich
pink light of autumn in the plains filtered down on the city not
through a mist but through a delicate haze. Vincenzo was twenty-
five that day and he felt his youth glowing on him as he put on
his ceremonial robe of white satin, edged and embroidered with
gold, and felt the ducal mantle of white ermine round his shoulders,
hung here and there with black tails, which punctuated the transition from the wonderful, gentle white of the fur to the unrelenting
white of the thick, gleaming material. In fact, the theatrical satin
robe might almost have seemed excessive had it not been intended
to express the allegorical and dynastic reasons for his appearance.
It was only right that, above such a robe, he should wear the

ducal cap of maintenance with its ermine trimming on which there gleamed the crown, all studded with gems and lit by the red gleams of a famous carbuncle. And it was natural that when Vincenzo rose up, all in white, catching every gleam of light with his jewels, he should be recognized as sovereign lord even before he had received the ivory sceptre. He was already a duke, and with his crown he took on a new serenity which stilled his intolerance and his fears and gave him the slow, thoughtful majesty of a prince. Thus he took as his right the procession of churchmen, bishops, canons and clerics and still more as his right the magnificent array of cavaliers, in whose company he intended to present his subjects with the image of a great sovereign on this, the first day of his reign.

After the sacred ceremony in San Pietro and the symbolical ceremony of the handing over of power, it was the people's turn with the great cavalcade. The crowd had already decided that the men-at-arms, drawn up in the public squares, were superb—handsome men, all tall in stature with gleaming weapons and hung about with scarves of white, red and yellow silk—and now, with a joyful tremor of excitement, it hailed the vanguard of the procession, mounted arquebusiers in long cloaks of black velvet. Immediately after them came the most noble corps of guards who had no officers and obeyed only the Duke, they too in black velvet, but trimmed with gold, with loose scarves embroidered with mottoes on themes of love, with jewelled chains, hats laden with plumes, dangling ribbons, fringes, pearls, silver and gold lace and, at their saddlebows, the pistols which were to be used only for the defence of the sovereign. The vassals from the lands of Mantua and Monferrato, the ducal chamberlains, the gentlemen in waiting wore no livery, except that of a rich ordered elegance. Ten, twenty, thirty Gonzaga marquises who were recognized, by the crowd, one by one, which freely spread abroad the story of their impious lives, bore witness to the strength of blood ties and the weakness due to such subdivision of Mantuan territory. A luxuriously appointed Italian and German bodyguard preceded the twelve young pages who were so handsome that they might have served the first monarch in the world—all slim and eager in their suits of cloth-of-silver after the Spanish fashion, caparisoned in coloured silk with great embroideries of gold.

There were horses in plenty for the Mantuans to admire, for the pick of the famous Gonzaga stables were on show, ridden by the nimble court riding-masters who made them wheel, bridle and caper. And they had changed the uniform of the archers, who no longer wore yellow stockings and yellow doublets but scarlet stockings and doublets trimmed with yellow and ornamented with white and yellow ribbons. They wore in their caps long scarlet, white and yellow feathers and their commander was Guido Gonzaga, a veteran of Flanders, all patched with scars. The archers were the troops closest to the Duke. Immediately after them came the ducal canopy, preceded by the treasurer who, from two great pouches of white satin wrought with gold, drew handfuls of gold and silver coins to scatter to the crowd.

And there, under the gleaming, wavering silver canopy, carried by merchant citizens, was Vincenzo Gonzaga, Duke of Mantua and Monferrato, on his white horse, the jewel of the ducal stables, the famous Armellino, so full of fire, yet so responsive to the bit. He rode benignly and his face expressed a natural and unassumed look of thoughtful gravity. Everyone felt that he invited them directly, warmly and majestically to trust in him, and they would do so. They felt that, whatever his whims, whatever blinded him, whatever phantasms his senses called up, one thing would remain clear and unshakeable in their prince: his civil virtue, his interest in and love for his people.

Behind the Duke came the princes and dignitaries, the ambassador of Cardinal Scipione Gonzaga—the others had been dispensed with after the wearisome battle over precedence—the statesmen, the councillors, the senators, secretaries and officers of justice, the mayor, officials and nobleman. The procession was closed by two fiery companies of horsemen with little square banners of silk on their tall lances.

The immense chamber where the banquet was held was all yellow velvet and gold brocade. Gold brocade and yellow velvet made up the baldaquin which marked and covered the Duke's chair. This banquet was long talked of throughout Italy, with its jewelled crystal beakers, rimmed with gold, with its services of silver and gilt, with its lace tablecloths and its regal courses. The transparent porcelain services used on the tables of the barons and gentlemen—for the Duke only gold and silver was used—were not carried back to the kitchen but broken 'out of high spirits', says a chronicler, and quickly replaced with others, lighter and more delicate. On high, behind a gilt balcony, the musicians poured down on the guests consorts of instruments or of voices. The banquet lasted six hours.

It was night; at a given signal, everyone crowded to the windows and balconies. A beflagged castle, bristling with towers and bulwarks, advanced over the lake, and fireworks made a gay display for the set pieces of the assault on the castle, the fire and the final triumph. Leaning on the balcony, Vincenzo laboured to subdue within him a heart overflowing with exultation. Perhaps only his wife Leonora, who was still ill in bed, saw, when he entered her chamber to salute her as Duchess, that his blue eyes were full of dangerous dreams, and felt, not only uneasiness, but tenderness mingled with doubts for the future—that essentially feminine anguish of domestic Cassandras who cannot even warn the man they love to be on his guard against himself. To the others, he was more than a happy man, he was a demi-god who could make others happy.

Vincenzo's first gesture as a ruler was a handsome one—the pacification of the factious families of Casale who filled the capital of Monferrato with blood and fights. It was a cordial and magnanimous gesture which announced to the people of Monferrato, so sorely tried by Guglielmo's asperities, that they were to enjoy the blessing of a mild government. Still more indicative of his wise intentions was the Court list on which there admittedly figured young gentlemen of his own age and temperament—but only the more mature of them. It included, too, some of

Guglielmo's old ministers—those who had been the young Duke's teachers, who had more than once set him right, who knew both his strength and his weaknesses: Aurelio Pomponazzi and Marcello Donati.

The truth was that instinct, which both guided and betrayed Vincenzo, warned him that he needed more than one source of help when attempting to deal with his own impulsiveness. Not that he was unaware of how he was placed—so much he had absorbed from the age he lived in—or did not know that whatever he did he must bear foreign powers in mind—Spain, Austria and France, with the Pope there to act as mediator when and as best he could. But he would have dearly liked to be able to look forward to a sturdily independent future. However, a brave volition is not in itself a means to an end. That was why he was casting about for some means of dispelling from Mantuan territory the dark shadow of Spanish domination which was cast over him from Milan. Yet what answer could his ministers give except the one word which had been Guglielmo's motto—equilibrium?

This was the period when the Spain of Philip II, replete with the gold of the Indies, was moving towards that maturity which so untimely turned into decrepitude. The obstinate, unending wars in Flanders, the war against Elizabeth of England culminating in the defeat of the Invincible Armada, the internal wounds inflicted by the Inquisition, the nobility's high-handed ways and intrigues, the neglect of commerce and industry, which were no longer under the sovereign's care and protection—all these factors were already condemning to paralysis the expansionist urge of a great kingdom. But the King of Spain was still all-powerful in Europe. He financed everything and had a finger in everything, supported by his cousin, the Emperor of Austria, whose family put its trust in the haughty motto of the Hapsburgs —AEIOU. *Austriae est imperare orbi universo.* In Italy Spanish dominion was firmly in the saddle in Sicily, the Kingdom of Naples and Milanese territory; the whole peninsula lay under the oppressive burden of a peace which admitted of no other solutions.

These were the years when writers, poets and political theorists, catching fire over Italy's lost freedom, talked so much of chains and wounds and tears and of bondage which must be redeemed. Hatred for Spain became daily more bitter but a confederation of Italian states against the foreigner was unthinkable. Venice was immured in its golden neutrality; Tuscany, shut off by the Medicis. In Ferrara the Estes were in decline; in Parma and Urbino, Farnese and Della Rovere were pensioners of King Philip. This division of minds and spirits, which Philip most ably provoked and cultivated, was aggravated by points of honour turned septic and by proud rivalries. Meanwhile the Pope, deep in the spiritual reform of the Church and in the struggle between Protestants and Catholics, with one eye on the age-old war in the East, needed the Spanish alliance and peace in Italy. Any prince who desired to live as a free man in his own right would have required more than intelligence and courage. These qualities, along with many others, such as lucidity, adaptability and energy, would have had to be fed by the fire of something approaching fanaticism—that voracious political fanaticism, for example, which was to be found in Piedmont, in Carlo Emanuele, Duke of Savoy.

As for Vincenzo Gonzaga, he knew that his state had an importance far in excess of its mere area. How often was he to repeat that Monferrato and Mantua were the two gateways to Italy? And it was true. It therefore seemed to him that he should take advantage of his key position to rise in the world—and his dynasty with him. It must be admitted that, with his quick intelligence, which unfortunately did not trust its own impulses, he was the first Italian prince to realize the potential strength of a French party which would aid the Italian cause by counterbalancing the power of Spain. This was an intuition which would have required to be decanted and examined as that fine politician, Ferdinando dei Medici, was attempting to do in Florence. But in Vincenzo's case it found tangible expression only in externals—in his dress, which, as the Spaniards noted suspiciously, he wore tight-cut in the French fashion.

But whatever his impatience with the arrogance and high-handedness of the Spaniards, Vincenzo knew he must keep on good terms with the insupportable Governor of Milan and on excellent terms with the King of Spain, that great dispenser of favours. Nor did he consider he was being crafty when he sent his ambassadors contemporaneously to France and Spain to announce Guglielmo's death. In France he bade them tell his uncle, the Duke of Nevers, that only his father's death had prevented him from accepting Henry III's proposal to go to war against the Huguenots at the head of a thousand horsemen. In the embassy to the King of Spain the number of horsemen was increased three-fold so that Philip might see the type of proposal the young Duke of Mantua was used to receiving. Vincenzo made a merit out of the fact that he had refused such a high command in France and on the strength of it asked to be made general in command of the infantry in Flanders—asked, too, for the Golden Fleece and the direct protection of the Governor of Milan for Mantua and Monferrato. No generalship was forthcoming but, in the heart of the Escorial, Philip decided to send him the Golden Fleece; more-over, he instructed the Governor of Milan to bear it to Mantua in person. The significance of his cold little smile as he benignly proceeded to grant the honour we find in a letter to Vincenzo from the Grand Duke of Tuscany—a letter too much hung about with congratulations not to be suspect. 'What a happy event,' said the Grand Duke, in a feigned outburst of enthusiasm, was this peace and good will towards his Catholic Majesty. How well the Golden Fleece became the House of Gonzaga—particularly when one knew—as did all the world—that courtesy had been repaid with courtesy, that is to say that the Duke of Mantua had requited the King of Spain with three thousand fat ducats. In other words, Vincenzo had bought the great decoration with money from the famous iron-bound strong-room where, on Guglielmo's death, they had found piles of newly-struck coins gleaming in the darkness of the chests; over a million in gold, not to mention bills of credit, jewels and silver plate.

The letter from Florence with its wonderfully malicious style came, as we have said, from the Grand Duke, who was no longer Francesco dei Medici but his brother Ferdinando, uncle of Leonora.

Soon after the death of Guglielmo Gonzaga, in October 1587, there had occurred the tragedy of Poggio a Caiano—the simultaneous deaths of Bianca Cappello and Francesco dei Medici, which have been so much and so long discussed without it being possible, even to-day, to decide whether it was chance or poisoning. The Grand Duke had taken to his bed with a fever after a hunting party and an imprudent drink of iced water. Some days later the Grand Duchess fell ill and in a few days both were dead—Francesco first—amidst a confused, watchful coming and going of doctors, confessors and courtiers.

Cardinal Ferdinando was at their bedside and certainly this arid, muscular intellect, this pitiless exploiter of opportunities, followed the last moments of his brother and sister-in-law with such relentless asperity that it would be logical if he had helped them to their end. Indeed it would almost be a wonder if, having found it necessary, he did not do so. But perhaps there was no need for that. The Grand Duke Francesco had long been ill. He was consumed by high fevers. The mixture of ice and pepper which he alternated in his drinks was already an indication that all was not well with him and in Bianca we could follow from day to day, for almost two years, the development of a slow disease, which was said to be hydropsy and was perhaps nephritis. She recovered from the exhausting hallucinations, from the fierce delirium and the terrible fatigue, at the price of nervous efforts which were as short as lightning flashes. The bravest thing about her was that, although worn by suffering and bitterly afraid, she contrived to control herself and rediscover the tone of her old Venetian light-heartedness. Her physical illness was nothing in comparison to the moral tortures she had to undergo—for example, Francesco's constant mad conviction that she was pregnant, whereas she knew that the swelling of her belly was a sign of illness and a bad sign at that. 'This tiresome ambiguity of mine' is the admirable definition she herself gives of her physical and moral suffering in an autograph letter.

When, in October 1587, she took to her bed after tending her sick husband for some days, Bianca was a done woman who had already come to terms with·her thoughts of death, had already accepted them and was prepared. Francesco kept her alive by means of that mysterious stimulus his love for her had always been; for he was a man no one else could read and intelligible to her alone. Obviously it would have sufficed for her to know that he had preceded her, and she would no longer wish to remain here alone. Perhaps Ferdinando's crime, which is all the more terrible because it lies outside the scope of human law, lay precisely in the fact that he informed his sister-in-law that she was a widow, that he kept reminding her of the fact and drove home its truth, that he made her aware of it through the odour of incense, the muffled footsteps of the bearers, the trampling of the funeral horses and the priests' long prayers. Perhaps he drove it home so hard in his inhuman, waspish way that Bianca felt the thought of escaping him by accepting death too pleasant to resist.

The funeral of the Grand Duchess ended in an obscure tomb, for Ferdinando said of her in one of his outbursts of unconcealed ill-nature, 'We do not wish her amongst us,' and abandoned her to her servants. Disregarding Francesco's will, which named his mysterious son, Don Antonio, as his heir, Ferdinando quickly shook off the purple and crowned himself Grand Duke. ('What will the heretics say?' asked Pope Sixtus in alarm, for even he was unable to anticipate or restrain Ferdinando's rapid, biting tongue.) As for Ferdinando, he at once felt that to reign was an activity which gave him room for his plans, ideas and theories.

Perhaps he had too many ideas and theories; his political instinct was to become the prisoner of his schemes. But at least with him there was a more lively atmosphere. In the Palazzo Vecchio the Chancellery was hard at work and it seemed that something new might happen in Italy. Belisario Vinta travelled through France and Germany, arranging the careful and astute schemes of his lord. His nieces, Leonora and Maria, Ferdinando loved, both because they served his political game and because of an old family feud; for he was a champion of Giovanna of Austria against Bianca Cappello. Besides, he recognized that Leonora was a Medici. He valued her precise, reserved elegance, the incisive quality of her judgment and the tacit way in which she observed the limits of her own personality. He knew that she alone could restrain her husband and keep him firm on a political course. Uncle and niece would understand each other. She was already expressing herself with freedom and familiarity in her first letters in which she replied to Ferdinando's somewhat chilly account of her father's death, writing in all sorrow and seriousness that she could only survive by a miracle of God. Ferdinando's nature was such that, even when he wished to be affectionate, he succeeded only in being clumsy, but he instructed Marcello Donati to give him detailed information on how Leonora lived. From Florence there would come letters, invitations and gifts—no longer the little, finely-made, fantastic caskets or the little elegant boxes full of fruit, crystallized flowers, amulets and antidotes for poison which Francesco had sent daily to his daughter—but jewels and pictures and perfumes. For Vincenzo, too, there came letters, frequently full of comments and veiled disapproval.

For example, Ferdinando could not understand what aberration led Vincenzo to quarrel with his neighbouring princes. He had the impression—and said so without beating about the bush—that the Mantuan government was trying to make its weight felt by its neighbours. This he could understand in the case of the Duke of Savoy because Carlo Emanuele seemed to toss and turn and pass sleepless nights out of sheer desire to pick a quarrel with someone; and it was nothing new for Savoy to cast eyes on the territory of Monferrato. But why should Vincenzo quarrel with his brother-in-law, Alfonso d'Este, Duke of Ferrara? From Alfonso Vincenzo had always received help and, one might almost say, support in his wild escapades. Alfonso had trained him in the use of arms, in hunting and swimming. With Alfonso he had grown up in a true school of chivalry. But it was this very word 'school' which had been irking Vincenzo ever since he had begun to suspect that his brother-in-law was treating him with the condescending air of a benevolent but clear-sighted schoolmaster and passing judgment on him from the remote heights and gleaming, sterile atmosphere of his sixty years. Admittedly, if Vincenzo compared his own devious life with the rectilinear morals of Alfonso d'Este he was bound to feel himself not so much slighted as completely negated by a mode of life so different from his own. Besides, his councillors had begun to have their say, for they saw which way the wind was blowing, and were whispering in his ear about certain designs of Alfonso's on the territory of Monferrato—designs which had apparently been no secret to Duke Guglielmo. It did not require much to complicate matters—the usual sort of questions that come up between neighbouring states over watercourses, boundaries and customs-duties. And there was no lack of hotheads to precipitate matters. Men caught up in a net of partisan hatred, of quarrels and vendettas, seized the opportunity to go to and fro across the River Po under the orders of both Gonzaga and Este. The Fantoccis, in particular, who were a rascally lot, finished up by taking shelter on Mantuan territory. One day at the beginning of May, just as the market was opening, a certain Alessandro dell'Ambrosia attacked the chief of the family, Alfonso Fantocci, and cut his head clean off. It was then carried in triumph into Ferrarese territory amidst the rejoicing of the people.

Being very young, not to say raw, in government, Vincenzo expressed his annoyance in vivid terms. *His* jurisdiction had been violated. His territory had been entered. The ambassadors haggled with each other, alternately casting light on the subject and obscuring it. Vincenzo got his revenge for Fantocci's death by holding in prison certain members of the Bellentani family, who were closely connected with the Estes. There he examined them and went thoroughly into their plots—and how boldly daring they were! They had, for example, planned to kill the Bishop of Ostiglia while the Good Friday procession was passing through the streets.

The names of the Fantoccis and the Bellentanis, along with others more obscure, keep coming up in the course of a highly emotional correspondence. To offset the Duke of Ferrara's patient contempt there was the cold wrath of the Grand Duke Ferdinando, who had been called to act as arbiter. He condemned the extreme stupidity of Vincenzo's outbursts and tried with elaborate arguments, which had often a touch of bitterness in them, to bring him round to a reconciliation. Unfortunately some men have not the knack of getting out of difficult situations. Thus Vincenzo, for instance, once crossed through Ferrarese territory in disguise, had an unfortunate encounter and then actually stated that his brother-in-law had laid an ambush to kill him. But even Vincenzo saw that the accusation was too serious and the affair tailed off in a bad fit of the sulks.

At Christmas-time the atmosphere became clearer. Margherita Gonzaga was recovering her high spirits because her beloved brother had sent her an affectionate message. An agreement was quickly signed. Then everything seemed to boil up again when the Gonzagas of Novellara, an unruly branch of the family who had long been in rebellion against the main branch and were friends of the Estes, made various raids and forays into Mantuan territory. The time had come for Vincenzo to pronounce the word 'war'. While he was secretly savouring it, Leonora of Austria was hard at work between son and son-in-law until one day, suddenly, Vincenzo discovered that he had agreed to a reconciliation and a peace.

The key which the Duke of Mantua provides to his own character is sometimes surprising. For example, he required a new motto to be embroidered on his surcoat for jousting and desired Muzio Manfredi, a literary man about the court and a friend of Tasso, to invent something new for him. It is not the poetaster's suggestion—a struggle between a lion and an eagle, which is a very trite allegory—that makes us reflect but the symbol which lay concealed beneath this emblem. Manfredi had to change the accompanying motto, *Victor victus*, for another, *Quid si concordes?* because Vincenzo felt that his character was not clearly expressed in the first version. It might seem logical to find in this tussle between two wild creatures a martial symbol or a political allusion. Instead Manfredi, who explains the allusion in a most elegant and courtly hand, says that the lion and the eagle represent two Lovers (the capital L is his) and explains that if two 'Lovers' of such beauty could but agree they would start a great blaze in the world, for beauty is love's stronghold.

Twisted in this way, the symbol acquires—admittedly with some difficulty—the significance of an oddly strained conceit; but it is useful to us for, thanks to similar clues, we will continue to find Vincenzo's days overlaid and obscured by an excessive number of amorous references. His garland of reputation is not so much enriched as weighed down by ladies' names. Understandably no trace is left of mere caprices and still less of various encounters with innkeepers' daughters whom he enjoyed when he broke his journeys; but the story would not be complete without his court ladies—Signora Orizia, who was always in the clouds, the Marchioness Felicità Gonzaga, Signora Barbara Guerrieri, Signora Francesca and Signora Fulvia. It was not true that the ladies were alarmed at the Duke's intemperance and inconstancy or that they hated each other—we shall see under whose influence they disciplined themselves. But they did not tolerate that others should intrude between them and Vincenzo. Anyone reckless enough to do so might share the fate of that great favourite of the Duke, Alfonso Boschetti, who when speaking to certain gentlewomen invited to a festivity by the Duke's barber, beseeched them 'by the resting-place of the True Cross' not to go because the barber, as he was in a position to tell them, was His Royal Highness's procurer. Whereupon one of the ladies immediately went off to denounce the rash man, who lost both rank and favour.

Leonora dei Medici made no move. She was surrounded by her children of whom, in 1591, there were four—Francesco, Ferdinando, Guglielmo and Margherita—and she felt increasingly secure in her position as reigning duchess. Vincenzo loved his wife, wished to be loved by her and even wrote to her frequently when he was away. He had the affectionate trick of saying 'Love me a little' and, to read his conjugal letters, one would imagine him the most faithful of husbands. Instead of which not one but two passions concurrently inflamed his dreams—or at least a passion and a fancy, both of them made more tender perhaps by an amorous friendship. Leonora knew it all. In fact, when unexpected catastrophes occurred and various men started up threatening scandal and death, Vincenzo turned to his wife, who immediately with skill and unerring authority protected, concealed and aided him.

How Leonora had arrived at such a broadminded view is a long story. One day she had noticed that Vincenzo's first fire was fading and that, whereas he had loved her, he now liked her. This simple and logical fact is one that women rarely truly pardon even when they accept it. But Leonora pardoned him—not only that, but she rediscovered her integrity and strength of will and moved on through life at her husband's side, observing him, respecting him and sometimes pitying him.

She had fallen back on the defences she had elaborated during her thoughtful adolescence when her mother, Giovanna of Austria, so often betrayed by her husband, had seemed to Leonora to be a victim indeed, but one guilty of weakness, and her father, Francesco, a guilty party but one who must be acquitted on the double score of being a man and her father. Now, after this long time, Leonora had once more to test the validity of what she considered the fundamental and practical rule in a woman's life as a wife—that what she must fear in her husband is not many loves but one love. What she must avoid is the favourite, the Bianca Cappello, the one passion, the woman who can subvert everything. This is the wisdom of an old woman but she arrived at it when she was twenty-five; but she had felt a cold shudder the day she had to tell herself she was a betrayed wife, and had felt the temptation of losing her self-confidence. She had sought the aid of religion, which had comforted and supported her; above all she used her powers of reasoning, which derived from her princely pride and the slightly arid assurance of those skilled dialecticians, the ladies of Tuscany.

So let the women come, Leonora concluded, and all the better if they come in numbers. So we find her informing her husband of the beauty of certain ladies of Casale—admittedly putting a gentle note of irony into her information. She did not keep from the court the women Vincenzo loved; on the contrary, she protected them, formed ties of affection with them without falling into complicity but maintaining her distance with all her moral authority as a princess. Meantime she watched over their affairs and, without appearing to do so, conducted the concert of loves. Thus she contrived that the various participants were in league with her against the danger of a solo performance which would have dispossessed them all.

Naturally every now and again one of them would evade her and friction would occur. The moment would even come when she could no longer control the situation. Naturally, too, the part she played cost Leonora dearly—just as all her successes cost her dearly, including her motherhood, which was so necessary for her rank and so greatly desired by all the Gonzagas. She had not been able to accept the unpleasantness of it without—at least in the early days—passing through moments of difficult rebellion, and had reached the point of writing to her little sister Maria, the future queen of France, advising her not to marry so as not to taste 'the bitter fruits' of marriage. A grave indiscretion this for a princess of these times who was bound by custom to conduct her correspondence according to the rules of etiquette. Maria, who was eleven, laughed at the matter—she was a big blonde girl, vigorous and phlegmatic—and made a jest of her sister's advice by drawing on the letter a whole series of dolls in swaddling clothes. Later, when experience of maternity had refined and matured her, Leonora would hold hard to status but in a sober fashion. She was a most careful and intelligent mother; her aim with her children was to maintain an attitude which would be at once gentle, severe and of a piece but without excessive emotion. And in secret she would always love their father in her children even if—and this points to the underlying difference between them—she tried to educate them on an entirely different model from Vincenzo Gonzaga.

CHAPTER SEVEN

Agnese

YET the disturbing phenomenon of a royal favourite rose like a constellation over Vincenzo's horizon. It did so round about 1589 —or perhaps earlier—in the most unsettled period of his reign when everything was in a ferment and external events did not seem to correspond to the fiery internal urges of the young Duke. At this time Leonora was passing her days in bed, caught in the coils of fever, and into her eyes there came the cloudy over-patient look of those who have been gravely ill in their youth. Vincenzo had probably gone off on one of his journeys—to his Hapsburg relatives in Innsbruck—and brought back his luggage full of stones, carved wood, prints and little Flemish paintings. When he came back, he found his wife cured, but he was no sooner returned than she fell ill again, which led the Grand Duke Ferdinando dei Medici to write highly secret and most urgent letters, bristling with dark queries on delicate problems of the bedchamber. Did they require, he asked, a Mantuan friar with great skill in certain operations and a first-class exorcism?

Had an exorcism sufficed, Leonora would have invoked it against the woman whom Vincenzo loved and who took the liberty of evading her control. This was Agnese, daughter of a certain Don Ferrante de Argotta of Cordoba—a lady from the south, from Naples with its Spanish ties and customs. She had made her appearance in Lombardy, summoned there by a great wielder of enchantments, the Countess of Sala; for it was Barbara Sanseverino who had brought the young girl to Colorno round about 1582, had kept her by her side for six years and initiated, her by a continual infusion of carefully moulded thoughts into her own free, lively way of inventing life. This education, falling on the vivacious Spanish temperament, had borne fruit and made Agnese, as her teacher said, the most charming woman in the world. For she was not averse to recognizing herself in her pupil.

It was among the roses of Colorno, with Barbara looking on and smiling, indulgent to the point of affectionate cynicism, that Agnese must have felt Vincenzo's love descend upon her like a nebulous, gleaming meteor. Like Hippolita in her time, she must have walked through the rooms of the villa in a heedless reverie, perhaps addressing as sister the Saint Catherine in Correggio's Mystic Marriage and seeing in the saint's delightful fears the mirror of her own ecstasy. Perhaps Hippolita Torrelli still came to Colorno as Barbara's guest. Perhaps the two women met. Did Hippolita recognize that the moment of her eclipse had come when she saw the other woman falter as if struck down in midflight? Who can tell with what weapons she faced the inexorable pang—tears, rebellion, prayers, resignation, or the sigh of a human being who has been set free and who sorrows over the discovery of the price a woman pays for liberation.

Meantime Agnese had responded to Vincenzo with the intensity and fickleness of southern women, sweetening it all with her youthful grace. She put herself entirely in her lover's hands and gave him sovereign powers. It was under his patronage that her marriage took place to Prospero del Carretto, a gentleman of Monferrato, to whom she was later to bear a child, Francesco. (Perhaps another Francesco, to whom the documents refer as having been born between 1588 and 1589 of Vincenzo and a Neapolitan gentlewoman, and who later was a most worthy friar and bishop of Nola, was Agnese's also.) We do not know the precise date of the meeting between the Spanish lady and Vincenzo but since, in 1589, Agnese begins to receive gifts and privileges from the Duke, we may deduce that their relationship had by then lasted at least a year. The letters patent of marchioness and her investment with a fief were to allow Agnese to climb from one privilege to another. The Countess of Sala enjoyed the spectacle, for it was a success for her school at Colorno, although the friendship between the two of them was to pass through periods of indifference and even of ambiguity before it took on the complexion and the intensity which was to make them tragically united. Certainly at the moment when Agnese arrived on the scene, Vincenzo could see in her no mark of ill-omen. Nothing suggested it—neither the warm gaiety of their relationship nor her character, for she seemed to come to the front of the stage with a quick nimble dancer's step and allowed herself to be caught up in Vincenzo's enthusiasm which, at this moment, was so decidedly constructive that it sought expression materially in limestone and brick. The result was the immense fortress of Casale which, instead of defending the territory at Monferrato, was destined to attract to it the attention of the great foreign powers.

While the plans for its construction, with its great towers, its communication system and its breastworks, was taking ghostly shape in his imagination, Vincenzo's minister, Petrozzani, was busy with words of excessive wisdom, trying to convince his master that the fortress ought not to be built. Monferrato, said the old councillor, was not in free communication with Mantua and it was impossible to move the smallest garrison there without passing through Milanese territory—that is to say, without Spain's permission. The fortress, therefore, would be of no avail, either against Spain, or against Spain's friends. Would it not end up by becoming a Spanish stronghold? And here Petrozzani repeated a truth which history has always faithfully borne out—that the defence of small states against greater states lies less in arms than in diplomatic and political intelligence. It was in vain; Vincenzo was determined to have guns and mount them on the vast platforms of what would be the greatest fortress in Italy in order to salute his independence. The fact that this did not correspond to reality was something which for the moment did not affect the wholeheartedness and impetus of his fantasy.

But we must not represent Vincenzo as more divorced from

reality than he was. In fact, let it be said at once that he was in no wise given to abstractions and that in order to arrive at those unexpected conclusions of his he always set out from something real and palpable. It was only in the process of reasoning that he went astray after the phantasms of his imagination. In this case, the idea of the fortress had arisen not so much as part of a train of argument, but as a defensive measure against a threat which Vincenzo felt to be imminent—the mad desire of his neighbour, Carlo Emanuele I, to acquire more territory. Had not this little Duke of Savoy defied the King of France and taken the liberty of occupying the marquisate of Saluzzo and annexing it without more ado? They had called him 'the Savoyard freebooter' and the Italian princes had turned on him with fear and envy—perhaps because they felt that he was the only one of them whose sword had in it the virtue of allowing him to expand. To Vincenzo it seemed that to raise up this vast structure, the fortress of Casale, against Carlo Emanuele, was to contain him; he genuinely felt that each brick played its part in opposing the designs of his dangerous neighbour. So when he accepted Germanico Savorgnan's great project, approved the expenditure and ordered the work to begin, Vincenzo felt himself inspired by such lovely joy that the woman he loved could not but be caught up in it. For him, too, it was a happy hour.

In May 1592, we find Agnese at Mantua in the Palazzo del Te. Perhaps she had been living there for some time as had another famous Gonzaga favourite, Isabella Boschetti, fifty years before. The Palazzo del Te is well suited as a residence for favourites. It is distinguished by the sensual paintings of Giulio Romano and by the sensuous, gay elegance of its rooms, by the conniving grace of its alcoves and by certain rather overwrought secrets in the decoration. Thus there is a grotto with a bathroom, encrusted with shells and with a scheme of lighting worked out in terms of daring scenography—an example of the terrible results even a well-educated taste may produce if it allows itself to be contaminated by certain subtle temptations. In the Palazzo del Te Agnese reigned with the full powers of womanhood when it is recognized as a power—reigned with the authority and assurance which, in some women of amorous intelligence, take the place of modesty. Light-hearted by nature, she presided over a most elegant company, composed of the finest gentlemen in Mantua— the kind of court one finds in a poem of chivalry, where such questions may be proposed and discussed as whether love is destiny or design. Destiny, said Agnese, in answer to an unknown cavalier—perhaps Vincenzo himself—who opposed her with the casuistical argument that, if it were destiny, what merit could lie in his free choice and constancy? She called in as umpire Battista Guarini, who was even then about to come to Mantua from Ferrara and arrange for a special performance of his 'Pastor Fido'.

The 'Pastor Fido' had been Agnese's choice. Applauded by Vincenzo, she appointed as her aide Count Buldassare Castiglione, great-grandson of the author of The Courtier. The author of the pastoral, Battista Guarini, man of letters, poet, diplomat and courtier, was then summoned to the palace. It was a good choice, the 'Pastor Fido'. It was true that we do not find in it the airy, crystalline qualities of Tasso's Aminta, that lightness and harmony which brings our emotions to bear on its verses with the same sudden astonishment as we derive from a tender-leaved tree in April under a windless blue sky, but Guarini's work is more colourful and more sensitive. It recognizes its own limits and uses them to draw with lively precision its conventional characters, now glancing at its Greek models, now discarding them; and it has a quality which matches the climate of love.

Nine years had passed since Guarini had read the first pages of his work to a gathering of literary men presided over by the madcap Countess of Sala at the little court of Guastalla. Now in one court after another everyone was demanding the story of Mirtillo and Amaryllis. It is beside the point that the courtiers, always prone to fall victim to new modes, were particularly enthusiastic over the mosaics of conceits which later formed the starting-point for Marino's exuberant seventeenth-century style. The voluptuous languor of certain scenes, such as the kissing-match between the girl and the young shepherd disguised as a woman or the dialogue between the wounded nymph and the swain who has wounded her or the contest in magic between Corisca and the satyr, together with the theatrical truth of the characters and the harmonious web of the verses, give the work such vigour that it withstood the centuries and crossed the seas, bearing as far as Persia and India the adventures of the faithful shepherd.

We can understand how, in the Palazzo del Te, Agnese felt herself ripen in the milky warmth of verses which speak of love smiling and triumphant on land, in the sea and in the air.

> . . . amante è il cielo, amante
> la terra, amante il mare . . .

It was not for nothing that people were to tell of young girls led astray by this amorous song or that Bellarmino made the severe accusation that the 'Pastor Fido' had corrupted more sons of the Church than Luther or Calvin. At Mantua the rehearsals came thick and fast. Sometimes, it would happen that in between times the youths who played the women's parts would change their treble voices for baritone. Then the lady and the poet had to look about them to find another Amaryllis or another Corisca, arranging with a patience which descended to the minutest details the intonation of the voices, the control of the gestures, the cadence of the entries and exits in a controlled production from which they hoped the work of art might emerge in the round.

From the ducal palace Leonora looked over to the Palazzo del Te and a shadow came over her brow. She said nothing, however, and played her own part in preparing for the performance in accordance with her husband's orders, for Vincenzo was anxious that it should be a brilliant success. The rustic courtyard of the palace was to be roofed over and lit by a thousand torches. Everywhere there would be lights, tapestries, pictures and·garlands which would make the richness of the settings extend out into the audience. The ladies were to prepare their most elaborate *toilettes.* Leonora said yes to it all, but something negative must have emanated from the ducal palace if, in spite of the fact that workers, musicians, dancers and actors hurried on the work and although there was no relaxation of the rehearsals, Guarini wrote confidentially to Cardinal Scipione Gonzaga that he had reason to believe that the performance would not take place—a conviction he repeated to a friend a few days later. The diplomat in the poet had foreseen things clearly, for the *Pastor Fido* was not given at Mantua at this time and had to wait until 1598. Almost certainly Leonora had a hand in this, being too deeply hurt at feeling herself subject to the will of Agnese.

For she had to admit that the Spanish lady, while respectfully constant in her deference to Her Most Serene Highness, was equally firm in asserting her own independence. Meanwhile Vincenzo gave her not only gifts and honours but watched over her. If there was a hint of scarcity, he sent her sacks of wheat from his own granary. When she had a lawsuit with a cousin on her husband's side, Aleramo del Carretto, he forced the hands of the judges by requesting them to consider the Marchioness as one with his own person. Leonora still said nothing and intelligently, but with malice, made her silence fall heavily on the only person who could take some action in the matter—on her namesake, Vincenzo's mother.

The Duchess Leonora, now old and extremely fat, had been unable to resist the vanity of signing herself 'born Archduchess of Austria', the moment her husband was dead. From her son she had received tokens of recognition which she had long foregone because of her husband's suspicious jealousy of titles. These were a magnificent apartment, a large court and much state. She was a woman entirely given over to religion who liked to declare her own virtue in sentences culled from some pious work. Then she lent her carriage horses to transport the bricks for the Jesuits' new church, and replied to those who pointed out how unsuited the fine beasts were for the task with the great empty commonplace that if they transported her own body, so soon destined to corruption, they could, with greater glory, transport the bricks for the house of God. She considered the sensual splendours of the Palazzo del Te to be works of the devil. She saw Vincenzo surrounded by hell fire and as for Agnese, she could have sworn that under her skirt she concealed the cloven hoof of the tempter. She approved the virtuous silence of her daughter-in-law and being unable, without causing scandal, to proceed against the sinners, took action indirectly against them by siding with Aleramo in his lawsuit, giving him her lawyers, her protection and assistance.

At first, Vincenzo was only mildly worried—perhaps it was merely a woman's whim—but when he saw that his mother was unrelenting, he began to storm and almost made Aleramo del Carretto pay dearly for the Archduchess's interest in him. Arrested and imprisoned, he had more than once to protest his obedience and devotion to the Duke in order to be set free, which he perhaps was so that the scandal might not fall too openly upon Agnese's head. Mother and son did not speak to each other for a time. Secret messages, if not actual letters, went from Leonora of Austria to the Pope. In a tone of fatherly disappointment, Gregory XIV warned the young Duke that he must not continue to offend against the sacrament of matrimony.

Everything was against Agnese, who saw reasons for uneasiness multiplying around her. She must overcome them one by one. Vincenzo still loved her openly—with bravado—and was eager to grant her active sovereignty, being amazed by the self-revelation of himself she afforded him and at hearing his own confession of passion coincide with hers. He had at last found that rare thing, equality on a sensual and sentimental plane, which gives the illusion of similarity and which sometimes even creates it, and is undoubtedly the prime condition for an attempt at a closer understanding between lovers. And he felt a sensation of exaltation. Not only did he catch fire in Agnese's presence, but in her absence as well, when suddenly the sensation of her spread through his whole being. Although, being compelled to live apart, they felt in their separation how their mutual images grew in their memories and took arbitrary form, yet so well attuned were they that they had only to exchange a glance to feel close to each other again and ready to resume the interrupted dialogue.

In Agnese there was, over and above her beauty, warmth and vitality. It was this abundance, this richness, this trembling movement of the heart, her voice always on the point of dying away, constricted by emotion, this emotional substratum in a woman who flowered so brightly, which perpetually renewed in Vincenzo the element of surprise, that fountain in which love renews its youth. Having become Marchioness, Agnese did not wear her ambition like a crown but showed that she knew how to carry her rank. Although her influence was discreet, how powerful it was is shown by those who used her to gain access to the Duke, including men of the first rank, such as Cardinal Sforza. At this time, too, Vincenzo placed so much trust in her advice that he let her open even the most jealously guarded of official despatches. Yet even the fact that she contrived to give so much of herself and that she was recognized at her true worth, could not ensure her lover's faithfulness. A person like him may fall victim to what seems to be, and indeed is, a kind of deviation—namely, that feeling his vitality increase he cannot always contain it, and in his intoxication listens to other voices, other allurements.

It is not surprising, therefore, to find evidence, dated 1591, of a relationship between Vincenzo and a certain Signora Orizia, whom he tries to represent as an impatient creature but who was perhaps merely annoyed at having to wait her turn. She had taken her revenge by obliging the Duke to follow her through various tortuous mazes of caprice. Then, realizing that she had lost the day, she forced herself on his attention, skirmishing with all those weapons which wound the user rather than the person aimed at. In the end it was she who had to repeat the wretchedly undignified gesture of women of all times and all conditions when their love is not returned—in other words, she asked for her letters back and insisted that she wanted them all. At this point we find an exasperated Vincenzo beseeching his friend and confidant, Fabio Gonzaga, to take over the tiresome task of collecting the letters and sending them to the wrathful lady. He warns him to make haste to settle the whole affair and stresses, using a word which was to be prophetic for him, that he wishes 'once and for all to emerge from this intricate labyrinth'.

It is difficult to discover by what complicated steps September 1590 brought the Countess of Sala back to him, independently of the link with Agnese. The name of Barbara Sanseverino continually came to the surface in Vincenzo's memory, even if he no longer purred over the words, as he had once done when he wrote: 'Signora Mamma, remember from time to time us your unhappy and miserable servants, and let not your grace depart from us, for we value it as life itself.' Now he describes her with tender enthusiasm to an envoy from Ferrara as 'more beautiful and more youthful than ever'.

At this time Barbara was approaching forty. She persuaded Vincenzo to invite her to Maderno, where she joined him in an elegant pavilion on the lake and enjoyed the keen exciting air of Garda along with three beautiful young women whom she had brought with her from Parma in her usual cunning and ambiguous way. Indeed, we might easily consider her habits unduly ambiguous and even verging on perversity if we remembered that she must have been well aware of the relationship between Vincenzo and Agnese, which had begun under her auspices some years before. Was it merely distraction she offered the Duke, now that she knew the position of her friend to be secure? Was there in her gesture a challenge to Agnese, which expressed the secret resentment of teacher for pupil? Or did she simply want, by presenting Vincenzo with something fresh, to open up a new chapter for him and see how he proceeded with the experiment? We might even ask ourselves once again whether the Countess confined herself to playing the part of intermediary, although Vincenzo himself informs us that his interest was aroused only by the three young girls; but perhaps it is better not to attempt to disentangle certain amorous complications.

Now that her affairs at Parma were beginning to suffer eclipse, the Countess began to feel the need of the Duke of Mantua as a friend. She had separated from her husband in an outburst of impatience which had earned her confinement in a convent by order of the Bishop of Parma until, fortunately widowed in 1485, she had succeeded in creating for herself a daringly free life—the life she required. It is a wonderful sight for those who rejoice in female victories to see how calumny was unavailing against her and even turned into pæans of praise. Thus Count Orazio Simonetta, master of horse to the Duke of Parma, who had previously described her as the greatest courtesan in the world, would willingly have married her at forty-five and adored her. Similarly her son, a rebel against his mother, who had received one of her envoys saying that he wanted to get rid of all the cuckolds who served his mother, in the end surrendered at the feet of the fascinating creature.

Where the Countess was concerned, the house of Farnese alternated between keeping watch with her and keeping watch on her. When the old Duke Ottavio died, the new Duke, General Alessandro, protected her from distant Flanders; she had found it a fine sport to keep the two of them on a lead. Yet when Alessandro was away, she already descried in Prince Ranuccio, his regent at Parma, a power hostile to herself. Her gambler's nature had suggested to her that she must maintain a close connection with the Duke of Mantua as one who might be useful to her in the future, but it was a false move. The meeting between them at Maderno was extremely imprudent, since it probably presupposes others and because it was precisely from that moment that Ranuccio could begin to associate, in his obsessed mind, her image with the hated figure of Vincenzo and thus condemn them both. Nor could she imagine that this gallant reunion amid consorts of music and amorous conversations, with garlands and feasting and all the gaiety of the wine harvest, would cost her her life.

From this period date Vincenzo's protests against the King of Spain for allowing his governor in Milan to threaten to invade the Duchy of Mantua if it did not bend entirely to his will. The territory of Mantua, Vincenzo wrote, is not such an easy prey to the would-be invader, 'because we do not lack that popular devotion nor that strength in men and arms nor that courage and resolution of spirit which our ancestors possessed in order to acquire it and keep it, even in times more turbulent than those.' These are the words of an armed challenge which, when loosed by a princeling against an armed power, have a touch of temerity about them. By the cold light of logic it seems difficult to reconcile this protest with the active attempts made by Mantua at the Spanish court to obtain the post of general in Flanders which the Duke so greatly desired. (Naturally Philip II did not dream of granting it.) But in the case of Vincenzo there was no levity and no illogicality in this request. There was instead a sense of freedom, a deep conviction that he could treat as an equal with anyone on any question. In view of his desire to prove himself bravely there was nothing which did not seem possible to him, if he but willed it. The Spaniards were not so much suspicious as highly scandalized. They understood nothing of a character which was ingenuous out of sheer generosity. They stood by and watched the mysterious movements of the French ambassador, who time and again announced his arrival in Mantua and then suddenly disappeared, thus creating an atmosphere even more mysterious than his conversations with the Duke.

Better proofs of his growing maturity were the measures Vincenzo took in internal affairs, whether during the Po flood of 1588 or the terrible famine which ravaged Italy in 1591. In order to help his subjects, he hit on the plan of building an arsenal in the little port on the lower lake at Mantua and he arranged that any citizen who needed to earn money could work on the building of it and be well paid. The bread was mixed with rice, which had grown in immense quantities because of the heavy rains that had rotted the grain. It was decreed that less vintage wine be made and more light wine so that the poor should not lack it. Guards were put on the frontiers, on the bridges, and at the ports so that strangers should not come and upset Mantua's long-sighted distribution system. In this way hunger did not descend upon

Mantua—nor did plague enter its walls, although it was running rife through the peninsula and in Rome carried away a
youthful Jesuit, the Duke's most famous kinsman, San Luigi
Gonzaga.

Vincenzo had been nurtured in a stronghold of the Catholic
religion which was at the same time the most intransigent centre
of the Counter-Reformation. It must not be forgotten that he
was born in the last year of the Council of Trent. He did not so
much respect friars and priests as love them—a dangerous state of
affairs which led him to give them more than his cautious father
had granted in the way of privileges and benefits, for Guglielmo
had always prevented excessive ecclesiastical gains on his territory.
Vincenzo went to Mass. In procession he wore the tunic of a
religious brotherhood. On Good Friday he hoisted the Cross on
his shoulders and asked for the heaviest one, glad to drag it from
church to church. And undoubtedly his inner colloquy with God
had an emotional and heartfelt note. He had felt, as we have seen,
the fascination of Carlo Borromeo, but without being affected by
it. Nor was he touched, except in his affections, by the moral
pressure of his cousin, for whom he felt such humble admiration.

It had been a truly memorable day in 1585 when Luigi Gonzaga
had renounced the title of marquis, his rights of primogeniture
and the domain of Castiglione to his brother Rudolfo, who was
incredulous of so great a gift. Then, seeing his brother's face shine,
Luigi had asked with his tiny bloodless smile: 'Which of us do
you think is happier, you or I? Certainly I am.' Then he went his
way without turning back. In 1589, the year of young Vincenzo's
love for Agnese, the long-nosed profile of the pale young Jesuit
had reappeared in Mantua for the last time. Leonora of Austria
had called him in as umpire in a most complicated affair between
the Duke and his relations at Castiglione, who were always ready
to pruduce thorny problems for the head of their family. Vincenzo did not so much let himself be caught in the toils of the
young man's serious analysis, or be swayed by his incisive
arguments, as allow himself to be fascinated. And while he handed
over to his relatives what was his by right, he felt, with joy spread

through his being, the sense of lightness and calm of a man who recognizes and submits entirely to a superior judgment.

When the news arrived that Luigi had died in an odour of sanctity in Rome, serving those stricken by the plague, Vincenzo was quick to preserve his memory, not only out of family pride, but because he found in that exemplary life heroism to kindle him and a spectacle to move him. Miracles not only filled him with enthusiasm but moved him deeply; but if he listened to the voices of the saints, he was naturally even more easily affected by the voices of those possessed by spirits with their admixture of magic. At the very time when his liaison with Agnese was at its height, he entered into a spiritual pact with a woman from Lucca, Antea dei Morti, who enjoyed a reputation for saintliness and had consecrated her life to the souls in purgatory and went begging from door to door so that masses and prayers might be said for them. Having learnt that Vincenzo suffered from a per-petual headache, she offered to take his affliction upon herself in return for a certain number of masses to be said for the souls she held so dear. The Duke's pain did, in fact, disappear and Antea suffered it joyfully instead. The miracle pious women relate is that one day, when the treasurer forgot to pay the Masses, the pain returned to the Duke and remained until his accounts were cleared.

Being disproportionately bigger than the little state of Mantua, the foreign powers which then dominated Italy were unaffected by Vincenzo's pinpricks, however sharp. This was a guarantee of peace; but he considered it a sign of impotence, and would have been cast down by it had he not had an infallible method of regaining his spirits when the mists of melancholy clouded his faith in the future. He would stride through the magnificent Gonzaga armoury, hung with flags and standards and pennants, going over to himself this evidence of his forebears' military glories.

One entered the armoury by passing through the court theatre and this proximity led to a disaster. One winter night a fire broke out among the scenery piled up at the back of the stage; the light wooden framework and the pasteboard of the sets burst into flames. Theatre and armoury burned together. The ancient trophies were destroyed and the lances, the inlaid armour, the halberds, the pikes, the maces, the bombards and all the armament for thousands of soldiers were reduced to scrap.

To wander about among the heaps of red-hot iron with their sinister little plumes of smoke caused Vincenzo bitter pain. He had not sufficient patience to contemplate the sight of so much destruction. The clouds of smoke cast a shadow over his thoughts and awoke in him a mixture of suspicion and doubts. He rejected as too simple the hypothesis of an accidental fire. The courtiers said yes, someone had started the flames, but who and why? Was it a case of vendetta or envy? When the Mantuan police said that suspicion pointed to a bandit, Ruggero Pantara by name— he had taken refuge in the Duchy of Parma—Vincenzo felt that he was listening to a revelation.

CHAPTER EIGHT

Quarrel with a Straw

AT Parma, after old Duke Ottavio's death in the arms of the Jesuits, Alessandro Farnese now reigned—but from afar, from his camp in Flanders where, year in, year out, he soldiered in the service of Philip II. He was represented in the Duchy by his son Ranuccio, who was nearly twenty. Age had taken any roundness from his face together with any capacity for adapting himself to life. It seemed as if relations between the Farneses and the Gonzagas had calmed down after Margherita's assumption of the veil and Vincenzo's marriage into the Medici family. But the calm was manufactured in the chancelleries and laboriously furbished with compliments. It is noteworthy that Vincenzo, who was always ready to start all kinds of disputes with his neighbours, was restrained towards Parma, although he knew of the humiliating accusations which the Farneses did not spare him. Perhaps, even without realizing it, he respected Parma's sense of undying pain and, in himself, a memory which still awoke in moments of bitterness—the memory of a certain Sister Maura Lucenia, the little nun in the convent of San Paolo. But precisely because his relations with the Farneses were so delicate and touchy, his reactions were all the more lively when provoked. The Mantuan police had no sooner enough evidence in their hands to be able to make out a case against Ruggero Pantara, than Vincenzo requested his cousin, the Marquis del Vasto of Casalmaggiore, to procure the bandit for him at all costs.

The young Marquis, who was one of Vincenzo's more reckless companions and had all the plumed haughtiness of his Spanish descent, adopted altogether too resolute an air when he proceeded to look into the obscure affair. The accusation against Ranuccio Farnese had as yet not been formulated in words. Count Alessandro of Correggio, who had a lawsuit with the Duke of Mantua over his little territory, was suspected to be the instigator of the crime. So far Ranuccio was blamed only for protecting the Count. The Marquis of Casalmaggiore, who considered that Parma would never hand over a friend's retainer, resorted to the stratagem of engaging another bandit, who trapped Pantara. Once captured, the wretched man was brought to Mantua and put to the question. Since this meant torture, the confession was forthcoming. The armoury had been set on fire, he said, on the orders of the Prince of Parma, Ranuccio Farnese.

We do not know how much truth there was in this. Not only did Pantara alternate between confirming and denying his assertions, but he kept varying them so much that it is impossible to discover any basis of truth in them. The fact is that no sooner had he pronounced Ranuccio's name than all Vincenzo's painful resentment was concentrated on it and the prisoner became a valuable prize. It was the gay Carnival time of 1591—a headlong tide of frivolous gaiety. That year little masks of gold and silver became the fashion and one evening, having perhaps that moment removed the gleaming mask from their faces and thrown a cloak over their festival dress, Vincenzo and the Marquis of Casalmaggiore went down into the prison to be present at the interrogation of the bandit, who produced a tangle of words and evidence under the pressure of pain and fear. This time, protesting his innocence, he eventually told a long story. A few days after the fire in the armoury, he said, he left Mantua, where he had come on business, and took the Parma road in the company of two merchants, who spoke of nothing but the great blaze in the ducal palace. The latter, warming to the journey and gaining confidence, had let it be understood that they were responsible for the fire—in fact, they ended up by boasting of having started it in the Court theatre so that it might spread to the armoury. Continuing their journey, the three of them had lodged for the night in an inn.

During the night one of the merchants had felt ill and sent for a confessor. From his bed, Pantara had heard the confession of the dying man and in it the denunciation of the Prince of Parma as the man who had ordered the fire.

Urged on by the horrors of prison and by torture, the bandit's imagination knew no bounds; probably even in Mantua they did not entirely believe him, however much they felt inclined to do so. Shortly after, Ruggero Pantara died, either through illness or from excessive torture. Taking advantage of the fact that the Marquis del Vasto was leaving for Flanders, where he was joining Ranuccio Farnese to serve with him under Alessandro's command, Vincenzo commissioned him to report the incident to the Prince of Parma and to make of it a candid warning from one gentleman to another. The Marquis was nothing loth to undertake the assignment. He discharged his embassy with haughty punctiliousness and did not realize that he had touched a sore point to the quick. Repressing his intense disgust, Ranuccio replied that this was a slander and asked for the record of the trial and the bandit's statements to be sent to him from Mantua forthwith.

The scene now changes to France in 1592, to the camp at Château-Thierry where the French Catholics under the Duke of Mayenne were gathering for the struggle—it was already in its third year—against Henry IV who was at this time not yet converted to Catholicism. In the great conical and trapezoid tents were camped, side by side with the French, the Catholic troops of Philip II of Spain, sent by him, as he openly stated, in the hope that he might see his daughter Isabella, who was descended on the side of her mother, Elizabeth of Valois, from Henry II and Catherine dei Medici, ascend the throne of France. In military terms Philip's hopes were solidly represented by Alessandro Farnese and we can understand why the King, being used to see his general conquer, thought that he held a winning card. So, taking advantage of a period of quiet in Flanders, the troops of the Catholic king had descended from the Low Countries into northern France with all the Italian and Spanish captains soldiering there. Among them were the Marquis del Vasto and Ranuccio

Farnese, who had been summoned by his father who, being already a victim of dropsy and gout, wished to hand on to his son his inheritance of military glory.

One fine morning in early summer, shortly after the inconclusive siege of Rouen, the Marquis del Vasto decided to go back to Italy. He had already taken his leave of General Alessandro when he saw the Prince of Parma coming towards him from Mass with a group of gentlemen. They greeted each other; then Ranuccio, secretly encouraged by the proximity of his father, by the military air of the camp with its fluttering pennons and the gleam of swords and armour, spoke first, asking for news of the famous trial at Mantua. He was aware that there was nothing new but he wanted to hear it said before witnesses. 'Signor Marquis,' he then said on hearing the reply, 'I wish to repeat that if you or your lord the Duke have said or caused to be said that I had the armoury set on fire, or if you try to spread it abroad or give it out as true, then you are lying. I offer to uphold this challenge with arms here or wherever you may wish.'

The Marquis del Vasto saw in each word the fuse of a future explosion. He was delighted, but he got satisfaction from restraining himself and striking a grandiloquent pose. He was surprised, he replied, that a speech in this tone should be addressed to him, a friend of the Farneses. However, no one had ever said that the prince was responsible for the fire. At most, the Duke of Mantua and himself had repeated Pantara's statement and reported it to the prince. 'If anything more had been said by us,' the young man added, and his voice became firmer and sharper, 'I would uphold it, not only before your Highness, but before any other person from the Son of God downwards.'

Having thus, in broad daylight and in the heart of the Catholic camp, planted a winged barb in the shape of this allusion to the bastard descent of the Farneses from Pope Paul III, the Marquis allowed the insult to penetrate deep. Then, turning towards the company of gentlemen where the press was thickest, he stated: 'Whoever has attributed to the Duke of Mantua the words spoke by that bandit is lying in his throat, and I challenge him to a duel. This naturally I say merely for my own personal satisfaction.'

Choking with anger, Ranuccio contrived to find his voice and asked for an explanation of certain remarks, which seemed to originate from the Marquis, on help which had not been forthcoming at a certain point in the siege of Rouen. Perhaps he changed the subject in an attempt to find in military bickering grounds for extending the quarrel, but the Marquis was the more cunning of the two and did not allow himself to be trapped. His reply was neutral. He had not been at the siege of Rouen owing to illness and therefore could not speak of it at all. Naturally, if he had spoken, he would have maintained every word he said sword in hand.

Bowing low, each went off to his tent, swelling with triumph beneath his breastplate. That same day, the Marquis left, but so intoxicated was he by the fumes of honour and by the fine part he thought he had played that on the way he had an access of scruple. Had Ranuccio's challenge, he asked himself, also included those who had reported the bandit's testimony? Because in that case, he himself, having reported it, must fight. His company came to a halt, the regiment quickly bivouacked and an envoy was detached and sent to Ranuccio with the question posed by the sophistical Marquis. Not until the reply came back that the disavowal only concerned anyone who had considered the prince responsible for the fire that he set off once more towards Italy. When he got home and reported the incident to Vincenzo, the Marquis embodied his story in a document and at once the chancelleries set to work to send a copy to every court. 'Whoever,' the Marquis stated, 'tells the story differently, is lying and if anyone says that I have lied, the lie is his.'

It was a whole chain of challenges. But naturally they were ineffectual, because with the 'if' a loophole had been left open to the enemy, thus revealing Vincenzo's game. And yet in this false knightly interchange, we may see more than an empty clash of points of honour. It is a sign of real suffering. In the field of manner, too, the heyday of humanism is over, the Renaissance has come to a close and the unease, the injured melancholy, the fantastic spiritual lightnings of the seventeenth century are making themselves felt. The clash between Farnese and Gonzaga points, through the private affairs of the two princes, to a state of mind in which generosity and impotence, splendour and decadence, anger and ill-temper are mingled. With it went a longing for something which—so they felt—must surely now be imminent and which would put each of them to the proof.

The summer of 1592 was a season of vaunting. At Mantua the talk was all of challenges written and spoken. Together with his great favourite, the Marquis del Vasto, the young Duke wagered hard, drank, swaggered and put into words a wild impulse—one which impelled him to draw up a statement of his own on the Pantara affair. He tried to maintain a tone of elegant neutrality but attempted too hard to interpret and deck out his feelings; as a result the statement turned out naïve—so much so that Ranuccio Farnese, while recognizing with delicate irony Vincenzo's good intentions, let it be known in his reply that something approaching a retraction had been read into the Duke's words.

Now that old hatreds and new rancours were adding fuel to the quarrel between Parma and Mantua the adventurers—the unscrupulous bravos inured to the use of sword and dagger— saw their opportunity. Bold and cynical, with daggers in their belts, their only assets were dexterity and their lack of scruple. Since they particularly excelled as spies they put themselves at the disposal of the great lords. Each day there were men who crossed the Po and plunged into the woods on the frontier to reach the capitals of the two states by little-used paths. At the city gates they relied on their cunning. Having entered in disguise, they absorbed intelligence and came quickly away. One of these men provides us with a precious clue, which is confirmed by other documents. Having been sent on a mission to Parma, he had arrived there after an adventurous journey and had seen Ranuccio's return from Flanders. He reported that the prince's first visit—he still wore his spurs—had been to his brother, Cardinal

Odoardo. Immediately thereafter had come a long visit to his sister, the nun, Sister Maura Lucenia. We do not know what brother and sister said to each other, but certainly they spoke of Mantua, and presumably Margherita uttered those words of peace and reconciliation which alone befitted her habit and her nature. But the fact that he visited her did not mean that Ranuccio needed her advice. He required only to see this girl who had once been so high-spirited, the young woman of the masquerades, jokes, pranks and songs, mortified in her nun's habit, for his hatred against Gonzaga to deepen—Gonzaga who now radiated happiness, who had a prudent wife, sons and so many deplorable glittering ideas in his head. In Ranuccio, the drama of Margherita's life was always present and alive and something he saw in her eyes —a light which refused to resign itself to setting—renewed his hatred.

Meanwhile, suspicious characters were passing to and fro between Parma and Mantua in waves. Soon irregular bands, who said they were intent on private vendettas, made their appearance on the frontiers. There was talk of killings and great alarm. One suspicion gave birth to a thousand more. The Grand Duke, Ferdinando dei Medici, broke out with an oath, so exasperated was he at the heedlessness with which Vincenzo was about to upset the whole structure of Italy, doing so in ignorance of one of those plans for the future which the Grand Duke was secretly hatching with the aid of his chancellor, Belisario Vinta. 'Your Highness,' he wrote to his niece Leonora, 'should pray read this letter to my Lord, the Duke, and then burn it.' He said clearly that Vincenzo could help himself in one way only, by refraining from saying anything further. 'There is a rumour that there has been a movement of malcontents who are being stirred up to form bands. I will speak freely for, were it true, I could not approve of it for it seems to me, firstly, that this is unfitting in a prince and secondly, that more harm than good may come of it.' 'There should be no more writing of statements, he added. That sort of thing, he said, was fatally tempting. 'There is no doubt,' he concluded, 'that for the sake of honour, one has to risk one's very life, but there is no reason to do so or be induced to it by quibbling.'

All the peacemakers were in agreement with the Grand Duke's extremely intelligent view of the case—whether it was the Duke Alfonso d'Este, who was now completely reconciled with Vincenzo, or the Emperor, the Archduchess or Pope Clement VIII. The latter in his alarm had sent to Mantua one of the most powerful soldiers of the church, Claudio Aquaviva, the famous Spanish Vicar-General of the Jesuits.

By directing all his feelings into the exercises of prayer and meditation, this disciple of Ignatius Loyola had, as it were, decanted his human personality. No hint of passion had remained in the robust figure he presented, with his slow, calm gestures, and his shy dignity, which almost gave the impression of bloodlessness. That he was equally endowed with intelligence and firmness, he had demonstrated in recent years by fighting a battle —a fierce one, as battles between ecclesiastics can be—against the Jesuit Acosta and the Pope, who had in mind to reform the constitution of the order and limit the dictatorial powers of its Vicar-General. In the end Aquaviva had triumphed and won the Pope over by his arguments. Aquaviva was in Mantua in September while Vincenzo was enjoying the delights of Marmirolo. The mistake the Jesuit made was to go and try to talk to the Duke and summon him to reason.

This most nimble-witted Spanish dialectician concentrated firmly on externals and refused to allow himself to pry into the grounds for this tangle of hatreds. The argument he produced was wonderfully sophistical. Since the first challenge, it ran, came from the Marquis del Vasto and since he had spoken the offending words in the camp at Château-Thierry, it would be possible to discuss a reconciliation if only Vincenzo could be induced to disassociate himself from the Marquis. No real insults had passed between Ranuccio and Vincenzo. In other words, there would be a separate peace. But Vincenzo would not hear of it. He would never, he said, desert his cousin, who had compromised himself on his behalf. But it was precisely because he had compromised himself, Aquaviva declared, that he must be abandoned. In an attempt to escape from the pincers of such cold logic, Vincenzo put forward his own proposition—that he and the Marquis del Vasto constituted a single person.

There is no doubt that the evil one is attempting to stir up the fires, commented the Vicar-General, who extended his network to the Jesuits in Parma, instructing them to use their influence with Ranuccio, and to the Jesuits of Mantua who, in agreement with the two Leonoras—mother and wife—would bring their influence to bear on the Duke and the whole court. But by now Vincenzo lived his days to a secret roll of drums. Not even Agnese, for all that she inflamed him, could satisfy the Duke. Was it she he sought, or some other love, on the shores of Lake Garda, where the envoys followed him and pursued him from villa to villa? The atmosphere of danger excited and intoxicated him. Following his example, the established order of the court was being turned upside down. There were disorders. The proper management of the household rested entirely on the solid good sense of Leonora. Even Marcello Donati, with all his wisdom, lost control, as he demonstrated by having an enemy of his beaten and next day sending to the palace for money to pay the damages. The insolence of the gesture did not fail to provoke comment.

Understandably, a pure logician like Aquaviva was, as he confessed, unable to follow the whims of Vincenzo, who at one moment seemed to be prepared for a sensible settlement and the next was off into his own world of fantasy. It required another Jesuit, the famous Antonio Possevino, himself a Mantuan, who was more flexible, more indulgent and whose mind had a certain fresh psychological insight, to approach the Duke and persuade him at least to recognize the authority of the Pope in Alfonso d'Este and Ferdinando dei Medici, who had been appointed as Papal arbiters. This step towards reconciliation was timely, for one document was giving birth to another and they were becoming increasingly highly-charged. To one written by Ranuccio, which contained the testimony of the Seigneur Ligny and Haschincourt against the Marquis del Vasto, the latter replied with a corrosive text in which, reverting to the theme of his own immaculate genealogy, he hinted that everyone knew the shameful origins of the House of Farnese. He was undoubtedly hinting at the ancient passion of the Borgia Pope, Alexander VI, for Giulia Farnese, who had made the fortune of her brother, the Cardinal—the one who became in time Pope Paul III. (This was the period when, in the Vatican, the Farneses were constantly on the alert to see that a Madonna by Pintoricchio in the Borgia chambers, which was mistakenly said to represent the famous Giulia, was kept boarded up and covered with a panel of brocade.)

Certain of Vincenzo's retainers contrived to aggravate matters. Thus the Prince of Stigliano, who was heir to Sabionetta on his mother's side, showed signs of wishing to sell his rights in the inheritance of the fief to Ranuccio himself, who was holding himself ready to send in five hundred infantry. There were other troops from Parma in the pay of the Marquis of Castiglione, brother of San Luigi Gonzaga, a youth who, following the example of Caligula, declared he wished his subjects had but one head so that he could remove it at one blow. Finding himself surrounded at home by enemies and traitors, Vincenzo displayed a certain careless, joyful grace in showing no fear for them. Nothing ever happened to him, so he was more justified in running the risk, than Leonora in trembling when she saw him leave, without guards and only lightly armed, to visit some courtier, to sup with an actress, perhaps, or visit a tavern.

Unlike Vincenzo, Ranuccio Farnese was afraid even of shadows. He laid bare the deep roots of his hatred of Vincenzo by a revealing gesture. He had begun a secret trial against Vincenzo for what had happened ten years before with Margherita, calling as witness a certain court singer who had apparently been the first to hear various intimate details which weighed heavily against the Duke of Mantua.

So Margherita, with her excruciating problem, was once more called back to the front of the stage where even her nun's habit could not defend her. Her name and her person were bandied from court to court; when she appeared in all her innocence, even the most active peace-makers declared that there was no hope. However, at the very moment when the word war was beginning to be used in earnest, things changed rapidly. So busily did the Jesuits go to and fro, so strict were the orders of the Pope, so much did the Medicis and the Estes rage, reinforced by the Emperor of Austria, that at last Vincenzo gave in. Ranuccio could not but follow his example. The old Duke of Ferrara, Alfonso II, who had been appointed arbiter in the matter by both Pope and Emperor, summoned the two quarrelling parties together. On the 27th July, 1593, a reconciliation of a kind took place, exactly one year after the first written challenge.

'Not so much peace as reconciliation,' was the gloss of one anonymous commentator but, even considered as a reconciliation, it was cankered. In fact, while the Chancelleries were exchanging the usual compliments, both sides vied with each other in arresting retainers and citizens on the evidence of trifles. At Mantua letters had been intercepted with allusions to 'a stomach remedy' sent by Prince Ranuccio for two friends who were taken to be Vincenzo and the Marquis del Vasto. In the so-called remedy they guessed at poison. In Parma two faithful followers of the Gonzagas were treacherously arrested. They were described as 'not only in the pay of but very dear and intimate friends of His Highness' and at the arrest all Mantua was startled.

The agreements have been broken, they said, and added that not even among barbarians would a trap have been laid for a friend's retainers. To be quite sure where he stood, Vincenzo had put himself in the hands of a jurist, who must certainly have been his shrewd minister, Annibale Chieppio. The latter agreed that he had the right to feel injured but said it should be limited to breaking off the reconciliation and a request to liberate the arrested men. Then the unending round of envoys from Rome began again with cardinals and priests. All the women were on their knees busy in supplication—Vincenzo's sister, the Duchess of Ferrara, with all the fervour of her red hair, Leonora dei Medici elegantly persuasive, Leonora of Austria with a severity which was pathetic in its emotion, never wearying of doing penance for her son and of beseeching the saints in Paradise and her Hapsburg relations on earth to see to it that he was brought into the ways of righteousness.

The letters which Vincenzo wrote about this time reveal the monotonous exasperation of his days. He was perfectly capable of self-examination (this was the era of spiritual exercises) and even of confessing that, if looked at seriously, his method of facing the future was excessively light-hearted. He resolved to limit his expenses and to make every effort to soften his reactions in the quarrel with Parma, but instead he increased the luxury of the court and became more bitterly inflamed against Ranuccio. As for the rest he stated it clearly:

'No good will ever come of attempting to make me do anything against my will or of preventing me by force from doing what I want.' So let them not meddle in his loves. Agnese had had the experience not of finding her place taken but of having more than one companion in the Duke's love. It was from this time that she began to pray so often before a Madonna by Andrea del Sarto to whom, she tells us, she told her sorrows, day after day. Prayer, which always looks well in a woman, reawoke in Agnese a feeling of warmth which was troubled by the knowledge that she had sinned and was being punished. This in her was both attractive and piquant and so, for the very reason that he made her weep, Vincenzo loved her more than all the others without, however, being able to defend himself from their assaults, particularly when, for the sake of appearances, Agnese had to follow her husband to his lands in Monferrato. Vincenzo's distractions, whether women of the people or actresses, had mostly been fleeting, but finally they settled on the Marchioness Felicità Gonzaga, whom Leonora kept among the closest circle of her ladies.

Felicità was the daughter of Tullio Guerrieri, Vincenzo's Chamberlain. She was very young and a widow, her Gonzaga husband having died in 1590. The first gift love brought her was a daughter, Francesca, whom Vincenzo recognized as his and whom he later married off with a large dowry. Leonora continued to keep Felicità close to her, for she probably knew the child Francesca, protected the two of them and watched over them, sticking firmly to her plan of regularizing her husband's amours whenever possible. It is clear that Felicità Gonzaga caused Leonora no worry for she was one of those sweet women who are wrapped in a kind of affectionate stupidity and are, where men are concerned, a thoroughly charted land and a haven of rest.

Vincenzo tacitly agreed with Leonora. He was fond of Felicità but it was only of Agnese that he had a portrait made—a portrait in bronze, obviously a bust, the work of the Milanese artist, Giacomo Cario. He entrusted Agnese to his sister Margherita, and was highly pleased when she said that he had ruined the looks of the fair lady. The day that Agnese bore him a son, who was given the pastoral name of Silvio, he fell so much in love with the child that he wanted to recognize it as a Gonzaga and as soon as it had passed its early infancy, insisted on having it at Court to grow up with the legitimate Gonzagas. Their ranks, titles, honours, teachers and even their dress must be the same, Vincenzo commanded, and readily acknowledged his likeness in the child, who for his part took from his father the power of attracting affection and added to it his mother's emotional range, so that there was no one at court who did not love him—including his brothers and sisters.

Vincenzo strove for liberty with a kind of frenzy which fused the old struggle against the constrictions of his youth, his new struggle against the constrictions of the age and another, more deep and more obscure, which was the struggle of his spirit which, although led to find its solutions in sensuality, was unable to find there complete satisfaction. And like all men whom the immediate business of life distracts from a knowledge of themselves to the point where they can no longer recognize the origin of their own unease, he had found a way of distracting his obsession—a way which was becoming widely diffused at this period. He travelled, he changed country, horizon and company.

It might be said that he inherited this instinct from his father; but, while for Guglielmo Gonzaga to journey meant taking refuge in solitary villas, fleeing from his own image as seen in the eyes of others, for Vincenzo it meant finding in others' eyes a gleam of understanding and agreement. And since his vitality required the support of a plebiscite, he expanded from city to city, displaying himself, seizing at any pretext to prolong and give variety to his sojourns. In 1592, following a courteous sentence from the Pope, he trumped up a summons to talks with the Vatican, alarming all the courts of Italy who sent their envoys thick as hail to discover the non-existent political secret behind this summons. Having arrived at Rome, he stayed there, visiting ruins, buying antiquities, going to the play, betting, hunting, and amusing himself with princes and cardinals, all of whom were his friends.

One day he discovered Genoa and the sea intoxicated him. At Genoa he played high and lost heavily and had to leave jewels in pledge. It took him years to pay off the debts. He was greatly loved by the ladies, especially Giulia Grimaldi, but found so little favour with the men that some years later when he wanted to ask for a loan, he could not find the meanest trader ready to oblige him on his pledged word. He had therefore to put in pawn the incomes of Monferrato and the territory of Mantua. He always went willingly to visit the Grand Duke Ferdinando at Florence but this was replaced by a kind of alarmed caution, particularly after the Grand Duke married Christine of Lorraine. He went to Venice, he went on pilgrimage to Loreto; he went to Ferrara, Innsbruck and Augusta. There would be no end to the catalogue of what he brought back from his journeys—prints, precious stones, cloth, brocades, lace, tapestries, jewels, paintings, sculptures, miniatures, ivories, bronzes, books, works of art to decorate the immense ducal palace, already so ornate, and to distribute as gifts. He had a genius for the distribution of gifts, so instinctive and happy that we might almost call it pure. It corresponded to his most generous instinct, which was to radiate outwards towards life in a generous gesture so as to awaken in others the most intensely affectionate of feelings. Giving, for him, therefore, always indicated choice, a method of communication. If his sister Margherita asked him for Spanish songs, he had a whole book sung through for him so as to choose the most beautiful. He saw to the mating of the lapdogs of his favourites and friends. He went to endless trouble over a length of cloth or a jewel to present to his wife. Under his own supervision he had wigs combed to show his sister, the Archduchess, the latest female fashion. He had a passion for artificial flowers of gold or silk as well as for real ones, and had them sent from all over Italy to be distributed to the court ladies and rejoiced to see them arrive at the festivities, blooming with his gifts. One morning, as he went through one of the verdant vegetable gardens which alternated with the flower gardens round the ducal palace, he saw an immense cauliflower with its fresh frosted leaves clinging tightly to the firm head, and he at once decided to have it cut and sent to a lady. And so it was with the fruit from Garda, with the fish caught in the lake or the lagoon at Commacchio, which he distributed to his wife and his mistresses.

Naturally his mother was opposed to so much generous distribution of affection and was always quick to spy on her son whatever he did, noting it down and sighing. But when she died in 1594, honoured and lamented, Vincenzo was generous enough to allow the priests and friars to draw the legacies set out in his mother's will instead of pocketing them scornfully, as princes usually did in such cases. This respect for his mother's wishes was better proof of Vincenzo's filial piety than the immense funeral, the great occasion which the dynasty was obliged to observe and which presented to the people a catafalque in the form of a temple erected in the middle of the Basilica of Santa Barbara, an immense lugubrious affair of statues, draped velvets, torches, eagles, epithets and emblems.

CHAPTER NINE

The Crusader

AMIDST all these varying stimuli, Vincenzo's years piled up; yet he had not succeeded in giving to them that energetic impulse which should have been the beginning of his ascent to higher things. If he went over them, he saw that the first years of his reign were interspersed with sudden gleams each of which stood for a hope which had immediately lost its enchantment. Time had been lost over the petty quarrels with Ferrara, and the enmity with Parma, still alive and fermenting, was a pain growing malignantly inward which could not be translated into warlike deeds because too many people were pledged to restrain and suffocate him. As for the requests for generalships in foreign lands, no one had taken them up. And Vincenzo was beginning to withdraw into himself and set himself some doubting questions when the echo of a glorious trumpet call reached him—the Crusade.

It was indeed a terrible lightning-flash which came from the Turkish scimitars suspended over Eastern Europe in the last years of the sixteenth century. The Emperor Rudolf II of Hapsburg was threatened on his frontiers and felt that he could no longer hold out unaided in an Empire torn by the internal feuds between Lutherans and Catholics; for the terrible Muslim enemy had entered Hungary and taken up quarters in Budapest and from there threatened his territories far and wide. Turkish plans were limitless; their forces were compact, fresh and fierce. Although Sigismond Bathory attempted to contain them in Transylvania, they had succeeded in infiltrating into the Balkans, into Wallachia and Moldavia. They were expected soon to be seen making their appearance on the Dalmatian coast. Thus the victory of Lepanto, that gem of Catholic glory, had been of little avail and when Rudolf of Hapsburg, worn out by the continual calamitous news, asked aid from Rome in 1595, Clement VIII made a warm appeal to the Catholic princes of Europe and Italy to take up arms. It was a question of defending the West from the threat of the Prophet's green banner. Italy gave a poor response to the fervour of the request. France sent nothing, for she had been too sorely drained by the struggle between Catholic and Huguenot and was only now coming to herself under the intelligent guidance of Henry IV, who by now was converted to Catholicism and recognized as king. Poland took some time to make up her mind, for she was skirmishing with Tartars and Cossacks and unsure of Russia. Being involved in the Flanders war, Spain sent money and gave vague conditional promises. Venice was caught up in her commercial treaties with the East and was gingerly practising elastic neutrality. The Medicis sent money, a body of mercenaries and three captains of ducal blood. The Duke of Ferrara, a cavalier by nature as well as religion, found himself too old to take up the sword. Parma and Urbino made no move. Only Vincenzo felt the appeal of the Papal demand and replied to it.

It was against everybody's advice. As early as 1594, at the first news of the fresh Turkish wars in Hungary, Leonora had seen her husband's eyes gleam with an intense blue and had understood. Gently, with the flexibility and skill of women who foresee their husbands' moves and wish to limit them, Leonora was defeatist about the Crusade under her breath. The example of her uncle, Grand Duke Ferdinando, who sent relations of the family but stayed at home himself, seemed to her the best one to follow. There were so many quarrelsome Gonzagas in the territory of Mantua—could they not go off, a dozen at a time? For a while she succeeded in her manœuvres. In the middle of 1594, when it seemed as if the Spaniards, in league with the Duke of Savoy, were about to invade Monferrato in order to partition it, she almost gave a sigh of relief, thinking the matter so serious that it would make the Duke abandon for ever the idea of going on campaign in the East. Instead matters were cleared up over Monferrato, for the King of Spain had no interest in the aggrand- izement of Piedmont. Serious news suddenly came from Hungary and the Pope's voice became more charged with emotion. During the Mass of the 23rd September, 1594, he soaked five handker- chiefs with tears. Vincenzo declared that he was ready to leave.

It was an intoxicating transition to leave Agnese's arms and go down in front of the castle and see himself greeted by the hard faithful eyes of Carlo de Rossi, the young captain who was to command the three companies of mounted arquebusiers and who saw to their equipment. It was wonderful to visit the weapon store with him, to read over the list of soldiers and horsemen, to assist at the manœuvres and to make up the squadrons. Then a badge had to be chosen for the enterprise, the sign under which the Crusade would enfold. After long meditation Vincenzo chose the ancient *Sic* of the Gonzagas, set in a crescent moon; which caused much conjecture among the courtiers who found it highly confusing that the crescent should be unfurled by a Christian against the Turks. The explanation, which is quite simple, we are given by the chronicler Amadei. The horns of the moon point upwards in the crescent phase of the planet, indicating the waxing power of the house of Gonzaga.

The Mantuan cavalry made a magnificent impression; solidly equipped, it presented the flower of Mantuan youth, upright on their picked chargers with their white *sic* gleaming on their left arms. Seven marquises of the house of Gonzaga, together with gentlemen and courtiers and all the first names of the nobility, followed the Duke as he rode along in the midst of his picked bodyguard—a truly regal company. Vincenzo had obtained from the Pope, over and above a most ample blessing, permission to take with him a bishop, bearing in a tabernacle a tiny drop of the most precious blood of our Lord. He was followed by his com- plete court of cooks, carvers, pages, personal servants, doctors, druggists and even musicians, five of them, under the direction of Claudio Monteverdi. When the new crusaders passed through the

streets of Mantua after the Mass and solemn benediction in the
crypt of Sant'Andrea in the sunshine of late June, the music,
songs, the applause, the trumpets and the bells formed a symphony
in the heart of the young Duke. Then at last he departed, leaving
that warm nest where his wife, his mistresses and the ladies of the
court wept for him, 'wept for him,' as a courtier says, 'and
languished for him.' In Agnese's eyes he had caught a glimpse of
the impassioned query, the feminine questioning expressed in an
elementary 'why?' to which men who are leaving for the wars
cannot and must not reply. He left Mantua. As he passed through
the Lombard fields, yellow with grain which burned under the
ripe breath of summer, he might, like the country squire he was,
have reckoned up the crop, but the breastplates and the arms with
their glint and gleam brought to his mind the thought of war and
held him dazzled.

Let life overflow, he felt, let life overflow, now that he was on
the point of putting it to the proof of the Turkish scimitars. Now
that the past was abolished and with it the laborious mechanism
of everyday reactions, Vincenzo felt the human simplicity of the
good soldier for whom only essentials are important. All the rest
was a mere game. The painful sense of oppression from which all
the generous spirits of Italy suffered at this time, and from which
Vincenzo had suffered to the limit, was miraculously alleviated
the moment he took sword in hand. Yet he did not fight either
to increase his own territory or for money—he was to lose a hundred
thousand crowns in the crusade. He did not even fight from profound religious conviction. Indeed it may be said that he had no
heartfelt faith in the cause which summoned him; but this was the
very reason why he was able to reduce the reasons for his departure
to a bargain with himself and, by accepting it, feel that he was
responding to a rigorous demand—that of his own conscience.
The gleaming equipment, the coloured plumes, the fluttering
scarves, the Sibylline mottoes, the poetic word 'Crusade', the
emotions of the farewells, the exciting impulse of the break with
the past—all these sensuous elements fermented within him. But
for the first time in his life, it was pardonable, because he had

accepted the clearly defined moral duty of courage and dignity which is the basis of any military undertaking. For Vincenzo, the journey was a period of ripening and a liberation of the spirit. When he reached Innsbruck and his sister, the Archduchess Anna Caterina, he felt that he had been ransomed at last. He had an outburst of mad laughter when he saw his sister coming to meet him, for she had become so fat that she seemed to be twice her natural size and was, moreover, dressed in a German fashion, so incongruously that he and his gentlemen could barely keep a straight face. He was still laughing about it in his bedchamber. He was laughing about it when he wrote to his most elegant wife that he had had a dress made for her exactly like the Archduchess's. But it would be asking too much of Leonora to see in this letter the age-old childishness of the soldier. She was a woman left at home to her fears. Life to her was a drama and war a tragedy. She could not yet get used to the idea that her husband had gone off voluntarily in search of perils when the world was already so full of pitfalls. She gave vent to her feelings along with her ladies in prayer and weeping. When she wrote, she confessed to Vincenzo that she was unable to get used to his absence. The Bishop of Avila, who was passing through Mantua to take the reliquary with the most precious blood of our Lord, arrived in time to give her a little emotional consolation; for he swore to follow the Duke into battle, cross in hand. This was a moment when even the bishop felt fall upon himself a reflected gleam from the spirit of Peter the Hermit.

But at Innsbruck Vincenzo had a bad day. A Mantuan was the cause of it, an astrologer, a certain Panizza who had confided to some gentlemen that, according to the stars, the Duke would not return alive from the Crusade. On the journey someone had reported the prophecy to Vincenzo, who was only too susceptible to the suggestions of necromancy—besides, what man in war does not believe in malignant or benign influences? The Duke took quick action on the prophecy of Panizza, this 'gentle spirit' as he called him laughing wryly, and quickly had a letter sent to his minister Petrozzani instructing him to have him arrested and to get out of him in one way or another what grounds there were for his prophecy. 'Not that I believe in it, but I do not like silly talk of this kind,' he stated and added with a reference to Ranuccio Farnese, 'I would not wish to give pleasure to someone who cannot bear me.' So they were to make him talk and deal with him firmly because 'I confess to you that I am burning with impatience'.

What became of the imprudent astrologer is of little importance. As soon as he had resumed his journey, Vincenzo quickly recovered his spirits and was warm and gay once more. Reaching the Danube, he was met by the Archdukes Ferdinand and Maximilian in a state barge. With them he travelled on to Linz and entered Prague, where he found the Emperor Rudolf II, who had so much in common with the enthusiastic and mystical spirit of that city. Rudolf of Hapsburg, a sovereign without consort—his people had never pardoned him for having refused the Infanta Isabella, daughter of Philip II, with the fat dowry of Flanders—was a constant prey to a nervous anxiety which he attempted to alleviate by country houses, palaces, gardens, artistic collections, stars, jewels and books. He was one of those men who pass from infancy to adolescence without finding a point where they can insert the reality of their fantasy into human reality and thus render possible their own adaptation —which may be no more than a convention—to the world as others know it. He therefore cast a sadness over his days by his attempt to find a way of accepting existence. He was inaccessible to conferences and communications; his hesitancy and his intense dislikes were looked upon in his court as signs of indifference. He was unloved and unpopular and although his culture made it possible for him to recognize and protect the genius of Kepler, it deteriorated into a love of over-subtlety which led him in the end into the most complicated abstractions.

His calling of emperor did not please him and he endured it only from an atavistic sense of duty. He was, quite apart from his obsession against the Turks, who threatened him from Hungary and had claimed tribute from Austria, impatient with the political

and religious discord in the German states and the constantly
recurring enmity of his brother Matthias. Both the Archduke
Matthias and the Archduke Maximilian had gone off to fight
against the Turks. No matter how much the Pope might exhort
him, he, Rudolf, would never take up the sword.

Help from the west was arriving. The papal auxiliaries, commanded by Gian Francesco Aldobrandini, were joining up with
those of Archduke Matthias near Gràn. And it was towards Gràn
that Vincenzo set out, taking his leave of Prague without much
haste. He had struck the delicate and lively imagination of the
people, for he had shone at the feasts, at the hunting-parties and
receptions with his easy gaiety. He arrived in Vienna in a carriage
with six horses, upholstered in black velvet, the present of
Rudolf II: there was no end to the Viennese festivities, all of
which he accepted gracefully. There was also a display by the
Mantuan militia, which rode past to the admiration of all on a
day when the air spoke of early autumn, with fine horses and
handsome soldiers, in the confident harmony of elegant uniforms,
controlled pace and measured movement. And finally they left
for camp.

To meet the Duke, there came Carlo de Rossi with his three
companies of arquebusiers, who had already been tested under
fire, to tell how hard the Turks fought. The tents arose with
their gleaming *Sic*, high up between the horns of the crescent.
Paolo Sforza and Monsignor Doria came to greet him, and later
the Archdukes Matthias and Maximilian and all the rest were
invited to solemn vespers sung by the Italian musicians under the
direction of Claudio Monteverdi. Almost certainly the music was
composed by him. How pleasant it would be to track it down
and follow the lofty emotion of the great musician who was the
only immortal there among so many princes, archdukes and
generals; the man, who, on the eve of battle and under the
Hungarian sky, made the sublime decision to transport his
listeners into a civilized world of his own where the element of
the eternal is fixed for ever in pure sound.

The first engagement in which Vincenzo took part was

favoured by fortune. Fighting night and day, they attacked
Plintenburg, a strongpoint important because of its position on
the river and because it was the centre of a region containing four
hundred villages. The attackers struck so hard and so often that
the siege ended on the 22nd September with the surrender of the
place. The fact that the besieged sent word that they wished only
to surrender themselves into the hands of the Pasha of Mantua
proves not only the high renown which Vincenzo had won but
also the shrewdness of the Turks, who must have learnt something
of his knightly grandness of manner. In fact, having received
their bows and praises, Vincenzo promised to spare their lives,
received their leaders in his tent, was filled with admiration for
their fine appearance and sent them off to Budapest in safety with
their families.

If, on the one hand, the gossip which bedevilled the life of the
camp related that Don Giovanni dei Medici, and with him Don
Antonio and Don Virginio, had lain in wait at the gates of the
town to rob the prisoners and considered this a successful joke,
there were stories on the other hand of Vincenzo's prodigality—
of how he had lent from his own pocket twenty-five thousand
florins to the Archduke Matthias and paid ten thousand crowns to
some Walloon soldiers who, being without their regular pay, had
left the camp and were pillaging the countryside. But the expedition began to lose impetus because of jealousies between the
captains. It is difficult to give an idea of the kind of thing these
crusading *condottieri* said of each other—one was a miser, another
consumed with pride, a third was a rogue, a fourth a horrible
Huguenot. 'They speak ill of each other in a terrible way,' wrote
Vincenzo, who, for his part, went on speaking ill of all in great
good humour. One scandal he had to relate was the following:
the cathedral at Gràn, which had been so many years in the hands
of the Turks, had been respected by them—it was not so respected
by the German Lutherans, who no sooner entered it than they
overthrew the altars and gouged the eyes out of the images.

But Vincenzo's military days were coming to an end. On the
26th September, he could no longer resist the desire to distinguish

himself, and seized upon the opportunity offered by Turkish skirmishers who were raiding between Plintenburg and Buda. He let it be known that he would issue forth and purge the country of this *canaille*. The trumpets sounded the fall-in. The Mantuan and Walloon horsemen gathered, and the body of tried troops moved off behind their guide through the damp Hungarian landscape with its little swelling hills, and advanced to meet the enemy with care-free hearts, persuaded that they saw the gleam of Turkish scimitars behind each tree.

They rode eight hours in silence. Of the Turks, there was not even a shadow to be seen. Evening came, and the tired horsemen halted in a wood where they consulted amongst themselves, unwilling to admit that they felt a suspicion that it was a trap. In the pauses between the speeches, there was a bewildered feeling that they were waiting for something. Meantime, in the camp, they had learnt about the expedition, and a Hungarian captain, either because he knew that the Turks had been seen in great numbers, or, as the Mantuans said later, out of envy of Vincenzo, sent men to stop the Duke, and himself came post-haste to join him. He found Vincenzo in the wood, and persuaded him to fall back on a safe position. Next morning, having sent out scouts, who reported the advance of a large Turkish army, they decided together to return to the camp.

On the evening of that same day, Vincenzo, Don Antonio and Don Giovanni, together with Gian Francesco Aldobrandini, were supping together in Don Antonio's tent, and speaking of the war. The talk became very free. Suddenly, Vincenzo declared that, with all this empty talk and scheming, he felt that time was being wasted, and that he was tempted to go back home. The words were no sooner said than they created a sense of uneasiness in which their enthusiasm and interest in the expedition melted away. Vincenzo tried to remedy his error, and to work up some hope and trust. He called for a conference of commanders, but they did not respond. Things were complicated by the first signs of bad weather, by mortality among the soldiers, and an attack of erysipelas which kept him in bed with fever and delirium. He was well tended, and he recovered, but by now he had a distaste for German territory, on which he felt so insecure that he requested permission to pass through Venetia; for he was afraid of ambushes. Without consulting the Emperor, and with a scanty greeting from the Archdukes, he gave orders for the tents with their gleaming crescents to be struck. Very soon, on the 1st November, the Mantuan crusaders were gathered round their hearths amid a thick aroma of autumn with truffles, new wine, mushrooms, and roasted chestnuts, to tell the story of their Oriental adventure.

The expedition, it must be confessed, had been a failure. Had this been admitted, Vincenzo might have found a tonic in the bitter dregs of confession. Men and officers had fallen in the field, a hundred thousand crowns had been squandered—that was the tribute of blood and gold which the East had taken, a heavy tribute for the little state of Mantua—yet the adventure had not led to higher things. Once more, Vincenzo was betrayed by his own fascinating sensibility. What he required was a stern glance; what he found everywhere in Mantua were eyes lit with joy. Naturally, his children were wild with admiration, and on the evening of his arrival clung to the corners of his bed, almost overcome by excessive love, resisting their tutor, who was trying to lead them away, as stubbornly as Spanish mules. What was lacking was Leonora's perspicacity. Seeing him back safe and sound, and thinking that he had learnt his lesson, she smiled at him knowingly, with that tempting feeling of ownership, common to wives when their husbands come home from afar. Ministers and councillors, including even those who had lately disapproved of the war, could not refrain from fêting the Duke— not to mention the ladies in their great stiff gowns, and the courtiers, musicians, singers, painters, and actors and all the colourful throng of his boon companions.

The Carnival was brilliant. Vincenzo's two eldest sons, Francesco, the heir-apparent, and Ferdinand, the future cardinal, acted in a pastoral, and the players acted, too, led by the fair Diana, who greatly pleased the Duke. Another actress, and a famous writer of comedies, Isabella Andreini, wrote him impudent and mannered letters, requesting his favour in a style which hinted at hands joined in prayer and bended knees. Then benedictions and congratulations rained down from a papal brief cordially couched. Why should Leonora be surprised if, for Vincenzo, the days spent in Hungary were becoming so transfigured that their bad moments were already cancelled out? Perhaps he would no longer have recognized as his the letter he wrote to Rudolf II on his return—a letter which reveals that he had left the camp without the permission of the Emperor. As the days passed the war to him became a kind of fresco in his honour, and since there was one thing which never failed in him, whatever else he lacked, namely a precise feeling for popular favour, he realized that he had risen in the esteem of his subjects from the moment they had seen him leave at the head of his soldiers. He felt therefore that he owed something to the image which the people were creating of their liege-lord. Encouraged by this excellent stimulus, he was highly successful in sorting out a bloody skein of crimes committed by the Gonzagas of the Castiglione branch.

Rudolfo Gonzaga, to whom San Luigi had surrendered all earthly privileges, had had his own uncle, Orazio, treacherously murdered, while he was peacefully fishing in a stream. He had then seized his estate, Castelgoffredo, imprisoning in a room of the castle the daughter and widow of the murdered man, while he attempted brutally to impose his rule on the peaceful populace. Nothing was too much to assuage the animal cruelty of Rudolfo Gonzaga, who heaped on monstrous taxes, tortured, mutilated and killed. But things went badly for him. One day, as he was going to Mass with his extremely beautiful twenty-year-old wife on his arm, a shot from an arquebus cut short the procession and his life.

The vendetta which followed and the massacre of the tyrant's guards, made up for the most part of men whom Rudolfo had hired in Parma in order to slight Vincenzo, were events over which the people rejoiced. Vincenzo sent a garrison post-haste to Castelgoffredo, where it arrived in time, two hours before a

Spanish garrison which found the positions occupied—a grave set-back for the governor of Milan. Vincenzo had the assassin arrested—a man of the people, who confessed with great nobility— and opened a trial for which he had been appointed judge by the Emperor Rudolf II. He brought it to an end by not only acquitting the assassin but praising him as the avenger of the people. This conclusion may have been suggested to Vincenzo by a desire to score a hit against Ranuccio Farnese; but it also corresponded to his own interests; for he wished to have popular favour on his side now that he was attempting to take the place of his cousin as ruler of Castelgoffredo. However this may be, his was still a rare verdict, especially for those days when princes were tenacious in the defence of their own intransigent authority.

What was almost more difficult to resolve was the case of the beautiful and innocent widow, who made her eyes all swollen by weeping, not so much over the death of her husband, as because she feared that he had died in mortal sin. Was it not said that he had made a pact with Satan and that he kept a demon enclosed in the setting of a ring? In order to reassure herself, the widow related amid her tears a dream she had had the night before the murder, full of saintly voices and angelic *misereres*. As though the wife's visions were not enough, her mother added hers, and said that in a dream she had descended into hell and seen the devils gnashing their teeth and howling with rage because Rudolfo had evaded them, thanks to the powerful intercession and prayers of his sainted brother, Luigi, at the throne of God. It would be a wonderful example of maternal love if by chance she invented this vision to console her daughter's anguish. The wolfish brothers of San Luigi Gonzaga showed themselves even more so when Rudolfo's younger brother, having fallen heir to Castiglione, began to make his sister-in-law's life a misery. In order to make things easier for her, the Duke and Duchess, who had a kindly respect for her, invited her to Mantua. In the end she came, and frequented the court, displaying with innocent guile her mourning and her widowed beauty, which was calculated to move the hearts and awaken the senses of men. With the Duke's approval, she married another Gonzaga, Claudio by name, who was both respectable and extremely rich, and to whom in nine years she gave seven children, safely dividing her time between conjugal love and prayer. Perhaps she was one of the few women who succeeded in approving of herself throughout her whole life.

Although he had settled affairs at Castelgoffredo with a sentence worthy of Trajan, Vincenzo lacked the courage to overcome the insoluble quarrel with Parma. We must recognize that he would have required a detachment, partly scientific, partly philosophical, to state the problem in exact terms, because, even had he wished to forget the present grounds for offence, there was one thing Vincenzo would never be able to get rid of—the memory of Margherita—all the more since, from afar, Ranuccio used his influence to keep it alive, not only openly, by suggestive acts, but with unrelenting mental pressure. We hear no more talk of the legal process begun against Vincenzo's divorce of his sister, but perhaps it still went on in the secret rooms of the palace where Ranuccio, who had been duke since 1592 and his father's death in Flanders, wove at his web like a mad spider.

The eternal quarrel was nourished by runaway servants, by servants abducted, by confessions of plots, by men imprisoned and examined under torture—another good-for-nothing confessed he had been sent by Ranuccio to assassinate Vincenzo during a masked ball. And now the jurists had begun to manipulate affairs with that sophisticated subtlety which was so congenial to Ranuccio's character, but went far beyond Vincenzo's experience. And yet although the protocols containing discussion of the offences on either side were becoming innumerable, the quarrel was flagging; it was a secret illness, wasting away the hearts of the two contestants. It seemed they might even make peace, as they had done once before in 1597 amidst the joyful tears of their nearest relations, but both the submissiveness of Ranuccio and the levity of Vincenzo were deceptive. To the latter, everything seemed highly unimportant now that he had decided to recover once more the fullness of his days in the fields of Hungary.

The news of the Crusade had been becoming steadily worse for

the last two years. The Turks were thrusting to the north, and
bearing down upon the west. They were advancing as if possessed,
like a rocket-burst, darting out from a solid base in a swift, sweeping conquest which the imperial troops were unable to dam. In
the winter of 1596 Agria in Upper Hungary fell and the threat to
Austria came very near. In his phantasm-haunted nights, Rudolf
saw green banners advancing to rise up like a forest on Christian
ground. He appealed to the Pope; Clement VIII collected gold
and men. The offices of the Vatican sent out one after another
letters for help to the Christian princes, but few replied.

Such an appeal reached Mantua, and Vincenzo, as he read it,
found in its words a sense of returning life, which was too precious
for his reason to oppose. He said that he was preparing, and then
announced that he was ready. In accordance with his sterner
understanding of war, he left Mantua on the 28th July, 1597,
without pomp and show, but solidly equipped with arms mostly
from the workshops of Brescia.

On the 29th he bade farewell to his Lake Garda at Desenzano;
on the 30th he was at Riva di Trento, and then passed through
Bolzano and Bressanone to Innsbruck. After touching at Linz, he
went on by river to Vienna, where he once more found his
friends so determined to fête him that he was wearied. The
Viennese carnival lasted eight consecutive days, and the talk was
of nothing but hunting and amusement. On the 22nd August at
Papa, Vincenzo met the Archduke Maximilian and there was
more rejoicing. Between the 28th and the 30th August they reached
Javarrino and began to explore the terrain. At first there were
little clashes, a river-crossing, escort duties on the baggage-
wagons—none of them easy—and Vincenzo discharged his duties
well with his handy troops. Then, after further preparatory
actions and other delays for feasting and hunting in quarters at
Oedenburg, at the beginning of September close siege was laid
to Javarrino. On the 9th September, Vincenzo, the famous
captain Giorgo Basta and the Marquis of Borgau met together.
Having divided the terrain into sectors, they decided to take the
heights round the city by a simultaneous manœuvre; Vincenzo

studied his sector and divided his men into little groups to offer a smaller target. At the moment agreed, he gave the signal for the attack, and soon found himself face to face with the enemy—the real enemy who was both truculent and brave.

It was a wonderful day. Vincenzo at one moment saw that an isolated group of his horse commanded by Ercole Rossi had fallen into a trap and was disappearing under a fierce whirl of blows. Cesare Gonzaga, already wounded by a lance in the back, had fallen. Antonio Andreasi, with his head split open by the blow of a scimitar, was hanging half-dead from his horse's croup. The blood was streaming from the numerous wounds of the Count di Rivara and Frederico Gonzaga. Shouting a quick command, Vincenzo turned his horse and made towards the little troop. Plunging into the fight, he struck out and engaged himself with *élan*. He rescued his men, took back from the Turks the Mantuan prisoners, left dead and wounded on the ground, and did not himself get a scratch. Of those who were with him, someone was inevitably to swear that he had seen the figure of San Francesco di Paola hovering over the Duke and turning aside the blows aimed at him by his enemies. Vincenzo did not fail on his return to go in solemn procession to thank his protector in the church recently built for him in Mantua. His thanks were sung from the fullness of his heart, but those to the Marquis of Borgau he had ironically hissed, for, although he had been present at the engagement, the Marquis had kept aloof and arrived to Vincenzo's aid when all was over.

Now that things were warming up, the command was entrusted to Don John of Prininstein, a born soldier, and the kind of man who possesses authority as if by natural right; so they passed over to the assault on the hill which dominated the besieged city. With great ability, the Turks attempted to draw off the Imperial forces by pretending to send troops against Gràn. The crusaders did not take the bait, and decided on the assault in which Vincenzo, who had received fresh reinforcements from Mantua, was in the foremost ranks. But on the first day of the attack their commander on his white courser died under the Turkish lances and scimitars; his death brought to a stop the expedition to Javarrino, reduced the imperial camp to the usual morass of quarrels, and struck a blow at Vincenzo's laboriously achieved self-confidence. That Marquis of Borgau, who had watched the Mantuan cavalry being mown down without moving to their aid, was nominated general, and Vincenzo was unable to shake off a bitter sense of legitimate resentment. He found an excuse to take his leave of the Archduke Matthias, quickly struck camp, and went home. Javarrino, the Duke of Mantua's lost opportunity, was taken the next year, and it was a great victory for Christendom.

Vincenzo was not in the least in doubt over the end of his second Hungarian campaign; the blow he had struck in defence of his own dignity was too legitimate. He had fought. He had felt his own life threatened by enemy steel and he felt that he had given the world such a clear picture of himself that everyone must now see him as he saw himself, charging on horseback across a turbulent landscape through a horde of janizaries, while a pathetic saint, hovering on a cloud with his eyes turned to heaven, entrusted him to God's keeping. This, and not a list of bare facts and hard-won achievements, was what the military life meant for Vincenzo. From one apotheosis to another, it was an easy step; pushed on by the arm of a rosy and muscular goddess, such as Titian had painted for d'Avalos or Parmigianino for the Farneses, he felt himself called to higher things—so why not to a royal crown?

The idea was not new in Italy. Savoy, Este, Medici, Gonzaga, all of them would have liked to emerge 'from the bunch of Italian princes', as Carlo Emmanuele I used to say. If the Duke of Savoy tried out on himself the titles of King of Cyprus or King of Albania—for he seized at any political opportunity with an ardour and enthusiasm which in his case usually turned into a kind of cynical yet luminous fantasy—at the other extreme the Medicis aspired to wake up and find themselves kings of their circumscribed Tuscan territory. Alfonso d'Este, for his part, had reconciled imagination and fantasy by announcing his candidature to the throne of Poland by virtue of being son of Renée of France.

Vincenzo also aspired to that same throne, because of his connections with the house of Hapsburg and his descent from Leonora of Austria. On the basis of what little was known of the disagreements among Polish nobility and of the uneasy situation of the Polish king, Stefan Batory, Vincenzo caused his diplomats to construct a skilfully engineered scheme. Disguised as grain merchants and supported by the Jesuits, his envoys left for Poland in the utmost secrecy, studied the economic and social conditions of the country, and spoke with influential electors, some of whom—they were Jews—signed undertakings in Hebrew which have remained in the archives. Others, like Sigmund Mishowsky, had the privilege of adding to their own name the name of Gonzaga. Mantuan diplomacy, the house of Gonzaga's perfect instrument, which was not a whit inferior to the celebrated Venetian diplomacy, had gone into action once more, and once more demonstrated its customary intelligence, which left its mark even when it did not win the day.

The web of intrigue for the throne of Poland was spun. It is a great pity that neither the detailed list of gifts to be distributed to those influential electors who supported the Duke of Mantua has been preserved, nor the scrupulous report of one envoy, Cesare Spadari, who advised—as one of the certain means of succeeding with the populace—the despatch of a handful of literary men whom the centre of studies at Cracow greatly desired. The throne of Poland was to remain a throne set up in the chancelleries. As he waited to seize a new opportunity from among the great selection which, like a series of lightning flashes, kept revealing themselves to Europe, Vincenzo, who was always quick to share his ambitions with his children, drew up yet another project. He had sent a little portrait of his eldest daughter, who was now seventeen, to the Emperor Rudolf II, and because of certain expressions of admiration on the part of the Emperor, thought of making him marry her in a few years' time. As a project, it was as good as any other. More modest, but more surely based, was his demand for a military appointment near the person of the new King of Spain, Philip III, who seemed to be more responsive to negotiations than his exceedingly rigid father, Philip II. The Mantuan ambassador in Madrid believed he could obtain great things.

About this time, there died without issue the last Duke of Ferrara, Alfonso d'Este II, leaving his wife Margherita Gonzaga widowed and extremely rich. She was young—little more than thirty—plump and white, with abundant red hair. Then Ferrara, after centuries of the Estes' glorious suzerainty, was joined once more to the states of the Church, for the Popes had never been willing to recognize as legitimate Don Cesare d'Este, son of Alfonso I and Laura Dianti. To him Clement VIII conceded Modena and Reggio with their surrounding territory, together with the title of Duke, while he himself entered in triumph the city of Ferrara, whose possession had been for almost a century the constant desire of the Vatican. Month upon month of processions, of festivals and magnificent receptions, awoke in the Ferrarese the illusion that, far from losing its importance, their city would gain. Those whose optimism knew no bounds went so far as to say that Ferrara, the Church's outpost in North Italy, might become a second Rome.

Vincenzo welcomed his sister back to Mantua, decreeing that she was to receive all possible honours and offering her the support of his heart which abounded in family affection; but it cannot be said that the fall of the house of Este afflicted him overmuch in spite of his old bonds of boon companionship with Don Cesare. He took it into his head to go to Ferrara with a procession of two thousand nobles who were dressed, bejewelled and marshalled in accordance with a glittering choreography which led up to a crescendo of splendour. He held open court for three days and all were welcome to drink and banquet at his table. Clement VIII received him with all honours, and the populace— who could contrast the Gonzaga's cordial magnificence with the rigid bearing of Ranuccio Farnese, also come to pay his respects to the Pope with a great band of retainers—accorded Vincenzo the palm of affection. It was the same affection with which his own subjects pardoned his squandered wealth, his haphazard military expeditions, and even the taxes Vincenzo had occasionally to place on grain and wine when his difficulties were strangling him. Admittedly he imposed them only for a short time—barely long enough for him to get over the momentary crisis, for he was almost happier to abolish taxes than the people were at being relieved of them.

In that year of 1598, over and above a Carnival packed with plays and balls, in the course of which were to be seen masquerades of janizaries and Turks—a recurring theme in the Duke's mind—there were the festivities for the baptism of Leonora Anna Maria, the last daughter of Vincenzo and Leonora, and future Empress of Austria. She was held up for the baptism by Margherita of Austria, who was passing through Italy on her way to Spain, where she was to marry the new king, Philip III. It was a wonderful thing to see all the festive stir in Mantua in these rich September days. The most beautiful women of Ferrara and Monferrato were invited in great parties and arrived in the decorative setting of great Spanish collars tipped with airy layers of lace, of pearl-embroidered dresses, and bejewelled and plumed decorations. Religious celebrations mingled with dances, jousts and tourneys; but the event which left everyone breathless, and for which the nobility from Milan and Venice fought over the tickets, was the performance of Guarini's *Pastor Fido*.

We do not know what emotions the adventures of Mirtillo and Amarilli, of Silvio and Dorinda, awoke in one of the first persons invited to the spectacle, the Marchioness of Grana, who had such close bonds with the poetry which had measured out her most turbulent days. She must have had it in mind when she called the child born to her by Vincenzo, Silvio, and the years which had passed since that burning year 1592 could truly be called years of love. It was to them that she owed the state and title of favourite which, now that she had been a widow for two years, was discreetly accorded to her. But the fact remains that to reap wealth and benefits from her own amorous season can dry up the youth of a woman's heart. It is almost better for her to weep with empty hands. This Agnese guessed, for she knew the voluptuous power of prayer and weeping. Now that she was approaching her thirties she shuddered at the approaching years—not that they did not bring the temptation of ambition—but they could only be borne on the basis of a warm, secret passion. But she refused to accept the role of renunciation and, as this story proceeds, we will find her restlessly active, as are all women who have a great contribution to make to love. We will not be romancing too wildly if we imagine her, hearing certain cadences from the *Pastor Fido*— 'Sweet life of love, why did you come so late to my heart?'—tossed to and fro on a sea of emotion; for she felt the question like a summons. Perhaps it was from this time that the name which to her meant all the colour of the world began to be no longer that of Vincenzo.

With the performance of the *Pastor Fido* a promise was fulfilled which had hung over the Mantuan court since 1592. The Duke, who could hardly bear to think that the pastoral had already been performed at Capravola in 1596 by order of Cardinal Farnese, had commanded that a sumptuous production should be given. This was done, and the performance was repeated three times with additional intermezzos, which proved to be full of vague fantastic inventions on pedantic themes such as the marriage of Mercury and Philology. Margherita of Austria enjoyed it as much as her haughty bearing as Queen of Spain would allow her, and left Vincenzo so certain that he would obtain the governorship of Flanders or some other exalted post, that when the offer came from Spain of command over the Portuguese galleys— a rank lower than that held by Savoy—he felt more offended than disappointed. So he would not reveal the secrets of his theatrical machines to the Spanish technicians sent by the Governor of Milan. If they wanted, they could see the machinery half dismantled. But it was a miserable revenge. Vincenzo then pointedly left for Spa with the excuse that he was going to treat a badly ulcered leg in the baths there. In Spa he had long conversations with his cousin Charles de Nevers, and with Maurice of Nassau, son of the Duke of Orange, Spain's great enemy. 'These are gentlemen of whom one is a relation of mine,' Vincenzo was ready to say if the Governor of Milan should protest, for he was determined that these avaricious, faithless Spaniards should have something to knit their brows over.

At this time, it seemed as if the most intelligent persons in Italy were tending towards friendship with Henry IV of France. The cue was given by Tuscany, where Maria dei Medici, Leonora's younger sister, and the richest match in Europe—her dowry was a million gold crowns—had turned down the Archduke Matthias of Habspurg, after a pessimistic examination of his miniature. She said that she felt she saw there not only the Duke's ugliness, but his lack of spirit and health, and she had let it be understood, being a woman of abundant appetites, that she would have preferred that gallant and exuberant man, Henry IV. This was very timely because, now that his marriage with Margot de Valois was dissolved and his favourite Gabrielle d'Estrées dead, there was reason to believe that he was fancy-free. Maria's taste coincided with the projects of the Grand Duke Ferdinand, to whom the French alliance seemed an effective counter-balance to Spanish dominance in Italy. He therefore mobilized his ablest statesmen and ably conducted the marriage negotiations in which one of the leading roles was played by an old acquaintance of ours, Belisario Vinta. On the morning of 23rd April, 1600, Belisario read out the terms of the marriage contract of the new Queen of France; he continued to remain on the stage during September and October through the festivities and the marriage ceremonies.

From Mantua came both Duke and Duchess, who were in the front rank at every festivity close to the heavily-bejewelled bride. Perhaps it was then that Leonora invented the charming habit, in which she afterwards delighted, of wearing on her elegantly studied dresses only a few jewels—generally only one necklace of pearls, chosen piece by piece, so that each taken by itself was a perfect little world; but it was the purple, the golden lilies, the salvoes from the cannon, the titles, the royal privileges, and the thrones, which excited Vincenzo's fantasy. He reached some sort of equilibrium in his exultation only at the performance of the *Euridice* of Ottavio Rinuccini set to music by Iacopo Peri, the first opera to be seen on the stage, and one which was to mark the birth of a glorious new genre.

While Leonora, together with the Grand Duchess of Tuscany and her ladies, accompanied her sister to France, Vincenzo remained in Genoa and only at Christmas returned home with his wife. All the winter he attended to affairs of state, mingling them with amours, court intrigues, balls and theatricals, which he arranged along with his master of ceremonies, Frederico Follino. He was already beginning to plan political alliances on the basis of various marriages—thus he was thinking of giving his eldest son as bride the Marquis del Vasto's daughter, or alternatively the daughter of his sister, the Archduchess Anna Caterina, who would have brought a dowry of eight hundred thousand crowns —almost as much as the Queen of France. But in the intervals between one play and another, Vincenzo began to realize that shortly he would be forty. The new generation to which his children belonged was already hard at his heels, yet nothing had happened, and his youth was fading.

From the East there came the roll of war drums. In the spring of 1601, it was learnt that the Turks in Croatia had bribed their way into Canissa (Grosskirchen) thus opening the way to Vienna from the south. Rudolf II once more asked the Pope for aid and the Pope in turn asked Europe. Once again there were the usual vague replies for which the despatch of money and troops here and there was a poor compensation. The Grand Duke of Tuscany as usual put forward Don Giovanni dei Medici and stayed at home himself, and for the third time Vincenzo said he was ready to set out.

Undoubtedly this routine of appeal and response had something mechanical about it, as is often the case with the actions of men who are not given to clarity about their own motives. On the other hand we must recognize in it proof of Vincenzo's naïveté and of the enduring nature of his aspirations. It was not difficult for him to explain away the failure of the two other expeditions. He could tell himself that now he knew what war was, and what he felt like with armour and sword. If, up to now, his undertakings had not shown a credit balance, the blame lay entirely in circumstances, which had denied him the opportunity of achieving it. He would set out therefore but, profiting from past experience, would try to have his hands as free as possible, so that the war might really be his war. He would have preferred not to stir without the recognized title of Lieutenant-General and all the honours and attributes of the rank, but however much the Mantuan envoys at the Roman court laboured to obtain all this for him, they only half succeeded. But at least Vincenzo received the title and post of Lieutenant to the General Gian Francesco Aldobrandini, nephew of the Pope, and declared himself willing to rest content with it.

That Vincenzo meant this campaign to be a turning-point is proved by his preparations not in the military field and in the field of administration—both of his country and his household— but in other directions as well. Thus various artistic matters were carefully arranged for the date of his victorious return. And it is here, on the 18th July, 1601, that we meet for the first time the full-sounding name of Peter Paul Rubens. The twenty-year-old artist had newly come from Flanders to the Mantuan court and had been sent to Rome to copy the masterpieces in the great collections and acquire pictures of his own choosing. The Mantuan resident in Venice was to superintend the manufacture in Murano of the great crystal panes for the new ducal art gallery. The master of works received commissions to construct new loggias, new staterooms, new salons. The master of ceremonies was to organize splendid spectacles to celebrate the occasion. Even the troop of alchemists whom Vincenzo disputed with the other princes of his day and lodged in his palace received an assignment —to work away at their experiments and, if possible, produce their synthetic gold.

In charge of the government of Mantua Vincenzo left his sagacious wife, Leonora. If she looked into her heart she must have admitted to herself that the acceptance of this charge was no longer a burden but a reward—a fine one. However many sacrifices it had cost her in her first years of marriage to accustom herself to the unwomanly interests of state during her husband's irregular absences, now that she had tasted the power to command in its deepest sense—namely of understanding and foreseeing what must be done—she had become greatly attached to it and even loved it. One has only to look through her papers during the period when she was princess regent to agree with the historians in recognizing that she had both ability and finesse and the essentially political intelligence of the Medicis. Since his ministers already recognized this, Vincenzo was fully justified in looking to his wife. Unfortunately, shortly before Vincenzo left for the Croatian expedition, another woman had emerged to rival Leonora—not a favourite this time (there would have been means of dealing with her) but the Duke's own sister, Margherita Gonzaga.

Madam Her Serene Highness of Ferrara—such was the title the widow of Alfonso d'Este II had assumed in Mantua—was prone to say that she felt herself called to the meditative life of a cloister. So saying, she had withdrawn into a convent where she reigned over a little court of women picked by her and dependent on her. In fact, after her husband's death, Margherita Gonzaga had suddenly discovered her true nature. At Ferrara, she had never thought of busying herself with affairs of state, for her husband had the monopoly of thoughts and ideas, and had manœuvred her with an old man's sagacity, confining her organizing activity and ability to works of charity and the invention of those festivities and balls which had made the last days of the Duchy a fabulous period.

Flattered and spoilt, Margherita had for years accepted the part of the young woman married to a disproportionately old man, and had not realized that this role had kept her in a limbo of childhood and prolonged minority. Now, as she suddenly felt her thirty-five years give her new strength, she suspected that a trick had been played on her. But what was she to do with a vigour which suddenly matured at the very moment when she could no longer express herself? The life of a private lady, to which she was fated now that she was a widow, was repugnant

183

to her. Her brother's honours and aid, her sister-in-law's kind reception and esteem, were not sufficient for her; she felt that she was made for other things; she felt great natural abilities which made the power to command both a revelation and a necessity. If only Leonora had been weak, but instead she was sharp and tenacious; she held all the cards and there was no way of undermining her authority. A better plan would be to turn the flanks of the situation and lay siege to Vincenzo who, because he was a man and because his life held so few secrets, might well be vulnerable.

It is not easy to discover precisely how Her Most Serene Highness contrived to realize her schemes. We know that at court she had someone who was very faithful to her, and that she could rely in particular on a little loyal group among those solid conscientious people who admired in her the re-emergence of Duke Guglielmo's positive qualities. One thing is certain—in May 1601, Vincenzo wrote to his friend and confidant, Fabio Gonzaga, appointing him governor of Monferrato during his absence; then in July he relieved him of the office and entrusted it to his sister. She showed a certain reluctance at first, and then to please her dear lord and brother she accepted and left for Monferrato with the air of sacrificing herself on the altar of duty. We will see later what intrigues she contrived there on her own. Yet the result of the double female regency promised to be excellent. The two sisters-in-law did not so much rival as emulate each other, and put into their office the best of themselves. Both had good heads, Margherita being more fiery, and Leonora more given to reason. Let us put it this way, that if their intelligence was equal, it was on a qualitative plane. They both started off by paying homage and obedience to masculine authority; then at a certain point, without even admitting it to themselves, they freed themselves from vassalage and acted on their own, using their own judgment and their own understanding of things. And what emerged from their aristocratic hands became for each of them, once it was no longer an offering to Vincenzo, an individual mode of self-revelation and self-expression.

Vincenzo left Mantua on the 18th July, 1601. He was greatly fêted in Venice where the populace, feeling itself threatened by Turkish inroads into Croatia, acclaimed him as their defender. At the beginning of August, he arrived in Graz where he was cordially greeted by the Archdukes Maximilian and Ferdinand. Gian Francesco Aldobrandini, the Pope's nephew, and Don Giovanni dei Medici were already there, with the Papal troops and the Florentine mercenaries, turbulent and disorderly fellows who were disturbing the calm of the countryside. No sooner had he arrived, than Vincenzo found himself faced with a full-scale quarrel.

Not only did Aldobrandini, as generalissimo, not wish to recognize the Duke of Mantua as Lieutenant-General, but neither did Don Giovanni, who haughtily recalled that his house had never given way in questions of precedence to the Gonzagas since the days of Cosimo I. Furthermore, when he compared his own military qualities with those of Vincenzo, he found the advantage so much on his side that he felt it insufferable to have to accept the orders of a man whom he considered technically inferior. The leaders of the Crusade began to vie with each other in ferocious insults. From Mantua Leonora wrote to her uncle the Grand Duke of Tuscany, begging him to admonish his unruly relative. And time slipped by.

Paralleling the skill of their military strategy with a cunning political game, the Turks pretended to be overcome by the death in Belgrade of Ephraim Pasha and gave signs of being willing to treat for peace; meanwhile they reinforced and supplied Canissa. At Graz, on the other hand, when they were not quarrelling, the Crusaders were revelling in the soft breeze of autumn, spending their energies in amusements and jests, hunting and banquets, gallant adventures in town and country. The letters which reached Mantua with the frothy account of the Crusaders' gay life seemed to crinkle in one's hands with a sinister rustle.

Finally, on the 13th September, when the controversies had been stilled by dint of compromises, a general review was held, and on the 22nd, Vincenzo left for the field under a sky brave with clouds and sun at the head of his Lombards, whose generous and civil manners had made them so popular with the towns-people. They left amid songs, flowers, and garlands. 'In Gottes Namen, durchlauchtiger Herr' the people cried as they accompanied the departing Italian troops, chanting their greeting in the German manner. They followed him for a good league, singing all the time, fascinated by that handsome, affable, fair-haired commander, who laughed as if he came straight from a tale of knighthood.

But at Graz, there was someone who already had his doubts. It was Vincenzo's counsellor, his most intimate and quick-witted minister, Annibale Chieppio. It was on Chieppio, who had taken Marcello Donati's place—the latter was now out of touch with the court and given over entirely to his codices and his botanical and medical experiments—that Vincenzo's government was so solidly based. This excellent jurist, this far-sighted and most able administrator, this gifted politician, had risen from a modest condition and now merged all these qualities in devotion for his lord's splendid person. At first his thrifty nature was dazzled by Vincenzo's sense of the magnificence; but he became accustomed to it and could see where it fell short. Then he would come to the rescue, improvising, looking ahead, correcting mistakes. For his part, Vincenzo loved him, and although sometimes the counsellor felt estranged, and experienced the discouragement of an intelligent man embittered at finding further confirmation of his pessimistic view of human nature, yet he always contrived to re-establish communication with his master and climb back into his confidence. He was not dishonest, but on the other hand, he was not disinterested. For him wealth, besides being a means to an end, was a sign of power. And naturally, being the favourite and extremely rich, he was hated, feared and detested by the courtiers, particularly, as is the rule in courts, by those who declared themselves his friends. Thanks to them, he was more than once to experience the poison of pain beneath the layer of honey.

Still young—he was about thirty in 1601—Chieppio was with Vincenzo in Graz, and even before the Duke's departure for the field he had cautious doubts about the Crusade, for he had experienced the unruly tempers of the captains, which were reflected in their troops, and had made an accurate comparison of strengths. He went back to Mantua in a thoughtful mood, hoping he might be mistaken. He wished he could believe the optimists when news arrived that the plague had broken out in Canissa to thin the ranks of the defenders, so that it was thought that the city would make little resistance, and might even open its gates without a struggle. The news of the plague was a trick of Hannam Pasha, who was conducting the defence of the town—a tried veteran, equally adept in the use of arms and psychological shifts. Let the assailants come on confidently, the storm would be all the fiercer for them, thought the Turkish general, drawing up his small, plump body with a fierce smile in his bright, flashing eyes. Had he needed encouragement, he would have been cheered by the news of what was happening in the enemy camp.

The quarrels between the leaders of the expedition were beginning once more. What was the meaning of the fact that certain captains were coming under the direct commands of Don Giovanni dei Medici, and why did Colonel Orfeo, who was planning the strategy of the campaign, not communicate his plans to the Lieutenant-General? To avoid having to obey Vincenzo, Don Giovanni produced certain imperial patents which exempted him from dependence on any command. Then he went off with the van of the army and made it march at his will, or else took advantage of his appointment as quartermaster to distribute the billets in such a way that the muddy places and those exposed to the enemy always fell to the tents of the Duke of Mantua. The latter complained to the Archduke. Summoned to report, Don Giovanni relied on military authorities, quoting at length, splitting hairs, becoming eloquent. The Archduke said there was much to be said on both sides and next day the whole thing began again. It was already clear that the war did not have that constant secret *élan* which brings military operations to a happy conclusion.

When fighting began, a certain concord appeared to be reached. The Italian commanders to whom the imperial officers had surrendered command, perhaps because they foresaw the difficulty of the enterprise, for a moment felt the honour of their responsibility and acted in concert. The siege network was studied, the ground was measured out and the army carefully deployed, but so much time had been allowed the Turks that Canissa, which was bulging with munitions, food and troops, was now an unbroken ring of defences. Hannam Pasha leant from the walls and saw the enemy camp squatting among the muddy marshes of the plain and left them to the mercy of the seasons.

The end of August came and September began. The days were rainy and misty and broad grey lagoons spread round the city. Yet on the 12th September, after three days of preparation, with a rapidly executed move Vincenzo advanced under a heavy rattle of Turkish arquebuses, and seized a bridge which, crossing the widest of the lagoons, led on to dry ground near the city. He had the bridgehead fortified and next day put over men and guns. Then they were able to camp under the walls of Canissa. Hard fighting followed with a force of six hundred janizaries, who attempted to enter the city through the eastern gates under cover of a thick mist. It rained continually, but Vincenzo, who was always in the saddle ready, decided and thoughtful, took the hardships of the day as a reward, and at night his sleep was easy and profound, the sleep of a soldier. But when thanks to hard schooling he was on the point of finding his true capabilities, he fell ill and had to withdraw to his tent. He was suffering from the old sore on his knee which had been badly tended at Spa. Then everything became difficult to deal with.

They came to report that the Florentine soldiers refused to pull the guns because that work was beneath them, since they had come as artillery men and not as pioneers. As he lay in pain on his pallet, the Archduke Maximilian and others came and made long speeches on the various corps and their tasks. Every now and again the outposts seized a prisoner—a citizen of Canissa, an old woman, or a janizary in disguise—and led them to the Duke, who saw in their eyes only the same gleam of greed and mendacity.

From the walls of the city day and night cannon and arquebuses wrought continual damage, countered feebly by the besiegers' artillery. 'Here we are supplied with every possible discomfort,' wrote Vincenzo, 'and the abundance lies in the cannonades and musquetry.' The Lutheran Germans, into the bargain, lost no occasion of mocking the Crusaders, and were echoed by the Turks within Canissa with their satirical grimaces. The papal troops had received longer-range artillery, with which they began to batter at a massive tower which was one of the enemy's dangerous observation posts. At each shot the Turks applauded, ran up flags and lit fires, capering like madmen. 'Fire away!' they shouted, 'because all this stuff will come in useful to us,' adding that they thought less than nothing of their enemies, that they were determined to defend themselves, and that they were most amused at the simplicity of the Christians who put up with discomfort while at home their wives carried on with friars and priests.

What is surprising, and indeed almost distressing, is that in the Christian camp, they found this bloodthirsty exchange of insults amusing. 'We have both war and play-acting,' wrote one Mantuan with great good-humour which is altogether too close to cynicism, and which proves that if the soldiers were unscathed by the enemy's insults it was because none of them felt for the cause they were defending. They were almost all mercenaries and war for them was a trade like any other; but the fact that they did not even feel an urge to do their job well, as mercenaries had in other wars—and still did in Flanders, for example—was a grave indication that morale was disintegrating.

Of all of them Vincenzo Gonzaga was the only one who was soldiering without pay—the only one who had joined in the adventure of war because of a genuine impulse; but the hopes of the September days had been unfulfilled and now he too was beginning to feel lost. As always he was betrayed by his own weakness seconded by an external circumstance. Some urge had for long been at work within him, leading him away from the logic of war to the vagueness of an uncontrolled fantasy. It was an immensely insidious urge, for we find letters dating as far back as the good days of August addressed to certain Mantuan agents and doctors, who were instructed to pass on orders from the Duke to the band of alchemists at work in the apartments of the ducal palace and the Palazzo del Te.

The nature of these orders reveals the disturbed state of Vincenzo's mind, for the alchemists were not only to prepare poison —perhaps to poison the enemy's wells and foodstuffs—but also cannon-balls which, when shot from the bombards, would release poisonous or soporific clouds and make the Turks either lose their memory or fall down dead. Thus, from the beginning, his dream worked like a secret enchantment to dissolve practical requirements in riotous excesses of imagination. For unlike the other princes of his time, who were all more or less affected by the passion for alchemy, Vincenzo simply could not keep his thoughts and actions distinct from the temptations of the magic which rose with the fumes of the furnaces or dripped from the retorts. In this case it is more than ever obvious that for him dreams had become a substitute for life, and that this false life reached a pitch of excitement over deceptive and untrustworthy presentiments of the future. He was not even discouraged by the charlatanry of the alchemists who would promise immense discoveries, secrets which whole kingdoms could not repay and then, snatching a purse of ducats, would abscond in dressing-gown and slippers never to be seen again. Clearly those who stayed on were not very potent magicians. They did not even succeed in concocting a poison of any potency in spite of all the urgings from the Duke, who was fretting to receive the little box of powders which would make him feel that he had magic powers, however few. So much was he beset by the idea of poisons for use in war that he forgot his usual paternal humanity and gave orders for the toxic substances to be tried out on certain persons held for grave crimes in the Mantuan prisons. So one day the distiller of poisons, accompanied by a doctor, went down into the prison with his phial held gingerly in his fingers. The poison was poured into some meat balls and the plate presented to the wretch who, guessing at his fate, would not accept them. Finally they obliged him to eat and waited to see the effects. The only visible result during the course of the next few days was a high fever, but perhaps, says the narrator of the story, it was a fever brought on by fear.

In short, the alchemists failed not only with lethal or soporific ammunition but with the more common poisons as well. Any man truly born to the profession of arms would have told himself that he ought to return quickly to solid earth and be on his guard against further flights of imagination. But although he had recovered from his sore knee and rode out on a reconnaissance to prepare the siege of Canissa, Vincenzo was all the time indulging in fantasies; it therefore never occurred to him to wonder why Don Giovanni dei Medici was going home or why so many other captains were doing the same on one pretext or another. Gian Francesco Aldobrandini, the commander-in-chief of the Crusade, had died in October, and with each defection Vincenzo felt that he gained in authority. His pride swelled to think that soon he would be the victor of Canissa and that all the glory of the enterprise would centre on him. No lesson was harsh enough to warn him—not even the defeat of the 30th September when, wishing to use the newly arrived and newly sited artillery, he gave orders for an assault. In unpractised hands the artillery mistook its target and was unable to cover the attackers, who died in their hundreds under the accurate Turkish fire. They had to withdraw without the least advantage gained.

'Canissa will not give in to us nor we to the cold and the seasons,' said Count Alessandro Siggi, a man of letters, writing home with an elegant and dejected phrase; but from now on his letters, usually so supple in their narrative, become short, omit any news of the campaign or summarize it cautiously with frequent appeals to God's justice and wisdom. What restrained the Mantuan's lively pen could not yet be described as pessimism but was certainly a presentiment of it. Vincenzo, however, was not only hopeful; he was certain he would win the day. He had asked to be reinforced by German troops which the Archduke Matthias was sending under the command of Colonel Hermann Christoph Roswurn. Vincenzo planned to wait for them and then, having concentrated his forces, they would move together to the last

assault. We can fix on the date of 13th November, 1601, as the
last day when Vincenzo was able to believe in his own vocation
as a soldier. He recognized the sensation of pure joy flowing
through his being and knew that it brought confidence. In this
way he was able to abandon himself to the rhythm of a secret
motto which he had borne with him ever since he left Mantua for
the Croatian war: *Forse che sì, forse che no*—Maybe yes, maybe no.
Perhaps it was an old proverb out of the mouth of the people;
certainly a poet had elaborated it in an amusing trifle a hundred
years before and in the ducal palace everyone probably knew by
heart the graceful song in which indolent, ironic elegance sways
to the pendulum movement of the verse.

> *Forse che sì, forse che no*
> *il tacer nuocer non può;*
> *forse che no, forse che sì*
> *non fia il mondo ognor così.*

> Maybe yes, maybe no
> silence cannot hurt us so;
> maybe no, maybe yes,
> the world won't always be like this.

It had pleased Vincenzo to detach the first line and take it as
his motto. Undoubtedly, in his usual chivalrous way, he associated
it with a lady—perhaps a lady of the court who had brought it to
his mind by the accomplished coquettishness of her behaviour.
Perhaps she thought that Vincenzo, that unrepentant lover, would
wish to storm Canissa with his lady's colours on his arm and sash.
Certainly it is to misread an easily read character to think as people
have done, that he chose the motto with an eye to the uncertain
outcome of the war, and because he had foreseen the probability
of defeat. For how could he, an ardent enthusiast and a faithful
Catholic, have doubts, yet persevere, sure of himself, and heaven's
aid?

Until the 13th November, 1601, Vincenzo was sure that

Hannam Pasha could be defeated, and that the gates of Canissa would open for the triumphal entry of the Christian troops. The German reinforcements were beginning to arrive. There were innumerable rumours that in the city they were suffering from hunger, while in the store-rooms provisions were rotting, flooded by the heavy rain. So it was easy for him to cheer on the soldiers by offering them calm, sympathy and confidence. And so little did he suspect that he was deceiving others as well as himself, that he took up the pen that very day, and wrote to Mantua to his master of revels, Federico Follino, telling him to prepare for the next Carnival a series of tableaux representing in colour the story of the siege and conquest of Canissa.

He did not think of a poet—a Tasso—to sing of this Crusade. Perhaps later he would think of an historian who would relate the episodes in elevated prose and adorn it with the embellishments of ornate seventeenth-century rhetoric. But his immediate and natural thought was for a dramatic commemoration—a celebration in terms of choreography. Follino no sooner received the Duke's letter than he collected all the despatches and spent the night at his desk, putting together the outline of a spectacle in five scenes. Patrols coming and going, regiments passing in review order, artillery going into position, prancing cavalry, victorious assaults, ballets of perfidious Turks and heroic Christians, allegorical scenes and waving banners—all this and much more besides was brought together on Follino's page, thrown down without any other logical thread than that required for a series of theatrical ideas which only later would reveal themselves on the stage. Four scenes were designed but not finished; the last, representing Vincenzo's apotheosis, was only sketched in a couple of lines. In order to commemorate his triumph to the full, said Follino, they would wait for details of the storming of Canissa. Dawn came, and the Master of Revels finished his work. Having handed over his letter for the Duke to a special courier, he went to bed, pale and satisfied. He certainly did not imagine that that very morning the Mantuan army was returning to the mists of Graz with all hope abandoned.

It had taken only a fortnight for things to come to a head. Once more it was not a question of a defeat in the field, which would have been hard but decisive and unequivocal. On the contrary, battle had not even been joined with the enemy. When Colonel Roswurn arrived, Vincenzo had gone to meet him and welcomed him as the man who brought him forces to put fresh blood into an army bled white. Naturally, they would come to an agreement on the final assault; Vincenzo asked for nothing better than for discussions to begin at once on the plan of battle, but the German colonel made it clear that he had brought with him a detailed programme which he unfolded gradually in his own military way —at once hypercritical and stern. After a great deal of preliminary courtesies, he had asked for a report on operations to date, and having called a Council of War, assailed the Lieutenant-General with dry, pitiless questions. It was nothing more or less than a court-martial and Vincenzo suddenly found that he was not so much condescending to supply information to a dependant as being thrust into the dock. He replied lackadaisically, saw that he was making a mistake, and tried to assert himself. Things went from bad to worse when Roswurn, on an inspection of the Christian camp, cast piercing glances on the equipment, the arms and the men, and followed them up with unvarnished criticisms. The Imperial captains, who could not believe their luck at being able to do so, took his side and said that they had disapproved of the campaign from the beginning, thus disowning any responsibility and throwing it all on to the Lieutenant-General.

The moral panic which beset Vincenzo depressed him and clouded his judgment. It was now that he began to feel the cost of all the effort, all the suffering, all the dead. He was ridden by the incubus of an error he had himself committed but had not suspected. Everything around him began to acquire a ghostly quality. Roswurn was not to be moved, and shook his head almost in pity when people talked to him of new battles; deep in his small, light blue eyes there was a gleam of crude, German irony— the same irony as set the tone of the humour at the Court of Rudolf II when they talked of Canissa in the Imperial chambers and ante-chambers. Not because the Croatian campaign was a failure, the Emperor's councillor, Charles of Lichtenstein, explained in an attempt to be subtle—the Imperial forces remembered only too well that for six years they had been suffering by the dozen much graver defeats at the hands of the Turks—but because the war was being conducted without skill and without order. No one admitted or indeed wished to admit that Vincenzo was an unlucky enthusiast. The accusation against him—the most humiliating for any man who thinks of himself as a commander in the field—was that of lack of military skill.

Drawn on by some treacherous, unseen power, Vincenzo seemed himself to give support to his critics. He had succeeded in persuading himself to resist the assaults of weariness and fatigue, but under the fire of criticism he was lost and felt the ground give way under his feet. Obeying what was undoubtedly a crude instinct of self-preservation, he suddenly, without explanation, without preparation, without even going through the motions of calling a council of war, said tents were to be struck. The order ran through the camp and gave rise not only to comments but also to searching, urgent questions on this important move.

They were leaving to go home—that was all very well, but they had not sufficient vehicles and horses, and how were they to transport all their sick and wounded, and what about the rations, including three thousand large loaves which had newly arrived? There were no ropes for manœuvring the heavy artillery. How was it to be shifted? It would be interesting to see how all these problems could be solved, said the Imperial Officers, implacable in their criticism. The Lieutenant-General solved the problems badly—that is to say did not solve them, but at each question withdrew further into himself, became curt and inaccessible, and passed everything on to his subordinates. So at last, after a clash of orders and counter-orders, the troops fell in in confusion. The invalids, the sick and wounded, followed on with God's aid. The rations were abandoned, the guns were destroyed and left on the marshy plain. The return of the Christian army, badly dressed and in disorder, had all the appearance of a retreat.

At Graz, the Lombards found rain, silence and frost, and grey hostility exuded from the sky and everything around them. They left quickly, as soon as they had put their ranks into some sort of order. They arrived in Mantua on the 18th December, and even the fires of home could not warm them. Those who had returned were few. There were a lot of weeping women, whom it was not possible to comfort with a brave story. At court Chieppio drew up the balance of the ill-fated venture. Leonora herself could not refrain from passing judgment on it although she tried not to discuss it. And every day something new and fascinating arrived. Now it was an account of the Croatian campaign presented to Rudolf II by the Imperial captains and backed up by a long, pedantic and ferocious letter by Colonel Roswurn. Now it was a series of stinging Roman pasquinades, now it was a malignant account from Florence. And each time the Duke and Duchess had to control themselves, to be calm and listen to it all, even the quick slights and commiserations of the courtiers.

It was more difficult to have to explain things to his friends and prove to them that Canissa could be and indeed was an honourable event in the life of a prince. The chancellery, headed by Chieppio, prepared reports, chose envoys and sent orators. One of the most able was sent to Venice and presented himself to the Council of Ten with a highly detailed account, recalling the episodes of the siege, one by one, boasting of the Duke's acts of valour and prudence, revealing his strategical plans, accusing the Imperial colonels of having acted on their own without making contact with the commander and dwelling on the illness, the discomforts and sufferings which had decimated and weakened the troops encamped among the marshes. The Venetians listened and appeared to understand and agree. At the end, the Doge replied amiably, assuring the spokesman that he was quite certain that the Duke had borne himself at Canissa like the brave man he was, that fortune in arms is variable and that Venice considered Vincenzo her dear son and so on. That same day the Spanish ambassador at Venice went from palace to palace proclaiming that, after so many demonstrations of bravery, the Duke of Mantua could carry his head high, even if the outcome of the war had not been favourable. These testimonials of adequacy were understood in Mantua in their true sense—as mortifications, yet they had to pretend to accept them as rewards and consolations.

Thus, for Vincenzo, Canissa was to be a dividing line. In his own brutal way, the Conte di Fuentes, the Spanish governor of Milan, was right when, three months after the Croatian campaign, on Vincenzo's asking for nothing less than the command at sea, he advised the Mantuan ambassador not to seek military appointments for his lord, since everyone had seen that he could not hold them. Let him instead take a pension like the Dukes of Parma, Modena, and Urbino, and stay quietly at home.

But Vincenzo would never accept being reduced to staying at home on a pension. After Canissa, he required some time to restore himself, but not very much. Carefully and avidly he listened to his courtiers who, distinguishing subtly between facts and possibilities, proved to him that everything in the war had been logical and destined by fate. He listened to Leonora who, out of wifely charity, had become tired of saying she was right and admitted that her husband was the most warlike of the Italian princes—indeed, the only warrior among them. Probably he listened to some woman like the Countess of Sala or Agnese, some expert in the art of comforting men by telling them of themselves and giving an interpretation of the story which runs parallel to the truth but, by means of a slight transposition, sounds more persuasive than truth itself. With the aid of this great deception, he was cured—was able to hope and believe in himself sufficiently once more to build kingdoms for himself, to sketch heroic adventures, to see himself a conquering hero and dream of glory and revenge. More than once we shall see him playing for high stakes. Yet precisely those things for which the historians reprove him, his lack of political incisiveness and the uncertainty of his actions, are for us sure signs of that instinctive caution which prompted him not to trust himself even when he was most applauded.'

Vincenzo's sensuality was never so splendid as after his return from Croatia, never so entire and intelligent, diffusing itself through love and art with a magnificence at once sagacious and deeply felt. All forms of art tempted him, first and foremost the theatre. In the documents we see him summoning around him actors and actresses and setting up his favourite companies, particularly the company of the Fideli, choosing comedies and distributing the parts which the actors were eager to receive from his hands, out of adulation or coquetry, but also out of homage to the taste of a man who understood affairs of the stage. Meanwhile Mantuan companies received, from his taste and encouragement, that cohesion and fire which made them highly sought after, not only in Italy but in France, where Maria dei Medici and Henry IV found them so much to their taste that they begged Vincenzo to send them to Paris. And at Paris, these same comedians, who had lost nothing of their anarchical nature and did not hesitate to draw sword on anyone, were to be the first to bring to the stage the openness, the freedom and the subtleness of the Commedia dell' Arte which later had the great good fortune to influence the formation of Molière's genius. From the documents we can easily get a picture of the Duke of Mantua in the palace one morning. The actors have left with their parts for the new comedy, and he is examining a picture sent to him from Rome, Venice or Florence. He knew how to enjoy them for he had been brought up since childhood in the school of the great Gonzaga collection and at sixteen had had a painter of his own in his pay. In Leonora dei Medici, he had found a companion who, with her polished Florentine taste, re-echoed his enthusiasm. Being more limited in her taste, Leonora had pictures by Andrea del Sarto specially sought out for her and Vincenzo, if he found them, gallantly handed them to her, but for his part, he gathered whatever was excellent and rare with affectionate zeal.

If we were to enumerate the great works of art which belonged to the Gonzagas at this time—Mantegna's Camera degli Sposi in the Castle, his Triumph of Cæsar in the Palace near San Sebastiano, Titian's Twelve Emperors, Michelangelo's Cupid and Tintoretto's Fasti Gonzageschi at Goito with works by Raphael, Titian, Tintoretto, Veronese, Correggio, Perugino, Costa, Parmagianino, Sebastiano del Piombo, Carpaccio, Romanino, and Giulio Romano scattered everywhere, we would have merely a bare catalogue. Let us say instead that Vincenzo considered his gallery not so much as a legacy but as another reason, and a most noble one at that, for exalting the life of the senses. There is an almost orgiastic quality in his passion for painting for, if all the Gonzagas were by tradition great patrons, none of them but Vincenzo had given away an estate—land, castle, title, rent and all—to the Count of Canossa in return for a Raphael Madonna.

When we find Rubens at Mantua in the pay of the Duke (he had recruited him as a very obscure young man in the course of a journey in Flanders in 1599) we cannot but feel pleasure over the happy accord of two temperaments which had in common abundance and magnificent vitality. Indeed, it would seem that no one could correspond so well to Vincenzo's temperament in his way of painting and his mode of life. Yet such was not the case. Admittedly we cannot ask from Vincenzo the critical capacity to see in an artist in his early twenties the great artist of the future, nor must we be surprised if to begin with he should have employed Rubens merely as a copyist and as an expert to advise him in his purchases. But when we see him prefer, both then and later, another Fleming, Pourbus, who is a master too, but a master in quite a different category, it is a sign that Vincenzo's intuition, initially so good, has not lasted, that it has been led astray. It is a pity, too, that we must explain the favours shown to Pourbus by the refined, elegant psychology, the caressing dignity and the airy liveliness of his portraits.

With the Gonzagas, however, Rubens was well off, as he stated himself many years later, when he summed up his youthful years in a sober, affectionate eulogy to the house of Gonzaga when it was foundering under the storm of the Imperial lances and he, now at the height of his fame, had no reason to flatter. The warm, loveable freedom of Lombard manners, a sense of swelling life which emanated wherever Vincenzo was, and almost absolute independence, allowed the painter to indulge in spiritual adventures—the only ones which counted for him—with the great painting of Italy in general and of Venice in particular. So it was willingly, after the manner of the man who picks the right time for everything, that in 1603 Rubens, who had and always retained diplomatic ability and finesse, accepted Vincenzo's proposal to go to Spain bearing messages and gifts to the court of Philip III.

Shortly before, it had become clear that in Madrid the Duke of Lerma enjoyed the position of favourite of the King. Vincenzo, who had not given up hope of getting something out of Spain, thought to win over the Spanish potentate, so he chose for him sophisticated jewels and prepared for the King and Queen a theatrical carriage built like a church with several façades and intricate projecting silverwork; and added perfumes and unguents. For the favourite who was said to be a lover and connoisseur of art, he ordered copies of the most famous paintings from Italian churches and galleries. It was to be Rubens's task to lead the convoy and offer the gifts. So the painter set off. His was an exciting journey which he was to retell in a fine colourful style in some very pleasant Italian letters of his. Whether the great carved and painted baroque carriage, all covered with scrolls and little gold cupids, appears swaying on the backs of mules in the narrow Apennine ravines; whether, on his arrival at Florence, the Grand Duke Ferdinand asks to speak to him and unfolds to Rubens, who must keep his mission secret, Vincenzo's actual instructions and the list of gifts shut up in the coffers; whether he is having difficulty in getting on board ship at Leghorn, or is at sea, tempest-tossed, or finally arriving in Madrid where the Duke of Lerma, clad in a dressing-gown of gold brocade, casts his eyes over the copies and approves of them with boorish condescension —for he took them for originals—the young Fleming always shows himself to be a wise man with a lively sense of humour, who is able to see with equal clarity the serious and the fantastic side of things.

His calm was particularly admirable when he opened the boxes and found the pictures ruined by the damp. Taking up his palette he patched them up on the spot, one after another, and repainted two of them entirely on virgin canvas under the eyes of the Mantuan ambassador, who was greatly excited by such rapid and splendid work. But it was a little later that the Fleming measured himself in human terms against the prince who paid him and showed himself the more solid character. Vincenzo had ordered him to go to France and paint the portraits of all the French-women—princesses, burghers' wives and women of the people—who were noted for their beauty. In reply Rubens wrote firmly but without ill-feeling, asking to be used for work which did greater honour to the artist and the Duke. Perhaps an indirect consequence of this exemplary refusal was the commissioning of three huge paintings—the Baptism, the Transfiguration and the Trinity—which Rubens painted in Mantua and which Vincenzo intended to donate in 1605 to the new Jesuit church which bore the name of the Trinity.

They are all on sacred subjects but in the picture of the Trinity, which was destined for the High Altar, Rubens set out the Gonzagas as Mantegna had before him in the Camera degli Sposi. High up we see the representation of the Trinity. Below, in adoration of the Dogma, Rubens sets out his Catholic dignitaries, posed and pompous, but without the least rigidity. A noble wind blows across the terrace, which is bounded by a low balustrade, and gives on to a background of trees and sky—the very image of a terrace in a garden by a lake. In the foreground, bent devoutly in prayer on two prie-dieux, are the Duke and Duchess with cloaks and great collars, diadems, trains and necklaces, flanked or rather assisted in the background by Leonora of Austria and Guglielmo the Hunchback. All have their hands clasped. Twisted, swelling, fluted columns bound the central scene and mark off in arcades to right and left the portraits of the Gonzaga children—three boys to the right and three girls to the left—which were later to be cut off and stolen. A quivering white greyhound and two ducal guards with uniforms, so bright they almost seem to sing, point to the luxuriant graces and dignity of a reigning court. And just as Mantegna had painted himself along with his masters, so Rubens included his portrait in the same picture with them.

Things have changed with the times, for Mantegna stands calmly speaking on equal terms with Frederico Gonzaga, the heir to the marquisate, with his hat firmly on his head; but Rubens must introduce himself disguised in the gay clothes of a halberdier in order to have the right to appear in the picture at all.

The great picture of the Trinity has reached us in a mutilated state with the top and the sides cut away so that the self-portrait of the painter is lost. Yet even to-day there is an expansive air about it. If the portraits are not so much human stories as princely biographies to mark an occasion, it is enough to notice Leonora's narrow Medicean nostrils or how Guglielmo's face (copied from previous portraits but recreated by the painter) is bowed in prayer to a degree that borders on the grotesque, to notice how the veil falls over the brow of the old Austrian duchess and almost obliterates her face, revealing her obstinate desire for humiliation —it is enough to notice these things, to realize that the picture is telling a story in psychological terms and that it is Rubens who gives us the truest portrait of Vincenzo. For he not only understood Gonzaga as a person, he also understood Vincenzo's projection of himself, as we may tell from the way he interprets the Duke—the way he comments on the over-lively turn of his head, that look which is more intent on terrestrial visions than on prayer, that princely figure which, through attempting to assert itself beyond all bounds, falls into caricature and loses all integrity, all human appeal.

One person must have understood Rubens on a spiritual plane and have been understood by him. That was Leonora, who, had she lived, could have boasted of having had her portrait done by Rubens even before her sister, the Queen of France. This portrait has come down to us in three originals with little variation between them. In it the painter, called upon to render a difficult character, responds magnificently; yet he makes no attempt to embellish his subject—indeed he accentuates certain defects like the corners of the jaws and the over-long chin. Honest respect for another person's personality just restrains him from giving a disconcerting quality to Leonora's direct gaze, which speaks of so many spiritual renunciations, so many courageous admissions and such bitter wisdom. Did she perhaps realize that in this image of herself she was rendered a just testimony, a delicate act of homage, of respect and comprehension?

So it is clear that Rubens could not have set out to look for these portraits of beautiful women which Vincenzo sent others all over Europe to paint. In an attempt to assuage the Duke's uneasy promptings by a visual orgy, Pourbus was to go on his travels for him and so were other minor painters; the assembly of the collection was to go on for a long time—even after Rubens had left Mantua and Italy itself, thus bringing to a close at the appropriate artistic moment his Italian period which had held him there through all the years of his youth. Vincenzo was unable to see that he had lost someone whom it would have been well to keep. He was busy having built in the palace a little room which he would go on filling with portraits of beautiful women, and a chapel where he collected copies of all the miraculous madonnas of this world. Nor did he feel that he was contaminating himself by this mixture, but rather fulfilling himself and finding absolution.

Like so many other men of a voluptuous disposition, he sinned by loving and did not realize that he was sinning *against* love by multiplying his adventures. So the number of his mistresses grew, and the story of the intrigues, which Leonora tried to deprive of their secret piquancy of the splendour of amorous pomp, repeated themselves monotonously. Leonora was so careful that few of the names of his many favourites have come down to us. Agnese still conserved a certain power which would remain even when she had agreed to call it friendship. Felicità Guerrieri's star had set and given way to another member of the house of Gonzaga, perhaps a woman called Francesca, by whom Vincenzo had a son whom he could not recognize as his, for then the child would lose the right of succession to his putative father. Perhaps it was to her that the motto *Forse che sì, forse che no* was dedicated—the motto Vincenzo brought back safely from Canissa, the motto which cast a glow of love even over those unlucky days. Now, on his

return, he desired that motto to be inserted in a maze, as an ornament to the gilded ceiling in the new apartment which was being
prepared for him near Leonora's airy rooms; he linked it to his
Croatian days by an inscription round the edge: *Dum sub arce
Canisiae contra Turcos pugnabat.*

The ceiling is still there and still retains the mystery of its
allusion, just as Vincenzo intended when he insisted on this
obscure communication to the uninitiated from out of his days of
chivalrous adventure. The pendulum swing of the motto and the
geometric outline of the maze confirm the mystery and the secret.
Perhaps the timid gleaming twigs of gold, which are set to punc-
tuate the mottoes as they repeat themselves in the windings of the
maze, represent a garden—possibly the labyrinthine garden which
was made about this time for Vincenzo. Perhaps some woman
was the nymph of the garden and suggested to her lover that he
celebrate her in the symbols which Vincenzo then ordered for the
central room of his suite—the finest room of all, whose walls are
covered by a lofty frieze and decorated with gilded Cordovan
leather, painted with landscapes by Tintoretto. Perhaps—but the
chain of evidence is lacking.

For Vincenzo everything had to be lit and illumined. Life
flowed through the rooms of the immense decorated and ornamented palace. It was a conglomeration of apartments which,
through the centuries, had spread between gardens and terraces,
linked together by winding corridors, steep stairs, back staircases
and secret passages. There we constantly find proof of how indis-
criminate Vincenzo was in his choice of stimuli. One such proof
is to be seen in the first room of Vincenzo's apartments—the so-
called Room of the Archers. The moment we enter it we are aware
of a sudden chill draught at our backs—a sensation that there is
something wrong with the dimensions of the room. It is difficult
to say whether it is too high or whether it has gone too much
to width. But we discover something suspicious only when we
look up to the distant ceiling. At the far end are caryatids in the
shape of harpies. Some are wholly or partly veiled by a material
which matches the tossing locks of their tempestuous heads;

others smile sarcastically; others again are sunk in bestial concentration. It would be of no account were this merely a decorative aberration; but in the harpies' breasts there is a trace of perversity of the imagination. Some hang pendulously like aubergines. Others are round and swollen with painful humours or misshapen as though they might, at any minute, burst and give forth an infected lymph. This gallery of bewitched creatures becomes positively evil in the case of the most obsessive of the caryatids, whose breasts are long, triangular and upraised like the blade of a scythe, fixed there in the diabolical moment of evocation. Certainly when such a ceiling is invented for its owner's pleasure, there is justification for stories of dark magic practices and tainted visions. Love itself, whipped up by an uncontrolled imagination, took its unbridled course until both feeling and intellect crumbled into corruption.

CHAPTER TEN

The Dynastic Marriage

IT was in vain that they had sent the Duke of Lerma a whole gallery of famous paintings copied and retouched by Rubens. Nothing had come of it except a vague plan for a marriage between Vincenzo's widowed sister, Madam Her Most Serene Highness of Ferrara, and the omnipotent Spanish minister himself; for he too was recently widowed. Such was the will of the Duke of Lerma—and on the favourite's will depended the whole of Spain with all its immense and delicate problems. Meanwhile Philip III displayed to the world the very picture of spiritual degeneration—of a king incapable, either from inertia or lack of courage, of using the power consigned to him, who drifted along instead of forcing himself and others to accept power as a guarantee of the future. So Vincenzo failed to ransom from Philip either Sabbioneta, which had passed on the female side to the Dukes of Mandragone, or the tiny domain of Coreggio. (Yet if Philip was cautious it was out of meanness of spirit rather than because he had a political programme.) And it was in vain that he took up once more Guglielmo's project of uniting under one rule the little fiefs into which the lands of Mantua were divided.

He was to return to another of his father's ideas—that of exchanging Monferrato, which lay far from Mantua, for Cremona and its territories. This was a sound idea, a solid project, on which ambassadors and envoys reported in copious documents. But this was something Spain would never allow him nor anyone else to achieve—the consolidation and expansion of territory which might mean the beginning of Italian power. Unwilling to recognize this harsh truth, Vincenzo tried to get round it by an astute manœuvre which bears the marks of his instigation even if it was carried out with caution and constant prudence by his great minister, Annibale Chieppio, with the aid of the two councillors, Tullio Petrozzani and Annibale Iberti. Vincenzo had reason to trust these three men. However spasmodic his bursts of energy might be, his ministers saw to it that they were disciplined and harnessed; thus they gave to the policy of the Gonzagas both coherence and logic. Yet even with such unstinting expenditure of ability, intelligence and labour, all they were to be able to achieve could be reduced to one melancholy word: equilibrium.

But poised over the equilibrium of Mantua and, worse still, over that of Italy, there perpetually hung a threat of destruction. It came from Piedmont, from Carlo Emanuele I, who was still consumed with a desire for the territory of Monferrato. You will remember that, in the very first years of his reign, Vincenzo had had the great fortress of Casale built against his Savoyard rival by Germanico Savorgnan, a fortress for which the fifty thousand crowns set aside in the budget had been exceeded and the figure of a million and half reached—an enormous expenditure which, while it did not cause Vincenzo the least concern, roused the wiseacres of the court, with Leonora at their head, to administer a severe rebuke. Nor did Leonora spare harsh criticism of the architect for the great divergence between estimate and cost.

But the fortress at Casale was not enough. At Turin Vincenzo had a number of extremely well-informed spies who, in letters signed with a variety of names, informed him of the Duke's every movement. Thus, with the aid of the Spanish governor, who was also quick to check Carlo Emanuele's future expansion, he had been able to keep the frontiers of Monferrato intact. But everyone foresaw that things would not always go on like this. From Rome the Borghese Pope Paul V, successor to Clement VIII, sent word insisting that the two rival houses should ally themselves by a pact to be sealed by the marriage of Margherita, Carlo Emanuele's eldest child, born in 1589, and Francesco, Vincenzo's first-born, three years her junior. The idea was that, if he were agreeable to the alliance, Vincenzo would forego a dowry and cede some of the Piedmontese lands of Monferrato. There would be a further exchange of territory in the interests of both states. But Carlo Emanuele replied to the first offer from Mantua with such a voracious gesture—he demanded no less than half of Monferrato —that for the moment the negotiations came to a standstill.

There was one person in Mantua, however, who had seen her opportunity, and meant to take it—Madam Her Most Serene Highness of Ferrara, Margherita Gonzaga. Three years of independent life—on condition that she accepted the seclusion of a cloister—were beginning to hang heavily on the still young widow who, with secret bitterness, saw herself slipping into the over-ripeness of a woman whom love has passed by. In her attempt to forget she looked into her own heart and discovered an unexpected quality—intelligence. Once she had removed the wrappings of sentimentality it shone with a crystalline gleam. She began therefore to divide her days between two passions— religion and politics, and from day to day revealed more clearly that keen intellect of hers, so dangerous to her rivals, which ambassadors were later unanimously to recognize. On Vincenzo's departure for Croatia—not of her own accord but undoubtedly at the suggestion of someone who supported her cause—she had been appointed regent of Monferrato. When she went there in June 1601 she brought with her a plan drawn up in agreement with the ducal councillors.

On her arrival at Casale she tested the temper of the place, had slighting things to say of the ladies, complained—but not excessively—of the heat and fatigue and acted a little as if she had been hard done by. But meanwhile she was receiving an envoy from Turin, with whom she was in constant close conference. Finally in August 1601 she sent off one of her confidants—a Benedictine monk called Father Valeriano—to Carlo Emanuele with this proposal: let Margherita of Savoy marry Francesco Gonzaga and she, Margherita Gonzaga, Carlo Emanuele, to whom she would bring a dowry of 500,000 gold crowns. Father Valeriano arrived in Turin, contrived to speak secretly with the Duke—

who formed an adverse opinion of him—and awaited a reply. Meantime the Spanish ambassador, having guessed the nature of the embassy, kept up ceaseless, lengthy talks in the hope of wrecking the negotiations. Were they not agreed that the eldest daughter of the house of Savoy deserved the honour of an imperial marriage? And how could the Duke, with nine children at home, think of marrying at a moment so inopportune for the father of such a large family?

Carlo Emanuele allowed himself to be given advice which he himself had probably instigated, and listened to each point with the keen attention of a politician trying to discern from the interchanges of a dialogue the speaker's motives and what advantage he himself may draw from them. Not that he thought marriage inopportune—so amorous was he that his natural children soon numbered eleven, and later he secretly married Marguerite de Rousillon—but he considered it better to be free, and not hampered, particularly not by a woman like Margherita Gonzaga, who was beginning to show that she was not only intelligent, but extremely self-centred. Father Valeriano returned to Casale with a refusal. In it Madam Her Most Serene Highness read her condemnation to widowhood and fell ill of silent disappointment. From that moment she realized that there was only one spot left where she could rule—Mantua—and only one way of ruling— indirectly and secretly. But she did not yet wish to resign herself to this. Next year, however, when she returned to rule Monferrato once again, she found in existence a party prepared to resist her orders. Then she smelt defeat, which would have robbed her of all her prestige, and, womanlike, took refuge in spinning a cocoon of dissimulation. Thenceforth—after a brief preparatory spell of meditation—Margherita Gonzaga was to cultivate religion with a kind of passionate intensity. Having left her first convent she had the church and convent of Sant'Orsola built for herself at Pradella and made of it a wonderful independent enclave, all finely painted and gilded, and protected by the high wall of the cloister. But a coming and going of friars and priests and laymen linked this fortress with the ducal palace and made it into a kind of observation post; from it she was to follow from day to day the doings of her family and intervene resolutely whenever the house of Gonzaga was in crisis.

The negotiations for the marriage of Francesco with Margherita of Savoy were resumed and seem to have been concluded in 1604. In September of that year Carlo Emanuele and Vincenzo, who had brought the eighteen-year-old Francesco with him, had met on the boundary between the realm of Savoy and Monferrato. There had been a long and apparently inconclusive conversation in a hunting pavilion. Promises of peace and friendship were made; the exchange of Monferrato territory for land round Asti was settled; but Carlo Emanuele, although he had covered the young heir of the Gonzagas with caresses and admired the way he sat a horse, had been unwilling to discuss which of his elder daughters, Margherita or Isabella, he would make the young man's partner. The second, if the Emperor of Austria wanted the first-born, the first-born if the Emperor wanted the second— that was what he said, and for a moment he stripped his words bare of their easy affability. Nor was he concerned if the Gonzagas felt mortified at this conditional promise.

On the contrary, all historians have described Carlo Emanuele as an affectionate father and we can accept their description of him on the strength of the delightfully lively letters he sent his children; but his affection took second place to a passion which transcended all other motives—his passion for politics. He moved his children about like pawns according to his own plans—and they were changeable plans which altered according to his own fleeting intuitions. He had sent the three eldest boys to Spain to be educated and to gain favour. The eldest, Filippo Emanuele, had died in his 'teens in Madrid; as for the other two, the Duke had had to admit that little attention was paid to them at the court of Philip III. So he had given orders for them to come home. He nourished internally a great disillusionment over Spain—for he had dreamt of its crown for his eldest son and then for his eldest daughter. To conjure up crowns for Margherita's head was an exercise suited to his gambler's mind. First of all he had almost concluded her marriage with the Prince of Condé, the heir-presumptive to the throne of France; but it had been broken off the moment Henry IV married Maria dei Medici. Then he had negotiated the Spanish marriage with Philip III; but Philip had chosen an Austrian princess instead. Now for Carlo Emanuele the air was thick with gleaming visions—such as the archducal, the almost royal, crown of the Hapsburgs and the imperial crown of Rudolf II.

Boredom had been the normal state of affairs at the court of Turin ever since Caterina, daughter of Philip II of Spain, had arrived there as Carlo Emanuele's bride; for she had brought with her, and had indeed accentuated out of pride in her origins, the stiff and rigid customs of the Spanish court. Being convinced that even the slightest demonstration of feeling on the part of a prince was a self-inflicted insult to his own image, and being accustomed to conceal the impulses of the heart—and in her they were both warm and lively—under an air of extreme haughtiness, Caterina had forced the whole court of Savoy to undergo a course of repression and self-torture; not so much Carlo Emanuele—although his close friends said he was not the same man as before his marriage—as her sons and, of course, her daughters. In order to mortify her own lively nature, which she had transmitted to the girls along with her own blood, Caterina had brought from Spain a lady of the court, Donna Mariana de Tassis, who had become mummified through the worship of etiquette and bigotry. A narrow-minded genius of the whipping school, she was one of those women of Philip II's generation who prayed in the front row at the *auto da fés* for the condemned men at the stake and exhorted them to thank God who was leading them to such a wonderful act of expiation.

Since she was continually engaged in an inhuman fight with herself, it is understandable that Caterina's heart broke. But she was permitted a husband by law and he had been allotted to her by her father with instructions to keep him firmly attached to Spain, so she had permitted herself to love him and loved him to the point of dying of it. She had given him ten children, had followed him, supported him, obeyed him, wearing herself away in the struggle between the love which aroused in her an intense and even joyous sense of vitality and her determination to dominate herself. At last, weakened by an unfortunate pregnancy while Carlo Emanuele was on campaign at Chambéry and sent no news of himself, she concluded that he was dead and gave herself up to a passion of grief. This, the first taste of liberty in her life, overwhelmed her, and led to her death in November 1597, at the age of thirty-two.

For the sake of the woman he had loved so much Carlo Emanuele tolerated in his castle the overweening haughtiness of Donna Mariana de Tassis—not to mention the fact that the governess's fame as a wardress relieved him from any worries during his daughters' youth. In a series of restrictive decrees, Donna Mariana gave orders that the four princesses, in their stiff bejewelled gowns, should be condemned to an airless life. They were to leave the castle once a month. In church they were to show the populace from a high dais their little heads bowed in prayer, dimly seen in the thick, gilded shadows of the chapel royal. Prayer and penitence were both permitted and advised, and the princesses subjected themselves to their rigours, even learning—a dangerous pleasure—the meaning of the hair shirt and flagellation. The pleasures necessary for a princely education were not prohibited, but on the contrary imposed with iron discipline. Dancing was, for instance, taught to them by numbers, so that the girls might find in the dash and whirl of the dance a lesson in mathematics.

Since Spanish pomp demanded that the court of the infantas should be inhabited by courtiers and gentlewomen, many Piedmontese lords and ladies, with their fair colouring and light eyes, moved in formal ranks through the salons of the castle amid the gilded twirls of the furnishings, bowing expertly under the pessimistic eye of the Spanish governess. It must be admitted, however, that if her relations with the Duke were not always friendly, Carlo Emanuele cared little. Indeed sometimes, when he had heard her speaking with too great severity and allowed himself a moment to reflect on the life the girls led under such despotism, he would suddenly appear in the princesses' rooms and choose for them plumed and bejewelled dresses. Then he, too, would disguise himself fantastically and go out with the young ladies—the elder ones with him, and the younger with the Duke of Nemours, all in gilded sledges, upholstered with red brocade, to the trot of fiery ponies, amid the excited cracking of whips and the joyful salutations of his adoring subjects.

It never occurred to their father to wonder what it meant to come back from such brief and exciting drives—or from the rare but exceedingly splendid court balls—nor how the memory of them went on fermenting in the children's minds. If the Infanta Isabella, the second daughter, found enough strength in herself to withdraw into gay starry pride, for the eldest Infanta, Margherita, pride alone was not sufficient to reduce her to neutrality. Passivity, woman's last weapon of defence, was repugnant to her—and how can we help seeing in that repugnance the mark of a life which had gone wrong?

Though the poets might sing of nymphs and goddesses—stressing her 'majestade'—Margherita was not beautiful. Not very tall, not very white-skinned, not very generous in her figure, she did, however, have the delicacy of build and, above all that intense vitality which is so charming at sixteen, and which made her so closely resemble her father. She was like him in character, too, compound of impulses, intensely proud and brave—qualities which, if allowed to flourish too liberally in a woman, are called excitability, arrogance and self-will. But Margherita would never, even at the price of her own peace of mind, be able to resist her determination to impose on others her own obstinate point of view. It was therefore natural that, in the autumn of 1605, having learned something of the negotiations with Mantua, she should choose from among the courtiers a gentleman friendly to the Gonzagas—Count Alessandro da Ro—and, making up to him without appearing to do so, begin to quiz him on the Mantuan court, on the family of her probable betrothed. At once the gentleman became her accomplice.

Boredom was banished. Margherita's head swarmed with pressing problems. That through the descriptions of Alessandro da Ro she came to know a man who might become her husband and after scrutinizing him, accepted him in her heart, was nothing in itself; to lead matters on from betrothal to marriage, although she herself was in a dependent position, to make her father bring her to the altar, to eclipse her sister (whom Carlo Emanuele seemed more inclined to designate), to intrigue unbeknown to Donna Mariana while preserving intact her reputation, her dignity and her conscience—all this Margherita contrived to do. Up and down the Po between Turin and the plains of Mantua went letters, embassies, secret gifts of scarves and embroideries; delicate sighs floated to and fro; showers of tears were shed. The Infanta had in fact for long been in control of the operation, when at last Alessandro gave a cry of triumph; he felt, he said, that he had succeeded in winning a bride for his lord.

Undoubtedly the hopes set on Mantua brought with them to Turin a touch of warmth. The winter of 1605 to 1606 was made gay by the Duke of Mantua's players, sent by Vincenzo with the task of entertaining and captivating his future daughter-in-law. It was no mean concession to have transferred from Mantua this famous company which all Italy longed to see and France insistently requested—the company in which the famous actors Pier Maria Cecchini and Tristano Martinelli played Fritellino and Arlecchino respectively. The actresses who took the parts of Flaminia, Flavia and Rizolina were light and piquant ladies and they provoked languid, highly spiced gossip. Don Amedio, natural brother of Carlo Emanuele, protected Flavia; Count Camillo Martinengo, Flaminia. Emblazoned coaches vied to carry the capricious charmers to and fro. High up on her chair of state Margherita was caught up in the vibrant atmosphere of this skein of love, though she herself had no part in it, and watched the spectacle with a feeling that she had been launched on a path strewn with new and lively ideas. The amorous words of Lelio and Flaminia did not so much move her as induce a state of icy intoxication while she secretly applied them to herself as if they had been invented for her. From her discovery of the theatre—as from all her other discoveries—she seemed to wring a meaning only because she saw in it another episode in the story of that eager self-examination which made up her day.

The little intrigue lasted almost three years and one might, if one wished, find in it all the elements of a romantic love-story—except that the tone is wrong. It was the two protagonists who, in unconscious agreement, disguised with tender tints the mutually convenient arrangement which led them to each other: on the one hand, Francesco, so mindful of the interests of the Gonzagas that he was willing to marry into the house of Savoy and, without knowing either of Carlo Emanuele's daughters—having been told in fact that the second was considerably prettier than the elder—let his choice fall on the girl who embodied the rights of primogeniture; on the other Margherita, who had sensed that in the Gonzagas and in her betrothed there was room for her to make further conquests, to widen her powers. Obviously, if set alongside these facts, their trepidations, their ardours, their appeals to each other are not an expression of love's delicious anarchy, but are dominated by a crude and disquieting secret rhythm of their own. They are part of a marriage conspiracy.

In 1606 it seemed that the Emperor Rudolf II was concentrating his lunatic desires on Margherita. So she wept in Turin, while in Mantua Francesco swore he would never marry the Infanta Isabella. But these were the prickings of self-will, not of pain. Meanwhile Donna Mariana discovered the intrigue, denounced to the Duke the Gonzagas' friends at court, and, rattling off long, excited, disapproving harangues, declared that the Infanta Margherita was a girl who demeaned herself by revealing her inclinations before being authorized—nay, commanded to do so by her father. Perhaps Carlo Emanuele might have taken umbrage, even though it was clear that his daughter's desires would never be an obstacle to his own plans, had he not discovered that Rudolf's proposals were merely a shift by his Hapsburg cousins in Austria and Spain to prevent the Gonzaga marriage; for the Emperor had no real intention of marrying into the house of Savoy. But

Carlo Emanuele had no intention of letting it be said that the Spaniards could deal lightly with him. Instead, he would present them with the following situation: he would marry the two Infantas off together, both to Italian princes—Margherita to Francesco Gonzaga, and Isabella to the young prince of Modena, Don Alfonso d'Este. And there would be great festivities.

The year 1606 was the year of the famous conflict between the Pope and Venice—the year of the two Pauls, Pope Paul V and Paolo Sarpi. And it was an unlucky year for Vincenzo—one which would lead to a period of moral blindness. He was to learn the meaning of betrayal, but he was to prove incapable of learning it thoroughly.

Admittedly 1606 had found Vincenzo in a bad case. He still felt the consequence of the risk he had run in 1604 and 1605 when he had threatened war with the Pope over a question of jurisdiction between himself and the cardinal legate of Ferrara. From Milan the Conte de Fuentes had thundered in the name of Spain against the disturber of the peace, and an agreement had been reached only through the mediation of Venice, which already foresaw much graver conflicts over similar questions. But the word 'war', like a sword, suddenly flourished and suddenly resheathed, and this sudden picking of an adversary in the Pope whom he had sincerely venerated up to that very moment, shows that there was something unbalanced in Vincenzo. It was in vain, therefore, that Chieppio employed all his intelligence and all his subtlety to turn the Duke's very errors to Mantua's benefit. In that same year, 1605, hard on the Venetian mediation, and at a time when Venice was showing great friendship for the Gonzagas, Vincenzo felt the moment had come to ask for the post of Captain-General of the troops of the Republic, which so many Gonzagas had held in past centuries. For Ascension Vincenzo went to Venice with his young son, Francesco, taking Chieppio with them. There were festivities, compliments, ornate and gracious speeches; but people like the Venetians were too well informed on the military skill of the Duke of Mantua ever to entrust to him the command of their troops on the mainland. If they went through the motions of conducting negotiations and produced from the Mantuan archives the parchment scrolls and the old treaties between the Gonzagas and Venice, they had only, with great caution, to air once more the rule which stipulated that the Captain-General of Venice must be free of tribute to other powers —let Vincenzo therefore send his Golden Fleece back to Spain— for any desire in his heart to lead the Venetian troops to be chilled.

At the beginning of August in that same year, Vincenzo, by now completely indifferent to the idea of becoming Captain-General of the Republic, suddenly descended on Rome after an affectionate pilgrimage to the holy places of Italy—Loreto, Assisi, Camaldoli and Vallombrosa.

He spent three days in the Vatican, warmly welcomed by Paul V. What had they said to each other? What had they agreed? What plans had they discussed? These were the questions the ambassadors asked themselves, for they could not accept the statement Chieppio put out from Mantua that 'there were none of these mysteries people keep talking about'. They could not be expected to believe that, they muttered. Perhaps the Duke had asked for a cardinal's hat for his second son, Ferdinando, or had discussed the marriage of his eldest boy with Margherita of Savoy, requesting papal support to bring it about. There were those who claimed to know that a war against the Turks had been discussed and in particular the possibility of a new campaign in Hungary, which was apparently very imminent. Indeed, on his return to Mantua Vincenzo more than once began to talk of the crusade and suggested to his representative in Rome that, should the Pope begin to think in concrete terms, he should put forward to him the idea that Vincenzo be appointed Captain-General of the new expedition. Let him remember that one hundred and fifty years before the Marquis Ludovico had been appointed to that rank by Pius II, the Piccolomini.

The idea came to nothing—in fact it was never even mentioned —and when in November 1605 the usual papal brief reached Mantua appealing for aid for Rudolf II against a new wave of Turkish invasion, Vincenzo replied sadly that he was too poor to be able to offer anything except his own person. He could take no more money from the public exchequer, which was already much diminished, nor could he take men from his lands.

Now that both the Venetian command and the command over the papal troops had fallen through, Vincenzo occupied himself chiefly with love, art and the theatre, music and alchemy, blending his passions with such loving fury that they were all raised to a high pitch. He was restless. He felt himself vulnerable in his body, his mind and his hopes. Travel was becoming a constant means of fleeing from himself, and even his family—that nucleus of fixed stars by which a man willingly lets himself be guided when he is uncertain of his course—was beginning to be affected by divergence of character and ambitions as well as by that slow decay to which marriages are subject.

The first to leave the paternal brood was Margherita, his young daughter, born in 1591, and married at fifteen to the Duke of Lorraine under the patronage of Maria dei Medici, who greatly loved this niece so like herself. This Margherita Gonzaga was a white- and rose-complexioned girl whom Rubens portrayed at a vivid moment of her adolescence; she had concentrated in her person much of the Austrian heritage of her two grandmothers— for example their tawny hair—but she had none of the Hapsburgs' haughty reserve. On the contrary, she was gay, very much of a Gonzaga, and Vincenzo would have loved her too much had Leonora not taken care to ration their father's love for her children. Loaded with pearls and jewels, to which the great diadem of the house of Lorraine would later be added, Margherita was brought to her husband by her mother; her father she had left at Augsburg with many tears and tender farewells.

Leonora journeyed on with her daughter, entered France, and reached Nancy, where a magnificent wedding was held, and the intelligent but discreet Gonzaga women dispelled the mistrust of the house of Lorraine. The progress of the Duchess of Mantua then continued splendidly through France to Paris where her sister, Maria dei Medici, fêted her royally and gave her the dauphin, the future Louis XIII, to hold at his baptism at Fontainebleau. This journey of Leonora's was like a holiday for her and she enjoyed it to the full, quick to note the various costumes and who wore them. However, since she moderated the sharpness of her tongue, which was that of a great Florentine lady, with a certain homely good temper, her remarks were sympathetic in tone. But even she discovered such excitement in the company of her brother-in-law, Henry IV, that she could not refrain from writing to her husband how understandable it was that even the stones adored the King. Henry IV, for his part, in accordance with his usual generous nature, fêted his sister-in-law and the ladies from Mantua—particularly Signora de Rossi, who had 'the most beautiful hands in the world', and a certain Signora Gondi. Neither his grey beard, nor his fifty-three years, nor the sadness which now and then cast a shadow on his most intelligent brow, could break him of his amorous ways.

With Leonora in France and Vincenzo on one of his inconclusive pleasure trips to Innsbruck and Munich, the regency of Mantua had been assumed by Madam Her Most Serene Highness of Ferrara, who had suddenly emerged from her monastery at Sant'Orsola, appeared in the ducal palace, and set herself firmly down at the council table with Chieppio at her side. They understood each other well, these experts in politic discussion, although they watched each other closely. Fate seemed to abet Madam's passion for ruling by giving her the regency at a difficult period; for while she held power the pontifical anathema on Venice burst forth, the Republic was excommunicated, and that obstinate struggle between the civil and religious powers which lay behind the papal interdict broke out. This is not the place to summarize such a burning and complex question, and we shall refer only to so much as is necessary for our story. Two loose-living priests— Canon Saraceni of Vicenza, who had been denounced by a married lady because she suspected him of wilfully defiling her doorstep, and Abbot Brandolino, who had been summoned to appear before the court at Treviso on suspicion of murder—were the immediate causes of a conflict which had its roots in old history. The Venetians said that the weal of the state must have precedence over everything else, including religion, and that crimes committed by anyone, whether layman or cleric, must be tried by the civil courts. Paul V replied that jurisdiction over the clergy belonged to the Roman court. It had been the good fortune of Leonardo Dona, Doge of Venice, who showed the kind of man he was by declaring that he was first born a citizen of Venice and then baptized a Christian, to find to hand in the monastery of the Servants of Mary a man like Paolo Sarpi. Naturally it seemed to him—for he was both dazzled and forti- fied by such intellectual vigour—a great gain for the Republic to nominate Sarpi its theologian; and so too it seemed to the Council of Ten.

Relying on Sarpi, Venice maintained that she had received from God liberty to deal with all her subjects even against the will of the Papacy. So after the exchange of innumerable letters and one incident after another over the most tortuous matters, the situa- tion finally took shape as follows.

In the last days of April 1606 the bull of excommunication was launched from Rome by Paul V. Mass was forbidden, as were the sacraments, the functions of the Church and all priestly offices. Within frontiers which God had abandoned the subjects of Venice were to be stifled by a life without spiritual comforts.

What happened then—the vigorous defence of the Republic, which forced the clergy to continue its offices under pain of death, the hesitations and then the submission of the bishops and priests, the resistance of the Jesuits inspired by a signal from Claudio Aquaviva, the General of the Order, their expulsion and their exodus from Venetian territory, followed immediately by the Capuchins and Theatines—is part of a great story which stirred the interest and passions not only of Italy, but of all Europe.

The voice of Paolo Sarpi thundered; as they listened to it, the Protestants thought to see in him the Luther of Italy and sent encouragement, letters, offers of support and men. In France, Henry IV, who was grateful to Venice for having recognized him as king before any other nation, could not take up its defence

without the Vatican doubting the genuineness of his recent con-
version; he therefore attempted to act as peace-maker by pro-
posing unemotional formulæ which his own ambassador respected
only in part. Spain did the same and sent plumed ambassadors,
but in secret she enjoyed the opportunity of fomenting war in
Italy, especially against the hated Venetian Republic. Of the
Italians, while the Grand Duke Ferdinand dei Medici was sincere
in his mediations, Carlo Emanuele of Savoy was busy reviving the
idea of a league between himself, Tuscany and Mantua, against
Spain; but at the same time he was sounding Spain in order to
obtain the territory of Monferrato and even sounding France to
obtain Milan. Everything was in complete disorder and confusion. Naturally such a high state of excitement, which would
have sufficed to make anyone else gasp, acted on Vincenzo Gonzaga as a stimulant—all the more so since Mantua, because it
marched with Venice, felt directly the consequences of whatever
happened in the Republic.

Thus scarcely had the decree expelling the Jesuits been signed in
Venice than they descended in flocks on the banks of the Mincio,
followed by the Capuchins and Theatine brothers. The swarm of
priests and friars in the streets of a city already so full of religious
establishments, their apocalyptic pessimism and general lack of
discretion, caused upheavals of conscience, and led to strange
reactions and equally strange factions. They went about both
prophesying and invoking war on Venice; they assumed the airs
of persecuted martyrs, lamenting and intriguing, and were prepared to go the length of masquerading as women in order to get
through to Verona and confer with the faithful. Vincenzo, for his
part, being by nature inclined to favour ecclesiastics, wrote to
Chieppio from Munich ordering him to lodge the Capuchins at
the Palazzo del Te along with the alchemists and the ducal mistresses, to dispense generous charity to the Jesuits and a warm
welcome to all. But soon he found himself gravely embarrassed.

Madam of Ferrara could hardly believe her good fortune at
having to deal with such important matters and such close contact
with friars, priests and cardinals. With joyful zeal she received the

fugitives and sheltered them for the love of God. What exultation there was on the festival of Corpus Christi when the great procession swayed along to the slow rhythm of a hundred and sixty Capuchins, walking two and two. There were masses every morning in all the churches and at all the altars, with sermons every day and spiritual conversions possible morning, noon or night. There is no need to add, however, that although Madam lived to the full her sacred Saturnalia she did not for a moment lose sight of her political interests. But even she could not restrain the Bolognese Jesuit Statera who, on the evening of 21st May, began to talk of princes and their duty of obedience to the Church in the Trinità, where Rubens's three brand-new pictures with portraits of the dukes and their children hung like banners full of air and colour and light. The result was a clamorous incident with Venice which was smoothed out partly by Madam Her Most Serene Highness, who amused herself by producing a series of lies, each one of them a jewel, which the Venetian diplomats admired even if they did not believe them—partly by Chieppio, and partly by Vincenzo himself on his return. A month had not passed before another Jesuit, Father Gagliardi, launched an attack from the same pulpit on the Republic and the writings of Paolo Sarpi and thus gave rise to an even more complicated diplomatic incident. Vincenzo was angry, Chieppio hastened to patch things up and once again matters were smoothed over. In fact they almost took a turn for the better, although the Duke was directly touched by a friar who began publicly to denounce the florid, voluptuous life led by the court at a time when the wrath of God loomed on the frontiers.

Thanks to Chieppio's able manœuvres, however, and his skill in tacking to and fro between Venice and Rome, Vincenzo contrived to behave with sangfroid. He had moreover refused the proposal to enter into a league with Spain and so earned the praise of the Republic. Meantime he kept an eye on the movements of Carlo Emanuele and the other powers, large and small. But he was overcome by the intoxication of the bustle of arms; he was bound to be drawn in. In October 1606, led on by his visions of grandeur, Vincenzo gave ear to some daring, unscrupulous captains. We know the name of one of them—Cristoforo Gualtieri, a sword for hire and a professional assassin. So he conceived a plan.

Chieppio was ill and absent from his desk. Vincenzo, who felt himself in full control of the state, took advantage of the fact to send a most secret dispatch to his representative at Rome with the following proposal to transmit to Paul V: What if Vincenzo were suddenly to enter Venetian territory and take by surprise the fortresses of Verona, Peschiera, Legnago? The operation promised to be easy provided the Pope approved. Those taking part would be men of quality and would include the captains of the fortresses themselves. Obviously such a raid would be a stab in the back for Venice.

We will not speculate how Vincenzo intended to justify the treachery he was plotting against Venice at the very moment when he was assuring her that he was an excellent friend, nor how he regarded it in the light of his conscience. Like many others with the same Machiavellian twist, he undoubtedly considered that anything could be justified by *raison d'état*. It would be more interesting to wonder with what arguments he faced the possible consequences of his actions—first and foremost, the opening of the floodgates of Spanish power, which was mounting in Milan under the fierce watchful eyes of the Conte de Fuentes, Venice's great enemy. It was a torrent which everyone in Italy, and indeed throughout Europe, feared, and it would spread quickly. His act of bravado, his whim, his outburst of temperament might cause a war which would involve all Italy and perhaps undermine the age-old existence of the Venetian Republic.

Yet Vincenzo did not succeed in realizing this great and ruinous adventure. The Pope was distrustful of the proposal; he was full of praise but had no intention of supporting it. It must, he said, be pondered carefully. Meantime Chieppio recovered and returned to his office, read through the documents, shuddered and felt, as he said, 'caught between the shears.' So he began to set things right—that is to say to whittle away at them—

and above all, knowing his Duke, to take time. In fact only a month needed to pass, bringing with it a reshuffle of commands in Venetian territory, for the plan to begin to crumble; meanwhile Vincenzo was brought back to reason by the arguments which Chieppio kept instilling into him indirectly. He saw his idea wither away, lost interest and barely gave it another thought.

At this point, however, the Pope once more took a hand. In his irritation over Venetian pride and intransigence he thought that by giving the Duke of Mantua a free hand, he might teach the proud Signora a lesson. So he took up the project once more, put new life into it and insisted that it produce results—and he promised to leave Vincenzo in possession of any conquests he might make in Venetian territory. To Vincenzo and Chieppio it seemed that they could no longer draw back; on the contrary, they must seem firm in their support of an idea already so far advanced and use this card to ask Rome that Vincenzo—rather than a Farnese—get command over the Pontifical troops. They spoke and acted correspondingly. But meantime they procrastinated—the Duke, for example, would go off hunting—and refused to come to the point. Then they introduced a new note into the negotiations by saying that while, of course, they were ready to take up arms they were in truth more inclined to peace than war.

When Cristoforo Gualtieri, the hothead who was to be Vincenzo's main accomplice in handing over the fortress of Verona, came to Mantua, his greatest enemy, Tomasso Canossa, a gentleman of the court who had lost many relatives to the Veronese Captain's sword, was inevitably warned. It was in vain that Gualtieri's arrival was kept a close secret, for the Republic of Venice had swarms of spies in the neighbouring territories. But it would be interesting to know who told Canossa that the Captain was in Mantua and who gave details of the route he was to take by night through certain lonely streets. The night of 17th January, 1607, was intensely cold. Led by Canossa, a small body of cloaked and masked men posted itself at a street corner. The hours passed and the streets rang in the frost. It was midnight when, warned by a mysterious signal, Canossa shifted his ground just in time to meet Gualtieri, force him to a duel and cut him down with a blow of his sword.

Along with the Veronese captain all Vincenzo's projects for attacking Venice in the rear collapsed. Vincenzo saw his last chance to figure in a huge misguided adventure fade away. Shortly afterwards a peaceful agreement was reached between Venice and Rome which was to leave Italy with a long, festering illness. The merchants of the Rialto had lost, through expenditure in arms and the standstill of all trade, six million gold crowns. Yet although Venice handed over the two ecclesiastics who had caused the conflict to the King of France for him to deliver them to the Pope, she had won. None of her laws had been altered and no new law had been introduced into her constitution. In Rome the peace satisfied no one. Perhaps, as an observer acutely remarked, because it had not been reached by war. But in Mantua, where they had felt war ready to flood over the Milanese frontier, there was no end to the Te Deums and the thanksgiving masses. Chieppio congratulated himself on his excellent navigation in the teeth of the wind, and with a sigh of satisfaction, he invited the courtiers to echo him as he praised the Duke's great wisdom.

Among the voluptuous products of Mantua which a censorious friar had denounced from the pulpit, calling down upon it the wrath of God, was Claudio Monteverdi's *Orfeo*, 'a tale in music', which that Cremonese musician had composed after hearing Peri's *Euridice* at the memorable performance given in 1600 when everyone had come to Florence for Maria dei Medici's marriage. Vincenzo was probably aware of the revolutionary quality of what has been defined as the masterpiece of the new school of opera—the first attempt at an opera in which music and poetry are firmly and logically connected. He certainly enjoyed it so much that, not content with being present at the long rehearsals, he had it repeated three times.

The librettist was Alessandro Striggi, the poet and nobleman. We could wish that the libretto of *Orfeo* were less cramped by the need to imitate Rinuccini and Chiabrera, and allowed us to see the grace and urbanity of a very modest genius. That is what *we* should like but Claudio Monteverdi, on the contrary, rose effortlessly above the meagre poetic talent of the libretto. He even effected the miracle of transcending Striggi's formal verse and saw the words as magic symbols which he brought forth one by one to shine afresh in his recitative, as if he had translated into music not the words but their evocative qualities. How can those who hear it fail to be moved by the dialogue between the Messenger and Orfeo with the unforgettable climax of sorrow which begins 'your lovely Euridice . . . your beloved wife is dead'? Vincenzo was among those who wept.

We can safely guess—the documents are really superfluous in this case—that the women singers were very often also Vincenzo's mistresses, even if we do not talk, as some have done, of a musical harem—if only out of respect for Claudia Cattaneo, Monteverdi's dear wife, who was one of the Duke's singers. But in the Duke's papers we can follow the whims of Madam Europa and Madam Sabina, together with descriptions of their merits, their rivalry and their difficult reconciliations. Until 1600, Vincenzo's favour was divided equally between singers and actresses, but when the new year began, immediately after the revealing performance at Florence, we find singers take precedence over actresses, and we can understand why. A woman who was capable of uniting the sensuality of a sweet voice with an actress's animation against a wonderful background of landscape and light —a woman disguised and finally transfigured in an allegory—was for Gonzaga an enchantress rich in love-potions. And who more disposed than he was to become intoxicated with them?

For a new art-form, new interpreters were needed and it was the moment for Madam Europa and Madam Sabina to slip into second place. Vincenzo, who envied the witty singers of the Medicean theatre, sought throughout Italy for a singer who would be trained entirely for him, and Paolo Facconi, a singer in the papal chapel, discovered one for him in Rome—Caterinuccia Martinelli, a little thirteen-year-old girl put forward by her father who guaranteed her virtue in words which were disconcertingly precise.

She was completely immature in voice and heart. Let her come soon, in fact at once, said Vincenzo, with his voice full of longing, and he gave orders that she should be brought to Mantua in spite of the extreme heat of the summer. But having revealed his impatience, he was now obliged to consent to the hard bargains driven by Caterina's parents. Yet if the idea of the child agitated him and stimulated his fancy, he was too fastidious to spoil in the bud a pleasure which he promised himself he would cultivate for the future. And so the little girl from Rome lived, as if she were at school, in Claudio Monteverdi's house, where she learnt to form herself musically under the musician's direction and his wife's careful guardianship. Who can blame her for the holidays she spent in the Duke's villas or palaces? Overwhelmed with favours and gifts, the little girl from Rome took everything with the ingenuous vanity of the very young who think the world is created especially for them. She was not the person to wonder at the meaning of the Duke's love, at once paternal and sensual, ardent and absent-minded, attentive and distant.

Perhaps it was by way of a sort of moral revenge, and not entirely for rigorous educational reasons, that Monteverdi at first set her to sing sacred music. Only at the Carnival of 1608 did Caterina appear on the stage with Cupid's wings on her shoulders and her bare legs in golden buskins, singing the part of Amore in Rinuccini's *Dafne*, set to music by Marco di Gagliano. She was now eighteen years old, at once plump and pleasing, and she had a high, pure voice which lent itself to the song with the trained sureness of a pupil who had spent five years in hard study under Monteverdi. Her graceful début was opportune. For at the court the little favourite, too young to be able to start a faction and too immature to make herself valued or feared, was not loved. The devotees of art began to forgive her and awaited with a benign curiosity her appearance in *Ariana*, which Monteverdi was preparing when an unexpected malady, either smallpox or scarlet fever, intervened, and she died in March 1608. Not mourned, hardly even pitied, said Chieppio; but Vincenzo, ever faithful to the memory of all his loves, ordered a splendid funeral for her, a tomb in the church of the Carmine and daily mass of intercession, and he had Monteverdi compose a musical elegy and a tender epitaph.

If singers had sufficed him and he had let the well-born ladies alone there would have been fewer gloomy faces in the palace, said the moral faction led by Leonora dei Medici and Vincenzo's eldest son, Francesco Gonzaga. Francesco, at this point in the story, was attracting the hopes—they were carefully canalized by his mother—of those thoughtful people who were tired of enumerating the scandals of the Duke's life. The young prince had the misfortune to know that this was so and yet he consented to it. Thus, at twenty-one, he posed as a virtuous youth and set himself up as a model in opposition to his father—became, in short, an amiable pedant. To this result his mother had contributed by an upbringing modelled on the ancients; but in this she was mistaken, as are almost all those whose educational standards derive from their own struggle with life. Leonora had been baulked of her wish to combat in her children the excesses of their father. She had shuddered unduly when Francesco, at seven years old, had incurred his first debt to a moneylender and then, calling for the whip, she would have beaten him with her own hand had she not been appeased by the tears of her other children kneeling in a row to beg mercy for their big brother. At this point she felt it necessary to take her son aside and begin to reveal to him the truth about his father's splendour, showing him that the suffering of others was the background against which the Duke's magnificence shone.

The lesson had taken root in his languid temperament and almost extinguished in him the natural propensity of the Gonzagas towards a voluptuous life; besides, although at sixteen he had been graceful and even handsome, at twenty he had already become excessively florid. His gentleness, developing thus on a puny foundation, soon revealed that as a man he was, if not exactly weak, at least mediocre. We can understand that at his mother's court the young man, being fair-haired, gallant and virtuous, was greatly loved, and that the girls and ladies jested with him after the free Lombard fashion, especially once the story of his disputed betrothal with Margherita of Savoy was known. Indeed, it was perhaps they who kept the secret warm with the fervent complicity of women in love with love. Since it was a question of a story with a matrimonial ending, Leonora agreed that jokes might be allowed. 'It's *his* day now,' said the Medici princess, laughing at the picture of her son with an indirectly critical glance at her husband's greying hairs.

Even she was of the general opinion that Vincenzo was pro-longing his youth beyond the bounds of decency and discretion. She was almost ashamed of it, not so much because she felt herself outlived and discarded by her husband's infidelities (his amatory life no longer concerned her) but because the flagrancy of all his amorous adventures offended her as a princess and as a mother. She was even willing to humour him, to weave out of a web of patience the veil which would shield him from the judgment of others. Her sorrow lay in the fact that she could not prevent someone like the Venetian ambassador, Francesco Morosini, from writing, 'His undisciplined life and the unfortunate outcome of his wars in the East have destroyed the Duke of Mantua's reputa-tion.'

'Ah, do not let them touch his reputation as a prince!' said Leonora passionately, caring deeply, not only for the family, for the dynasty and for the government, but for her husband as an individual who could be measured by the scale of human values. She, together with Chieppio, Madam of Ferrara, old Petrozzani, the mature Annibale Iberti and the young Marquis Vincenzo Guerrieri—one of the coming men of talent at the court and brother of Felicità Guerrieri, the Duke's favourite—were all united in defending him, even perhaps from himself. In a letter to Chieppio from France in 1606, Leonora was even able to give vent to her feelings against the astrologers who inhabited the basement of the ducal palace; there they made themselves com-fortable while they led the Duke astray and gave others the

opportunity to laugh at him. Leonora forgave her husband everything. Let him love, let him give orders for festivals and plays,
let him plan and build and express himself, but within certain
limits, not constraining her to an enforced tolerance which would
wither her heart; for instance, let him spare her from receiving
from her uncle the Grand Duke Ferdinand a note informing her
how Belisario Vinta, passing through Pavia, had heard someone
of low degree boast in an inn that he could sell the Duke of
Mantua's life to anyone since the Duke was spending his nights
with his beautiful stepdaughter. If she could have expressed herself
in words, Leonora might almost have entreated her husband to
show some restraint; but she kept silent. Perhaps she knew Vincenzo too well not to be aware that it was precisely this which
tempted him—the liberty to stop at every spring which might
reveal to him the intoxicating novelty of his thirst.

If his wife forgave him with sadness, his children judged him.
Francesco Gonzaga, who felt his importance had increased once
his marriage with Margherita di Savoia was settled, almost seemed
to be trying to set his father aside, while he himself strove to
attract the sympathy of the court. He gave full vent to his natural
affability and took pains to emphasize it; meantime he gloried in
his own exemplary life. On one point, however, father and son
were agreed for different reasons—namely that the festivities at
the marriage between the Houses of Savoy and Gonzaga should
be more than magnificent. It would be his moment of glory,
thought Francesco, little knowing that the temptation to give
expression to dreams which had still not lost their power was
active in his father and indeed gaining the upper hand over him.

From the moment that he was summoned to direct the wedding arrangements, Frederico Follino, the master of ceremonies,
a man used to translating life into choreography whether working or sleeping, was surrounded by a whirl of myths, as he
struggled with his allegories. The task of allotting the parts would
present no difficulties—that had been thought out beforehand.
The actors had been studying them for six months, the engineers
were busy with their designs, and the artisans were hard at work.

But what wore him down and almost drove him out of his mind was the task of keeping abreast of everything, of bringing everything together, of arranging the huge machinery as a harmonious whole. Claudio Monteverdi was to write a play set to music like the *Orfeo* which had pleased the Duke so much the year before. It was to be *Ariana*. The Florentine, Ottavio Rinuccini, had to provide him with the libretto and that quickly, Rinuccini being that delicate poet of the Medicis' court who wrote the play given in Florence for the marriage of Maria dei Medici with the King of France.

And then Monteverdi must write the music for the ballet, *Il Ballo delle Ingrate*, this too, on a theme invented by Rinuccini. And he was to write a prologue, too, to the intermezzos in the *Idropica* by Guarini on themes by Chiabrera, and the company of the Fideli was to come and act it. But who was to sing the part of Ariana now that the Roman girl, Caterinuccia Martinelli, was dead? After a moment's worry, they found a girl in Bergamo— apparently she had a divine voice—and a messenger was sent off to ask for her services. But the girl, who was ashamed because she had something wrong with one shoulder, quite rightly did not want to appear on the stage and sing sacred music as a soloist. So the hunchbacked girl was dropped, and Virginia Andreini, who went by the name of Florinda and belonged to the company of the Fideli, sang in *Ariana*, sang and danced in the *Ingrate* and acted in the *Idropica*. It was to be the triumph of this studious, fiery woman, who worked unremittingly to learn the scores under the stern direction of Claudio Monteverdi. Rehearsals were unending and those who had been to them came away with shining faces as if they had been initiated into a mystery.

And for all this the architects and the engineers drew, calculated and built! From their pencils were born grottoes, gardens, artificial wars, skies which came and went, winged cars, clouds, thunderbolts and stars. The elements were to dance in a display of wild fantasy. Money flowed in all directions and Chieppio was already pale at the thought of the accounts. Imitating the Duke, the nobility were bleeding themselves white to buy brocades and lace—not to mention jewels. Merchants with soft hands and hooked noses and heavy strongboxes were continually arriving from Venice. The theatrical costumes were all cloth of gold and silver. Everyone knew that for the ballet the ladies would wear grey silk, sewn with gold and silver filigree and scattered with little rubies, carbuncles and red gems to represent the ashes and the eternal fire to which ladies are condemned if they are cruel to their loves.

What a medley of invention this wedding was! In Venice Traiano Boccalini saw in the double alliance of the House of Savoy with the two Italian princes—Gonzaga in Mantua and Este in Modena—something approaching the beginning of real Italian unity. Chiabrera composed an elegant, trifling canzone on the glories of the House of Gonzaga and Gianbattista Marino, who had joined the court of Turin that year, divided the gleaming currency of his poetry impartially between the two sisters and brides. Abbés, secretaries, poetasters, all set their acclamations to verse and mingled them with the cheers of the court and the people of Turin who, on the 9th March, 1608, saw the Mantuan cavalcade arrive with the Duke and the Prince at its head, both handsome, gleaming and fair-haired—the father was the more attractive, said the ladies—with a train of ten marquises, thirty counts and a hundred gentlemen.

The meeting between Francesco and Margherita, after the three years of waiting, took place on the evening of 9th March, by torchlight, among bowing rows of courtiers and gentle-women. The two young people, who were drawn towards each other by a need for complete understanding which would justify their obstinate desire for each other, hesitated for a moment out of fear of not recognizing each other. Then they made an effort of will and had their reward in mutual pleasure. They were married on the 10th March in San Giovanni and next day bride-groom and father-in-law reported to Mantua on the young bride with the usual freedom of the Gonzagas. 'She is no Countess Flavia [a celebrated Mantuan beauty whom the Duke loved] but she is not ugly and she will suffice as a wife!' So Francesco concluded bluntly to his mother, and he jokingly warned his brother the cardinal that he had broken his Lenten fast by eating flesh, but that the dish was too fine and tasty not to partake of it. Vincenzo, for his part, attended the wedding and the elegant festivities in Turin with good humour tempered by melancholy. He had found Margherita 'not ugly but not very pretty either', was sure that the two young people had liked each other, and sealed this declaration with 'May God keep them always of the same mind', which came from his heart, accompanied by the muted cadence of a sigh.

It was a period of stifled sighs for Vincenzo. Having returned to Mantua to prepare a welcome for the bride and bridegroom, he threw himself into working on the great machinery for the festivities with an enthusiasm which bordered on despair. Whenever a limit was reached, the Duke urged things on, demanding that more should be done, and done better and more still. There was an almost frightening succession of symbols, an unbearable overflow of inventions which might seem to be the mark of extravagance or madness, yet in them we may see a pathetic human effort to assert himself at any price beyond the limits of his own destiny. It was a firm belief of Vincenzo's—one which had welled up in him from the earliest times—that the visual image brings with it the spirit of things and makes them real at the moment of evocation. So in the images, which would wring from the onlookers unconditional surprise and admiration, his humiliated pride, his disappointed ambition would have their revenge for all the satires, all the failures and mortifications of the past. He would present himself to the world as Vincenzo the prince, transformed into a hero, a hero in all respects, with his strength, his ripeness, his sensuality no longer threatened by time and mortified by error, but resplendent and his of right, come to life again in the colour, the energy and the whirl of dancers, the jousting and the banquets.

In cadence with this secret theme all Mantua flowed with verses, music, jewels, robes, talk and laughter—and with tears. While Claudio Monteverdi was giving dramatic vent in *Ariana* to his grief at the death of his beloved wife, a few months before, Gabriello Chiabrera arrived with his slightly oblique glance, his hair grey by now, a little cold as a person, but a most elegant inventor of challenges for tourneys, of ballets for ladies and cavaliers, the most exquisite person in the court.

Cardinal Ferdinando Gonzaga, the Duke's second son, laid hold of him at once—at least as far as he could get him away from his father. With his discriminating intelligence, his lively nature, his passion for music and literature, this young man of twenty was obviously one of the most genuine and cultured members of the dynasty. He was always in love and in this, too, was a true Gonzaga. At this moment he was in love with a Florentine lady to whom he sent verses, songs and sighs. Little did he think, the delicate young Cardinal, that the arrival of Margherita of Savoy would mean for him a tale of painful love, of suffering and remorse all his life long.

Meanwhile from the frontiers came word of the arrival of the Venetian ambassador, of the ambassadors of Lorraine and Bavaria, of the Archduke Matthias and the Archduke Ferdinand. As for Spain, it was incredible what jealousy consumed it at this Italian wedding which it had had to accept although it sent neither envoys nor gifts. Indeed, when Isabella of Savoy, on her way to Modena, passed through the state of Milan with her Este husband, the Conte di Fuentes did not prepare for her the least token of friendship or welcome. Hence the satisfaction all felt at arousing the wrath of the grizzled Spanish governor. He would see what the princes of the peninsula could contrive without him when all were gathered at the festivities in Mantua; for it would be no small thing to have there among them that personification of pride, Carlo Emanuele I.

But Carlo Emanuele did not move from Turin. He said he had to wait for the arrival of the French ambassador who had announced his departure from Paris. He said that boxes of munitions, destined for persons unknown, had been discovered in Savoy, the sign of obscure conspiracies. He said that he did not wish to expose himself to suffering the insult of Spanish indifference if, passing through the territory of Milan, he were not fittingly honoured by the Conte di Fuentes. With these and other arguments he excused his delay, but in reality he had already decided not to set out, either because he thought the Gonzagas so much beneath him that he could permit himself the luxury of neglecting them, or because of reasons of his own, derived from certain high-flown lines of thought. Following them up like the bold politician he was, he had begun to accept the idea of an Italian confederation against the foreigners, which in those days was not so much brilliant as positively mad. He advised his son-in-law to stop at Piacenza during the journey from Turin to Mantua and make a show of friendship to Ranuccio Farnese. It would be, he hinted, a unique opportunity to stress the peaceful relations between the two houses and to give birth to that union between the Italian princes which would allow them to defend themselves against all comers. The whole house of Gonzaga shuddered at the suggestion. Certainly Francesco had orders from Vincenzo not to halt for so much as one hour in Farnese territory.

The Duke was coming. The Duke was not. The Duke had put off his departure. The Duke was on the point of leaving. In Carlo Emanuele all this looked like mere caprice, and people might even have said that there were signs of hysteria had they not known that whatever Savoy did proceeded from a store of closely guarded secrets and followed a fiery subterranean logic. Meanwhile Margherita sat and waited to pick sides between her husband and her father. Francesco Gonzaga was becoming bored in Turin, for he was in no way interested in discovering in his wife, if not a soul, at least a character. He had, it is true, found Gianbattista Marino there, and this poet was the most gallant man in the world. But the compositions of a poet, which are very welcome in their time and place, do not suffice a prince. Besides, in the stiff court of Savoy where every step and every bow was counted (and woe betide those who made a slip) there was nothing to compare with life in Mantua—not merely its festivities, for there were these in Turin too, fine but infrequent, but because at Carlo Emanuele's court there was lacking that fervour, that freedom of manner which excites the pleasure of the company, stimulates the imagination, and overlaid the least festivity of the Gonzagas with a powdering of fantastic gaiety.

Francesco was roller-skating. It had been a heavy day and he was worn out by his father-in-law's indecision. As he continued this unexciting exercise, the very symbol of spiritual accidia, Francesco ruminated on his own ill-temper with this childish amusement, with Donna Mariana, Margherita's duenna, who still—indeed more than ever—instilled intransigent Spanish ideas into the young bride, and over the delays which kept him in Turin. His father was right, he thought, to be irritated by so many postponements. Mantua was already full of guests. Barges were coming alongside the banks of the lake. Coaches and companies on horseback were entering the city from north and south. The ambassadors were about to arrive, yet at court they had to confess that they still did not know the date when the bride and bridegroom would arrive. Vincenzo, with that likeable, fatherly, civilized way of his which made him so much loved by his subjects, was becoming angry, for he saw how the great stores of provisions, gathered for the wedding days, were going bad and how the price of grain and wine rose till it was a burden to the people. He was mortified by the pinpricks aimed at him from Lombardy by the Spaniards and their friends. Finally, he was offended by the lack of esteem Carlo Emanuele apparently had for him, although he knew Vincenzo's plans, first and foremost among them the journey to the waters of Spa his doctors had ordered him to make for that leg of his, where the old sore was now growing deeper and becoming discoloured. Francesco could not but take his father's side, but he did not dare to rebel against his father-in-law. When Count Alessandro Striggi came to Turin, however, with orders to make the bridegroom leave at once, with or without the Duke of Savoy, Francesco saw in him a true liberator.

Carlo Emanuele did not move but the bride and bridegroom set off with two of Margherita's brothers, the Princes Vittorio Amadeo and Emanuele Filiberto, and a glittering company of ladies and gentlemen, of poets, courtiers and musicians, all sailing along the river in a great state barge with a golden roof. Every so often along the banks of the Po a pavilion garlanded with flowers and wreathed about the name of the owner was to be seen, and boats of all sizes crowded round the barge. Then noblemen came to invite the princes in the name of their lord and of the ambassador of Milan himself to an alfresco lunch on the bank.

It was a gay progress, and Francesco's love profited by it, giving Margherita the chance to fill in the details of her husband's portrait. It was strange how his arrogance and listlessness changed to animation as they approached Mantuan territory, and how he showed his love for his country to be nothing short of adoration as he thanked the sky, the air, the water for bringing him to Lombardy. But was not this admiration too openly revealed— was it not a sign of weakness? Did it not show him to be a man whom timidity kept anchored to his home, as if he feared to lose his own identity if he went abroad in the world? Perhaps Margherita did not ask such a circumstantial question but she must have realized already something she later showed that she understood, namely that her husband had no strength of character. Perhaps the discovery both strengthened her and disappointed her. Finding him lacking in stature, she felt energy and the desire to expand mentally well up in her, and a predatory longing, duly repressed, filled out her slender corsage of cloth of gold.

On the morning of the 24th March, 1608, Vincenzo went down with Leonora to the Palazzo del Te. They were there again, Duke and Duchess, after twenty-four years, on a nuptial morning, on the very spot where Leonora had put on her bridal attire so long ago. At their side there stood, closely enveloped in copious widow's weeds, Margherita Gonzaga, her Most Serene Highness of Ferrara, who, seven years before, had offered to betroth herself to Carlo Emanuele and had been so firmly rebuffed. If the Duke and Duchess were moved, and therefore benevolent, she had no reason to be so. So when the bride arrived and knelt down to ask the blessing of her mother-in-law, and Leonora's eyes were full of pleasant tears, Margherita focused her intelligent eyes to examine her coldly. It was to be foreseen that the two Margheritas would not please each other, and the antipathy which later was to turn into enmity and then war, ending with the defeat of the young woman and the pitiless victory of the elder one, began perhaps with their first meeting. Margherita of Savoy was to be lost because of her pride, her energy and her unlimited opinion of herself and her own blood. It is not without significance that not only she, but her two brothers, had been instructed by their father before leaving Turin and his teaching had made them almost beside themselves with pride. The result was immediately visible. No sooner had they arrived, than the two princes of the House of Savoy declared their intentions. They meant always to have precedence at the festivities over everyone else, whether it was the Cardinal or the Duke himself. So Vincenzo, not to have his enjoyment poisoned, had to give up the idea of taking part in the bridal procession and returned to the palace in a closed carriage with his wife and sister.

The entry was effected with great solemnity. Margherita was on horseback with her great white gown covered with pearls and jewels. Her hair was unbound; she wore a crown on her head and a ducal mantle. The shadow of the canopy was disposed exactly round her. Her young face bore such an expression of majesty that it won over the populace; she took everything as her due—statues, triumphal arches, inscriptions and garlands. Followed by her bridegroom and brothers, she dismounted at the Duomo and was blessed by the bishop. Then she mounted again, putting as much dignity as she could into every movement. In front of the castle she did not start even at the sudden thunder of the artillery saluting her. She crossed the courtyard with its gay ornaments, and reached the archway leading into the castle. There she descended and found herself at the foot of the palace staircase where there stood Leonora, Margherita of Ferrara, and the young Gonzaga Cardinal with their courts. There were more salutes; then, accompanied by the Duchess, she went on, up the carpeted staircase between a double file of bowing and bejewelled ladies. Then her father-in-law came towards her. He had already recovered his composure and had patiently decided the part he was to play. So Vincenzo gallantly conducted the bride to her apartment, newly ornamented with gold, stuccoes, tapestries and paintings. There he left her to her ladies and while he returned to his own rooms, felt his heart touched once more by the solemn pleasure of the morrow.

For next day, being Whitsun, Vincenzo had prepared for himself an exceptional day which was to unfold itself in accordance with a theme conducive not only to admiration but veneration. On that 25th May, an order of knighthood which took its title from the Redeemer was being solemnly inaugurated; it was to receive gentlemen who had vowed themselves to fight against the Turks and prepare a picked army for the new Crusades. Eagerly petitioned, the Pope had in the end permitted the order to be set up, but without granting its knights the ten thousand crowns a year stipend which the Duke had asked for them from the benefices of the Church. Vincenzo who, however indolent, had an exceedingly practical cast of mind, was trying to give some sort of reality to his order of knighthood, and was negotiating with Genoa for the cession of a little port on the Riviera. He already saw the knights of the Redeemer appearing on the Ligurian horizon, cloaked in scarlet, sailing in the galleys of the Gonzagas to fight against the enemy of Christ.

What galleys? Where was the money to come from? Who was to pay for the port and the equipment and the soldiers? Such were the distrustful questions of the Genoese who had already lent Mantua more than 800,000 ducats—fortunately guaranteed by income from Vincenzo's estates. Like the Venetian ambassador when he reported on these schemes, they remained sceptical. Yet what might easily seem merely a decorative masquerade with all the vain refinements of its details—the gold and silver habit, the crimson cloak lined with white, the red shoes and stockings, the hat with the heron plumes, the motto *Probasti Domine* and the medal with the three drops of the most sacred blood—gives one a feeling not of unease but of solemn, measured melancholy. For the invention of the Order of the Redeemer belongs not so much to mankind's store of good intentions—although that, too, weighs in the balance with divine mercy—but rather to the painful heritage of man's defeats which, or so we feel, are illumined, and justified only when referred to God and absolved and granted His and our pardon. So it was right that all the onlookers were moved, as a sober witness informs us, when the Duke, having received the habit of the Order from the Dean of Sant'Andrea, in his turn enrobed eighteen knights. The populace already saw the air thick with trophies, scimitars and green banners, of lances and crescent moons and serried ranks of battle on land and sea.

Meanwhile for amusement there was the popular procession of the Guilds bringing gifts to the reliquary of the Redeemer. Most successful of all was the fishermen's tableau—a barge laden with laughing apostles in white gowns and gold haloes, throwing fish into the crowd which they drew still quivering from wicker baskets. Then they took out their nets and enmeshed the simple people as they passed. The barge heeled over and the farce became so merry that Margherita herself would have clapped her hands did she not feel herself such a great lady. In the afternoon there was a promenade, overflowing with people who took stock of each other and bowed. Then, greatly talked of in advance, came the evening of the first great spectacle. At the door of his new theatre Vincenzo himself received the six thousand people invited to this single performance of Claudio Monteverdi's *Ariana*. They had worked on it for eight months and spent more than two millions in gold coin.

Through *Ariana* I am achieving a true lament, Monteverdi was to say later, in his sober lapidary way. He was alluding to the famous *Lasciatemi morire* which even to-day makes us feel the effort of life fall away and leaves our souls bare and spotless and ready to take wings. The men found in it manly feeling, lucidity without sentimentality. The ladies, since to weep became a privilege, duly wept, while Florinda lamented melodiously on her rock and Caccini, the Florentine actress, put all her energies into the part of Venus. Behind the scenes Claudio Monteverdi listened, beating time to himself, full of harmonious melancholy.

When the spectacle was over and the great swish of six thousand silk robes had died away and the lights went out and it was time to go home, rain was falling. It was spring rain, now feverish, now caressing, which makes us think of the roses and how they drink it, still tightly enclosed in the firm buds, and distil from it their own red essence.

Thursday was, as it were, the apotheosis of the lake; it was after a day of sunshine; the evening was cool and the stars washed anew. At equal intervals along the banks they kindled great stacks of wood which made the dark burst into light, while three thousand lanterns, torches and flares transformed the regular design of the battlements into a perpetually moving pattern—a precise geometrical figure swaying to the caprices of light and wind. Through the people scattered along the grassy banks or on the bridge of San Giorgio, through the guests in the shrubberies of the ducal palace or standing on the balconies of the long rustic courtyard, there ran that overpowering feeling of trepidation which is caused by firework displays—as though we should respond to them by letting something flower within us and rise up in answer from loins to heart, as though we might, in a wild holiday spirit, feel impelled to catch at the hand of the stranger at our side. These are dangerous evenings. What irresistible intoxication it was to know that the fateful hour was about to strike when the triumphal chariot would arrive drawn by six sea-horses, who pawed the sea while flames sprang up around them. Tall sirens surrounded them with lighted torches in their hands. A beautiful armed woman sat in the highest point of the chariot and when she came ashore to where the princes sat, she arose and recited verses on the crystal Mincio and the joyful Dora. The chariot disappeared and there arose a fairy-tale castle with beflagged bastions, rock and towers—a Turkish fortress that the Christian fleet hastened to take by storm. What could be a more appropriate allegory for Vincenzo? The cannonades began and the Christians advanced to the attack. There were thick clusters of flashes, blows rained down and the fiery red apotheosis of the rockets made up for the colourless days of Canissa. Everything seemed to be on fire.

Then the flames died down and the fortress reappeared illuminated and intact. The dream had been restored and secured for the future.

From this moment it becomes difficult to follow the frantic rhythm of festivities at Mantua—the complicated ceremonies as they called on the bride to compliment her, and the comments of the ambassadors, who all accused Margherita of being stiffly Spanish and said that both Leonora and Francesco would have to work on her to make her beloved by the court and the people. But whether they were proud or affable, great lords or insignificant courtiers, the desire to amuse themselves gave them all strength and endurance—particularly the women. Seven hours it lasted, the *Idropica* of Guarini with its elaborate intermezzos in which they saw Ceres, Love, Europe, Fame, Juno, bevies of nymphs and winged horses—the whole apparatus of mythology in a framework of celestial arches, imperial mansions, gloomy woods and translucent seas.

That evening Cardinal Millini, bringing with him letters of salutation and goodwill from the Pope, stopped at Mantua to break his journey to Germany, where the Emperor Rudolf was beginning to feel his throne shake under pressure from his brother, the Archduke Matthias. The talk of discords in the Empire aroused Vincenzo's interest and, even more, the interest of Chieppio, for papers were passing thick and fast and most secretly, making their devious way through the Chancellery, preparing for an immense coup, the acquisition of the Imperial Throne for the Duke of Mantua. We do not know if they talked politics with the Cardinal or whether he knew of the crown Vincenzo was promising himself, but he too must have momentarily felt a wave of surprise when, at the tournament held by night in the presence of six thousand guests, Vincenzo was seen to arrive in an unexpected guise.

From a temple sacred to Eros, the greatest of the gods, there issued the Triumph of Love, as Petrarch had imagined it, with his slaves and his heroes about him. At the feet of the winged god they saw, not the young Francesco whose place it should have been, but his father clad in gold, armed and laughing—love's champion and almost fifty, with his hair turning from fair to grey. The most handsome gentlemen of Mantua, of Monferrato, Liguria and Piedmont, took part in the tournament, arriving on fantastic cars, leaping out of crags or from great rocks which suddenly opened up into caves. And since the roles were reversed, it was Francesco who appeared on the virtuous car of Honour. His train he had modelled on another famous original, the Triumph of Mantegna. There was a procession of elephants, camels and rhinoceroses, while cupids by the dozen fluttered through the theatre, throwing perfumed flowers. Venus descended from a luminous cloud and sang. From another came a scorpion bearing Mars in arms on its back to be received on earth by a group of Amazons. Then came the car of Pallas with, behind it, the Duke's third-born, the fifteen-year-old Don Vincenzo with his illegitimate brother, Don Silvio, the son of the Marchioness of Grana. (Agnese must have been present at the spectacle and must have bloomed secretly to see him, a handsome boy clad in silver, slim, serious and gentle, under his plumed crest, walking side by side with the Duke's legitimate son.) Meanwhile Apollo arrived with the four seasons, followed by ghosts. Then there arrived Bellona in arms on a car on which the Piedmontese were gathered with Vittorio Amadeo and Emanuele Filiberto at their head, splendid in cloaks and robes, sewn and stitched with gems. The tournament began and was still in progress when the first gleam of day made the sky grow pale. The sun rose. Jousters and spectators were still in their places and many remained there until far on in the morning.

Then they would go hunting or to the villas to feasts great and small, or to the ballet of the *Ungrateful Ladies* where they would find Vincenzo himself in the front rank among the dancers, together with his son, six knights and eight ladies, picked from among the most light-footed. Florinda sang that farewell to the world in which Claudio Monteverdi seems to express his dear wife's last farewell to life and warned the fair Mantuans not to be cruel on this earth to their lovers under pain of eternal suffering.

The populace was summoned to the public tournament. There were plays and great banquets during which Vincenzo displayed his services of silver and gold and bejewelled crystal. There were rustic feasts at the Palazzo del Te or at the Belfiore with swarms of masquers and of dwarfs singing and offering gifts.

When all was over and the ambassadors had left and the Piedmontese princes had given a last taste of their pride by returning a visit only to the Venetian ambassador, there was a smoky cloud of dust in the court. With his cold hands, Chieppio marshalled the catalogue of bills. Everyone was worn out with fatigue and lack of sleep. It never occurred to Vincenzo that things had been overdone. He at least was not satisfied, could not calm down, and felt his restlessness resist even his fatigue. Knight of the Redeemer, champion of love, king of revels which no monarch could have conjured up with more exquisite, more abundant magic—all this had already been cancelled from his mind by an overpowering worry. Instinctively he had prepared an alibi for himself—the course of treatment at Spa—for he had foreseen after the days of rejoicing the horrors of a period of vacuum. And since the wonderful dresses prepared for the wedding, the dramatic liveries, the fantastic ornaments, the plumes, embroideries and golden chains were there for him and for his court to use, he gave orders to set off.

Adriana

HE went to Trento, Innsbruck and Munich, trying in vain to
apply pressure to certain boorish German princes, deeply infected
by Lutherism, and make them return under the mantle of the
Church. He passed on to Nancy, to his pink-complexioned
daughter Margherita, who wept lovingly at the sight of him, and
then to Spa for his cure. Then came Antwerp and Malines, where
the nuns never ended working him airy collars of lace and embroidered shirts, and Brussels, where he was magnificently received
by the Archduke Albert and Isabella of Spain and gambled so
deeply that he had to leave in pawn a jewelled sword and a box
set with brilliants. At last, Vincenzo arrived in Paris. He and
Henry IV, the two veteran servants of love, understood each
other at once. We may recall that at this time Henry IV was
falling in love with the fifteen-year-old Charlotte de Montmorency, and was so inflamed with his passion that he could barely
think of anything else. Vincenzo, who was some years younger
than the King of France, might almost feel himself a novice in
love. Naturally, his escapades in Paris with such a sponsor could
well be the subject of a *conte galante*. With the Queen, Maria dei
Medici, who was becoming increasingly enormous in her white
and red obesity, the talk turned instead on family matters or dwelt
on the companies of Mantuan actors who were so sought-after
in France that the King and Queen themselves deigned to write in
the most intimate terms to the Harlequin, Tristano Martinelli,
and invite him to Paris.

But amidst all his escapades, Vincenzo, who never forgot his position as head of a state, attempted to talk politics. Here Henry IV showed his true nature, and while preserving his outward affability, withdrew behind an extremely detached air of prudence and wisdom. Being entirely given over to his great plans for mutilating the Hapsburg octopus which had Europe in its toils, he was only too willing to take any road which would lead him to deal a shrewd blow to Spain and Austria. Some months before he had agreed, but without believing in it greatly, to a project which in a moment of exaltation had appeared to Vincenzo like some wonderful new star. It was that he, the Duke of Mantua, might take advantage of the discords between Rudolf II and his brother the Archduke Matthias and be crowned King of the Romans. For in 1606 a secret family pact had been obscurely rigged between the various archdukes, brothers and nephews of the Hapsburg, whereby the Emperor Rudolf was declared unfit to rule because of mental illness. Thus the hope had awakened in the German Protestants of fratricidal war which would at last put an end to Hapsburg Catholicism. We can imagine how carefully Henry IV, who was busily feeding the discords in the Imperial House, watched the attacks mounted by the Archduke Matthias, who declared himself pretender to the throne and was making proselytes, even amongst the Protestants —not to mention the reactions of Rudolf and the moves made by the Vatican.

The idea of putting Vincenzo on the throne contested by the two brothers was not displeasing to Henry IV, although he considered it had but a slender foundation, and it was certainly with his consent that Carlo Gonzaga of Nevers went to Rome to sound Pope Paul V. Since no one could fail to believe in Vincenzo's romantic Catholicism, the Pope was obliged to receive the idea favourably, even if he shied at putting it into practice, once Nevers had left Rome. The French plan stated clearly, although not exactly in flattering terms, that Vincenzo's candidature would be in the best interests of Henry IV, since the Empire would have passed to a prince 'of not too exalted a rank' and one on whom the influence of France could make itself strongly felt. But a crown, the crown which had been Charles V's, was worth more than a mere exchange of words. And the Chancellery at Mantua, presided over by the tireless Chieppio, buzzed with hard work. Envoys departed and long neat reports arrived to take their place in the archives where we find them to-day. They cannot fail to move us, these dreams translated into positive words, passionately lived.

Vincenzo's imperial constellation set in January 1609 when the news arrived that Archduke Matthias had been elected King of Hungary and that his brother had been forced to agree to it; the last to see it in the Gonzaga sky was Carlo of Nevers who was still, in July 1609, sending envoys to the electors of Saxony and Brandenburg to keep alive negotiations already completely embalmed in time. Meanwhile a mission from the King of Persia revived in Vincenzo his taste for the Orient and made him order many-coloured turbans for all his pages. Colour from the Orient, but from a less distant part, was afforded by the arrival of certain Albanians sent by the chiefs and princes of their country which, well-nigh overwhelmed by Turkish expansion, had turned to Italy for help.

They stopped at Mantua, talked with Chieppio and Iberti in a highly elusive manner full of *double-entendres*, and disappeared, only to reappear at Carlo Emanuele's palace in Turin. There we hear them offering, in exchange for military help, that Albania which the Duke of Savoy would willingly have included in a list of projected conquests along with Cyprus, Rhodes and Macedonia. The project smacked so much of fairy-tale that the Venetians preferred to believe that it had been put together rather as a mental exercise than for any other reason; perhaps they were right, but it could easily be foreseen that a prince like Carlo Emanuele I would extract from these exercises a stimulus which must sooner or later be translated into action. And perhaps he let the Levantine expedition slip through his fingers only because, absorbed as he was in the more urgent and easily dominated European scene and by the war which Henry IV was about to wage against the House of Hapsburg, he understood that here, in the alliance with France against Spain, he would find a profitable vein to exploit. The Albanians were given leave to depart and returned to Mantua, where they set to work with speed and caution and instilled in Vincenzo's mind the idea of yet another crown.

Anything, anything, except renunciation, was the dramatic theme of Vincenzo's life as he moved about his splendid palace which left those Italians and foreigners who set foot in it mute with admiration. At this time there befell him one of those trials which mark the epochs in men's lives. It was July 1609, and his son's first daughter, little Maria, a beautiful baby who already gave promise of the beautiful woman Maria Gonzaga was to become, had been born. Vincenzo found great joy in being a grandfather and he tried to give it active expression as if it were a kind of lofty paternity. He treated his daughter-in-law with such friendly kindness that she, with her sharp-clawed egoism, felt she represented the future at court. So she gathered a faction around her, dared to enter the Duke's council chamber without being invited, took part in the discussions, and attempted to impose her will on them as she tried to impose her Spanish tastes. Her aim was to get the upper hand of her husband, her mother-in-law and the Duke.

There is something approaching candour in this twenty-year-old Fury with her youthful rapacity so openly revealed. But at court they saw in it only the intolerable pride of the children of Carlo Emanuele I. Was it not well known that Margherita's sister, the Infanta Isabella, wife of Alfonso d'Este, demanded that ambassadors to Modena should call on her before her husband? Besides, Margherita, with her Spanish strain, understood nothing of the political equilibrium of Mantua; this led her to cause incidents and receive doubtful envoys. Nor did she condescend to participate in Lombard life, as it had been hoped she would. She wanted to dominate her husband's languid nature, and sometimes he was dragged along in the wake of his wife's intrepidity so that there were those who could already detect her influence upon him. This was dangerous for her. If Francesco was weak it would be fatal for her to show herself the stronger. In that way she would provoke a reaction which might later find expression in a gesture, such as his wife's exclusion from everything connected with the government. She would have done well, too, to beware of Madam of Ferrara, who from the Convent of Sant' Orsola followed the doings of the court, noting one by one each occasion on which the young bride purposely showed lack of respect, interpreting her moves and marking them down for the future with intelligence and skill. Who knows—perhaps it was Madam of Ferrara who suggested that her brother send his son and daughter-in-law to govern Monferrato. She should be got out of the way, this girl who made trouble everywhere in the palace by forming factions of which no good could come. (It was to be hoped that the citizens of Monferrato, who had predicted so much evil from a marriage between Mantua and Turin, might yet be proved wrong.) Let the baby Princess Maria remain at Mantua with her doting grandmother and her little aunt Leonora who, barely ten years old, was delighted with her baby niece in her swaddling clothes—an exquisite animated toy.

When Margherita and Francesco had departed for Monferrato there was general relief. Leonora resumed her wise government, no longer pursued by the burning yet controlled envy of her daughter-in-law. Vincenzo abandoned himself with more ease of spirit and we see him enjoying himself in his famous little room thickly hung with portraits of beautiful women, indulging again through these pictures his worn but not yet spent imagination. *Worn* was the word that secretly saddened him on certain days which went on their limping way after a languid awakening. And none of the alchemists lurking in their dens in the Palazzo del Te, searching for gold and promising to change mercury into silver, could distil for him a philtre that would bring youthful prowess in love.

Someone whose identity we do not know promised the something better than a philtre—a guarantee of potent love—and advised him to take as a cure a wonderful little animal Spanish travellers had imported into Europe from Peru. It was called a *gusano* and it lived in the mountains of the Andes. He must have it, Vincenzo decided, and he would send his man of confidence, the chemist, Evangelista Marcobruno, who so excelled in his art that nothing in this world could daunt him. Let him leave at once, attached to the Marquis Vincenzo Guerrieri, who was at that very moment going to Spain to settle—if that were possible—the eternal question of the acquisition of Sabbioneta and other lesser matters. Obediently Evangelista set off.

How pleasant it is to contemplate this citizen without titles or arms, this traveller without escort or plumes, leaving Mantua in a mood of restrained joy. His was a mind which exercised itself in the free realm of scientific observation; he was a man with a passion for adventure which translated itself into such simple and unvarnished terms as these—that truly it seemed to him to take a thousand years to reach Peru. He was a true son of the scientific seventeenth century, this obscure Mantuan chemist, whom travellers' tales and the passion for research summoned to make discoveries in the new world beyond the seas. But he was without means and therefore without hope of travelling on his own account—so he had seized eagerly on his Duke's whim, for it would allow him to realize his adventure. He did not understand the Duke's feverish agony but he nursed it diligently, gave it rein and so assuaged it. In Segovia, without losing a day, he began to gather information by talking to people returned from the West Indies. He took notes and was able to describe the valley in the Andes where the *gusano* with its re-invigorating powers lived and to name the cities where it was marketed—cities whose very names are the promise of an exotic tale: Chuicago and Potosi. It is a pity that the story of the miracles performed with the *gusano* do not bear repetition; the language in which they are told is much too blunt. But it is certain that with the aid of a *gusano* a man remained twenty all his life, and so satisfied were the Peruvians with the practice that the exhortations of a Franciscan friar were of little avail there. Nor was this all. These cunning devils of natives added an antidote as well—a kind of sedative which countered the excesses of the stimulant. According to

Marcobruno it was in the ability to regulate it according to one's judgment that the virtue of the Peruvian cure lay.

But the Mantuan ambassador at Madrid, Cellario Bonati, shook his head. Such a long journey, he said, so much money to be spent. There was an element of foolishness about this whim that must be investigated, he said, for he was all commonsense from head to foot. He wrote to Mantua stating firmly that the same results could be obtained without going to so much trouble and he sent little animals picked up here and there by travellers who told him they were eminently suitable for his requirements. 'Ordinary beetles,' was Marcobruno's half-spoken comment, for he was very sure of his business. But he was worried, all the same, and exulted only when experiments had been carried out and it was learnt that the ambassador's little animals had not given proof of any particular virtue. Between the proposal and the reply the months went past. Meanwhile the chemist had learned how to handle the ambassador and now revealed himself to him as the true seeker of adventure he was. He talked to him of the herbs he would gather in order to discover their effect. He unfolded to him his passion for research and ended up by making a practical proposal. Let them give him the money for the journey, half in gold and half in goods. Not only would he recover the expenses by trading, but he would bring back so many strange and wonderful things that the expedition would not be a burden to the ducal budget. This, said Bonati, was plain speaking. He no longer opposed the urgings of the Duke and the apothecary—indeed he advised Marcobruno on what merchandise to buy and saw to it that it was packed properly for the voyage. 'The galleys leave at Christmas'—such was the news which Marcobruno sent to the Duke at the beginning of December and the words were like a gay trumpet call. He added that he wished to pass his life in the service of his lord and to return at once with all haste. The letter reached Mantua and found Vincenzo ill. It fell on his bed like a promise of youth. 'Our good apothecary,' as the ambassador called him, was to set sail from Seville in a Spanish galleon to reach Peru, collect a bagful of *gusanos* and come back to Europe.

laden with parrots, exotic plants, seeds, stones, spices and other strange objects. But fate ruled that in the port of Marseille he would be taken prisoner by the corsairs, led into slavery in Algiers and freed only much later. Vincenzo was never to have his *gusano* but he had only to think of it for a ray of hope to enliven his day, now that his health was failing. Leonora frequently found him at home and recognized in him that air of a shorn Samson which men of great vitality have when struck by illness. He was nearer to her in these intervals which made him an old man—perhaps older than his years.

Now Leonora was able to have long conversations with him about cures and medicines and plan a holiday at Madorno, the villa on the lake which Vincenzo had had built for his gay pleasures. It was the kind of project an old and slightly crazy married couple forms—a couple which takes a doctor about with them to help them to keep to a strict régime. But in the villa on Lake Garda, overhung with lemon trees and orange trees and roses, there awoke in Vincenzo the memory of all the voluptuous languor he had known. He returned to Mantua and found his court scantily supplied with women. Actresses and soubrettes did not satisfy him: he wanted something new and rare and asked for a real singer, for example that restless musician, composer and inventor of novelties Cecchina Caccini of Florence. But she could not leave the Medicean court and was too dear to the Grand duchess, whom it amused to have this rare plaything, this outstandingly intelligent woman, at her side. Then Vincenzo charged the cantor in the papal chapel, Paulo Facconi, who was an expert in whims and had procured for him the unforgettable Roman girl, Caterinuccia, to get him a collector's piece for Mantua. Who else could she be but Italy's most famous singer, the beautiful Neapolitan, Adriana Basile?

Adriana lived in Naples where everything aped Spain, where the richness and floridness of the seventeenth century seemed to coincide with the passionate flux, the philosophical upheavals and the melodramatic exuberance of men's hearts and minds. She had succeeded in creating for herself a high rank, in forming a court and a kingdom, and in her elegant house at Posillipo she received the foremost gentlemen of Naples. There was no great occasion to which she did not add lustre. Even the viceroy invited her to his palace or villa and bowed to the great lady. Since it had been difficult for her to attain such a privileged position unaided (although Adriana gave out that she was of noble birth and indeed descended from the kings of Crete, her family's true nobility lay, as she proved and as her brother, sisters and daughters were to prove, in their intelligence) she naturally defended this position tenaciously. So she played the part of the fine lady, got herself a husband, lived amidst the great family of sisters and brothers-in-law, chose a Jesuit confessor and followed the rules observed by those women who belong to the great sisterhood which lives by its wits—namely, to demand as much as possible and give nothing in return, except naturally when exceptions had to be made.

Her singing—and here astuteness gave way to generosity and artifice to sincerity—was a clear demonstration of her gifts. All Adriana's passion, all her voluptuous leanings, which were held in check by her will-power and vigilance, were released in her gay upward-soaring runs, in her daring intervals, in her sighing accents, whether she sat at her harp for grave and elegiac songs or took up the fiery Spanish guitar for light and jesting ditties. Then her admirers had a thousand reasons to swoon and rave and betray by their exclamations the ardour of their imagination. When her husband, Muzio Baroni, an easy-going and attentive Neapolitan, who shut his eyes to infidelity on condition that the decencies were observed, left Naples on behalf of Adriana's protector, Don Luigi Carafa, Prince of Stigliano, to inspect his lands and castles, the prince himself took up the pen and composed poems which spoke of voluptuous agonies and deep fervent sighs. He was echoed by a hundred poetasters, including one who attempted to excel all the rest and, passing in his exaltation into amorous invective, called her 'a deadly hyena' who 'sings and laughs' and 'a baneful basilisk which hisses and kills'. Such was the great prima donna singled out by Facconi. There followed a precipitate invitation from the Duke of Mantua, a rather brusque summons for Adriana's sophisticated ways for, like all women too prone to accept male advances, she felt hurt and offended. Besides, quite apart from the famous story of the Roman girl, who in Naples did not know how Vincenzo Gonzaga behaved? When he had come to Pozzuoli seven years before, they had seen him throw himself into such Bacchanalian exploits that they were still a legend. A charming seducer, the beautiful Neapolitan ladies had decided, and then vied with each other to send him their portraits to decorate the room of famous beauties at Mantua—sometimes not without risk, like Donna Emilia Spinelli who had posed unknown to her extremely jealous husband with a companion standing guard at the door.

Adriana did not wish to be one of their number but, being unable to refuse such an exalted personage, thought she had been very clever when she pretended to accept the invitation but laid down as one of the conditions of the bargain that the Duchess Leonora should write a letter summoning her to her own service, and another to the Vicereine of Naples, so that it might be clear to all the world that Adriana was not going to Mantua at the summons of a Duke but to serve a royal princess.

Surely his wife would not wound herself with her own hands and give way to her husband to the point of agreeing to summon her—so thought Adriana, a logical but not sufficiently subtle point of view. The Duke accepted her conditions as they stood and fixed a day for her departure. The date came round but since the Duchess's letters had not yet arrived when the moment came to set off, Adriana refused to budge and, with the excuse that the heavy, oppressive climate of Mantua did not suit her health, said she would not leave.

When he saw that she was about to escape him by this highly capricious gesture, Vincenzo became not only inflamed and piqued but completely recovered his energies. On the 5th March, 1601, no less than seven letters from Vincenzo left the secretary's office in Mantua. One was to his son, Cardinal Ferdinando, instructing him to send a trusty envoy, Ottavio Gentile, from Rome to Naples at once; another to Gentile—four close pages of explanations and impassioned argument which reveal injured vanity and slighted desire, and attribute to the Princess of Stigliano, Isabella Gonzaga, heiress to the domain of Sabbioneta which Vincenzo was in vain trying to assimilate to his dukedom, the blame for the fact that Adriana had not left. Yet another was to Father Gregorio Carbonelli, a relation of Adriana's husband— it was full of recriminations and protests at the way the singer and her husband had broken their word to a prince who, as everyone knew, 'required to be amused amid the grave affairs of his daily life'. Another still was to Adriana's husband; then came one to the Princess of Stigliano, beseeching her to be his friend and grant his wishes. Finally there was one to the Vicereine of Naples and one to the Viceroy himself.

All this for Adriana. Meanwhile Ottavio Gentile had at once left Rome and arrived at Naples, where he found all the traps set. The fact that the field seemed to be clear—Adriana's husband had left town—was a sure sign that the enemy was preparing secret positions. Vincenzo's envoy immediately grasped the significance of the husband's absence and saw that he must begin an out-flanking operation; so he went straight to the Princess of Stigliano with the Duke's letter. The lady explained to him, with some bitterness, that it was not she but her husband who protected Adriana, adding that she dearly wished the singer would leave Naples for then the prince would squander less of his ardour abroad. The envoy was then able to go on to visit the Viceroy and Vicereine and ensure that they were favourably disposed. Next he spoke to the Prince of Stigliano, who was forced to recall Muzio Baroni and proclaim himself—in words at least— deeply devoted to the Duke of Mantua.

Adriana's husband arrived crestfallen, torn between fear of his wife who had undoubtedly encouraged him to resist, and fear of the beatings or worse which some Neapolitan might perpetrate on orders from Mantua. He fenced with words, became confidential and then withdrew. He passed from protestations of devotion to passionate disapproval of his wife's behaviour. You had to deal with her, he said, to have an idea of how stupid and obstinate a woman could be. Gentile accepted the challenge, but when he climbed up to Adriana's villa at Posilipo he found himself met by a volley of caprices which defied logic, courage and commonsense. The more he insisted, the more she retreated. She was so pleased with the picture of herself in the allegorical garb of modesty fleeing from lasciviousness, and so much enjoyed the sensation of being the nymph pursued, that she thought she could try a bold gesture. Unknown to her husband and certainly unknown to Gentile, she wrote a letter to the Duchess Leonora. It was almost a letter from one woman to another, in which the singer expressed her sorrow that she could not come to Mantua because of her frail health and besought the Princess not to require her to set out at such danger to her good name and, in short, to help her to stay where she was, at home. But she had overestimated her strength, and the blow went awry.

We can almost see Leonora with Adriana's letter in her hand in the midst of her elegant court—a group of ladies in black, a group of young women in pink and silver velvet—she herself dressed in black with a string of perfect pearls on her neck and her favourite pendants of pear-shaped pearls, as a contemporary describes her at this time; worn but not defeated. Her face showed that she liked subtle mental processes. How did this woman, this singer, Leonora thought, dare to set herself on equal footing with a royal princess and above all how did she dare to resist someone like the Duke of Mantua and thus permit their enemies to make such a trifle a theme for conversation?

Leonora reflected, thought things over and reached her conclusion with a subtle smile which was half ironical and half melancholy. When Vincenzo came to ask her help, she had only to see his worried face to become his accomplice—an accomplice at once scornful and terrible who wrote a note to Gentile, assuring him that she greatly desired Adriana to come, and a letter on the same theme to the Vicereine of Naples. 'Since this young woman who sings'—it is thus that the princess refers to the singer, as if she were fending her off with the tip of a gloved hand—'has given her word to enter my service and that of this House and since I am desirous, because of the pleasure I promise myself, that she should come as soon as possible, I beg from my heart that your Excellency may be pleased, etc., etc.'

When these letters arrived they found Gentile almost out of his senses. With her instinct for behaving in life as she did on the stage, carrying her actions by mounting degrees towards a lofty catastrophe, Adriana was building up the telling scenes of the last act, fainting and begging with clasped hands, murmuring with a broken voice to spare her for pity's sake. This is quite sufficient to make any man feel like a butcher and be thoroughly ashamed of himself. Once he was forced to be ashamed of himself, Gentile became annoyed for he knew he had been outwitted. He had a great desire, he confided to a friend, to get things back into perspective with a couple of good slaps, but there was nothing you could do. The great scene was enacted on the 16th April. If the Mantuan had the imprudence to state that great lords like his Duke do not tolerate being made fools of, Adriana would launch into a pathetic heroic speech, interspersed with sobs and sighs, and prophesy that she might be maimed and slain at Vincenzo's orders but she would remain firm in her intention to defend her virtue to the point of martyrdom.

It was the peak of the melodrama. The desired effect had been achieved and there had been applause for it, so it was logical that the scene should come to an end, which it did hurriedly, to the astonishment of Gentile, who could not believe his senses when Adriana, forgetting her tears, began to smile and murmur that perhaps, who knows, she had made a mistake. A letter had arrived from Leonora, written in a princely tone which flattered her actress's snobbery—arrived at a time when there was no more material to continue the drama and Adriana was beginning to fear that the Duke would no longer invite her. Henceforth there was no point in trying to speak badly of Mantua. She had found another part to her taste, that of the woman who would go to the wolf's lair, and return immaculate and triumphant; she longed to play it. There was no holding her back. The Neapolitans had to rest content to say their adieux in poetry. It was her own brother,

Gianbattista, who spoke for all of them, saying he had discovered a mysterious link with something which went far back into the centuries. He claimed to see in the departure of the siren of Posilipo Mantua's revenge on Parthenope which, fifteen hundred years before, had stolen Virgil's body from the Mincio.

On the 24th May, Adriana, her husband, her small son, her sister, a brother-in-law who was a doctor, a brother and two of their children—a tiny fraction of her swarm of Neapolitan relatives—set off with an array of strong boxes and trunks in a whirl of velvet gowns and plumed hats, taking their places in a litter and a coach which were immediately transformed into a cage of pathetic coloured parrots. They left Naples among so many adieux, frowns, salutations and tears that it seemed as if the land of opera was indeed losing its *prima donna*.

Adriana's first meeting with the House of Gonzaga took place at Rome in the person of the young Cardinal Ferdinando, who came to visit her as soon as she arrived, and stayed to talk with her and make her sing. She is very fine, but a woman who knows what she is about, the intelligent young man said when he reported his impressions to his father. In the days that followed he invited her out in the city and to his villa and made a point of introducing her to a public of connoisseurs; everyone, including those who knew the singing of Cardinal Montalto's famous Ippolita, the touch-stone of every singer, declared her to be perfect. Ferdinando, meantime, went into ecstasies over her. He courted her with his delicate and gallant manner, made up of Lombard graces and Spanish charm, and began to feel a certain stirring in his blood. So when Adriana left a week later she had become for him what every woman is for the man who loves her, the most wonderful creature in the world.

How good-looking and courteous this Cardinal is, said Adriana on the 5th June, sitting back in the languorous shade of the litter as she went over the events of that delicious Roman week along with Gentile, who was accompanying her to Mantua. After so many storms, the two had become great friends and confided in each other. At Bracciano, where the company were guests in the

Orsini castle, she asked her friend in great secrecy what bed Cardinal Ferdinando had slept in when he was last there. Her accomplice told her and she said she wanted to sleep in it—to absorb the cardinal virtues, she stated, lowering her eyes, while Gentile remarked that if there was someone at Rome who had a warm heart, Adriana obviously wore a robe which set her on fire. So Father Gregorio Carbonelli was proved right. He had been secretly charged by Leonora to send her a confidential report on this famous Adriana and wrote that he had seen and examined her well when she passed through Rome. He had found her not exceedingly beautiful but certainly not ugly, above all 'wonderfully enticing and flattering, a true Neapolitan Armida'—in short a great flirt and all the more dangerous because of the wonderful way she played the part of an honest woman and kept it balanced on a continual exciting undercurrent of hints. 'I fell into a state of some apprehension,' concluded the shrewd friar, who at the same time indicated to the duchess the singer's two weak points— an overwhelming ambition to have a reputation for honesty and a peculiar greed for gifts. So Leonora should favour her and load her with presents; then perhaps she would be able to count on her.

At Florence Adriana sang for the Grand Duke and was a guest in the house of Giulio Caccini where she took part in a trying concert, a veritable tribunal of virtuosi. Adriana enchanted them all and accepted their splendid gifts. Those who had fine sentiments refused to hear her twice in order not to suffer too much when she left. Even Ottavio Gentile, who at Naples had felt his hands tingle with the desire to deal with her whims, was enslaved by her, even if he did not dare to fall in love. 'The more one hears of her the more one would like to hear,' he confided in one of his last letters as the party drew near to Mantua.

There they arrived on the 23rd June and were received like persons of quality. In the evening, at the invitation of the Duchess, a gilt coach brought the singer to the villa where Leonora was staying with her court and where Adriana gave her first concert. She was heard, not only by the ladies and gentlemen, but by the musicians of Mantua, first and foremost amongst them the master of music, Claudio Monteverdi. His judgment was sober. He recognized that Cardinal Montalto's Ippolita had a purer timbre but Adriana had perfect diction, a miraculous feeling for pauses and an emotional power which did not allow a single note to fall without expression; when she was silent and taking pitch, she had a beauty which exalted the soul and prepared it for the harmony to come.

Vincenzo, who was at Madorno, let a day pass. Then he came and saw Adriana under the eyes of his wife. He heard her sing and was moved by it. He cautiously cultivated his emotion but did not allow it to be spent. So there was Adriana installed as favourite and her life at Mantua began with holidays and concerts at the villa and in the gardens. And just as at Naples, so in Lombardy poems, madrigals and songs rained upon her saying that the most charming of all the sirens had landed on the banks of the Mincio. But in September, Vincenzo suddenly realized that he had reached the age of weariness—perhaps he was following a boat over the lake in which Adriana was toying with young Cardinal Ferdinando, who had arrived at Mantua the day before and was head over heels in love with the singer. Was he perhaps jealous of his son, this Vincenzo, who set such store by Adriana that he was unwilling to allow her a break of even a few days to go to Milan, where the Spanish governor was asking for her insistently and who wrote her letter after letter urgently 'in the middle of a meal'? Perhaps he was not jealous, for he knew the power of his ducal prestige on an ambitious woman like her. But perhaps at this moment when the rage of the blood had died away, if he looked about him in search of something to amuse and elude his sensibilities, he felt himself so caught by the indifference of things that he felt his pulses beat headlong with the terror of being alone.

CHAPTER TWELVE

The Albanian Interlude

IF only he had known the consolation which lies in work; but instead the greater part of public affairs and certainly all internal affairs he allowed to fall on his wife, who was still an object of furious envy to her daughter-in-law Margherita, for she took part in and indeed presided over the Council of State. Leonora's prudence and capabilities were now so well known that there was no ambassador who did not gladly recognize them. If we wish for reasons to admire her feminine elegance of manner we can point to the fact that although she was almost mistress of Mantua, she never said she was, nor permitted others to say so, but continued to give advice and assistance while appearing to retire into the background. This she did neither from timidity nor disdain but from a deep sense of freedom which had come to sit more easily each time an administrative measure, a business deal or a treaty was brought to a logical conclusion.

Naturally Leonora's virtual regency did not mean that Vincenzo's mind had become clouded. On the contrary, it had become clearer, but what did that avail him if, having gained so much experience, he could no longer relate it to the certainty of a future which would burgeon and flower? The future was marred in advance by his uneasiness, by all the delusions he had suffered. Clearly time made him more aware of his defeat by placing cause and effect in proper perspective. Determined to have it out with the gloomy power of the Imperial House of Austria, even at the cost of upsetting Europe, Henry IV was on the move against the Hapsburgs and Italy came into his plans as a territory to be liberated from Spanish hegemony. For any ruler who had the courage to take up the sword this could be a unique opportunity for extending his frontiers. But although Carlo Emanuele I of Savoy felt himself ready and was determined to take the field to attack the Spanish in Lombardy at a signal from the King of France, Vincenzo, in spite of encouragement, was unable to find in himself the energy to take sides. He was in two minds, as was Chieppio and even Venice, however hostile they might be to the house of Hapsburg. It was well known that in Milan that terrible old man, the Conte di Fuentes, was reinforcing his territories and fortresses and enlisting a great militia; so he would not be easily dealt with. Besides, all the Italian states were tainted with damnable prudence and accustomed for more than a century to be subject to foreign powers. Meanwhile in the village of Brozzolo in Val di Susa the High Constable of France, Lesdiguères, was giving concrete expression to the agreements reached between his king and Carlo Emanuele by a double treaty for a defensive and an offensive alliance. While France would attack from the north, Piedmont would attack Spain on the Milanese border; fifteen thousand French soldiers, commanded by Lesdiguères, would support the venture by thrusting straight at Milan. The Duke of Savoy could scarcely believe that he could at last utter his war-cry: 'Nunc pugnandum est'—the time for battle has come.

Vincenzo had not been summoned to Brozzolo and possibly he would not have wished to go. But he had had to return some sort of answer to Henry IV even if it were not enough to compromise him. Yet however little he said, someone overheard it; that person was Ranuccio Farnese who, true to his own guileful nature, denounced to Spain the treaty between Carlo Emanuele and France. Although there was no proof of Vincenzo's treachery, there were strong arguments in his undoubted French sympathies, in his family relationships with France and Savoy and in the name of Maria given to his newly-born grandchild. But obviously the destiny of Italy was subject to the dead hand of inertia. Scarcely a month after the meeting at Brozzolo, Henry IV fell dead, stabbed to the heart by Ravaillac. The anti-Spanish coalition fell apart.

Maria dei Medici, now regent of France and, like all her house, an enemy of Savoy, began a policy of *rapprochement* with Spain. Carlo Emanuele was left exposed to the threats of the Conte di Fuentes who was determined to give him a lesson which would clip his wings and check whatever idea of independence, however vague, Italians might cherish. The Duke of Savoy stood ready in arms on his frontiers and did not weaken for a moment in his warlike intentions. Then the Conte di Fuente died and Carlo Emanuele rapidly altered his objective. He deigned to ask pardon of Madrid and, gripped by his old idea of conquering Geneva, asked for the support of his old enemy, Spain, against France. When this plan, too, went awry, because of the Franco-Spanish alliance which Maria dei Medici decided on at this time, he went back to his scheme for an Italian league and began to negotiate the marriage of his heir-apparent, Vittorio Amadeo, with the daughter of the Grand Duke Ferdinando. Each day he found another idea to pin to his banner.

At Mantua the Duke of Savoy's dangerous political manœuvres were closely followed. Those who studied them most attentively were doubtful whether the marriage of Francesco to Margherita would really guarantee the territory of Monferrato for the Gon-zagas and protect it from the desires of their restless neighbour. Margherita was the first to become alarmed and, when the couple were staying in Turin, Vincenzo warned his son not to allow himself to be taken in by his father-in-law who 'the more he gives himself over to the merriment of carnival in order to lull people, the busier he is working out in his mind greater ploys. So you must observe the essence and not the appearances when dealing with men who feign one thing and do another and will never let themselves be caught unawares; thus your resolves will be made prudently and with maturity.' In these words we seem to hear the balanced judgment of a sage to whom it comes naturally to instruct others. Those who attempt to reduce the char-acters of men to a mere formula would be incapable of under-standing anything of Vincenzo, seeing him thus donning the guise of sober paternity which fits him as well as that of unbridled licence which made him send Marcobruno to Peru. But Vincenzo is an example of the extent to which an individual is a mixture of opposing and apparently irreconcilable elements, for he remained natural in every expression of his personality, even in those which falsified him, and was always true to his own instincts, whether physical or moral. It was from his instincts, from a last loyalty to his old dreams of glory, that he drew the strength to imagine himself on a throne—the throne of Albania which had already figured in the dreams of Carlo Emanuele I.

The Albanian who prostrated himself at Vincenzo's feet, endowing him reverently with the name of sovereign, was clearly an able intriguer and a subtle flatterer; but not even the sharpest wits could have distinguished at what precise moment he began to tell lies. He came on behalf of the patriarch of Serbia and of the greatest Albanian lords—one of whose chiefs, a certain Count Vuio, arrived in Mantua and seemed to confirm the proposals— and on behalf of various powerful leaders, all of whom invoked the intervention of a courageous prince to help them with arms, money and aid against the burden of Turkish domination. This time it was not Chieppio but Iberti who took the negotiations in hand and drew up the agreements. Albania was to rise in rebellion in October 1610. Vincenzo would disembark on the Adriatic coast with an army of ten thousand men. The chiefs would recognize him king and under their new monarch would move off together in a great common undertaking against the Turks.

So much was agreed and things took their course; but it was so clear that the agreements had little, or at least inadequate, foundation that when October came no one moved. Vincenzo was fêting Adriana from villa to villa and had almost ceased to think of the Levant expedition when more Albanians arrived at court to urge him on.

Their arguments seemed to acquire substance by sheer force of repetition. In a moment of high spirits Vincenzo allowed himself to be persuaded and gave orders that the concrete possibilities of the undertaking should be explored. Two envoys, Ippolito Dentelli and Laurenzo Barzo, were to leave along with Captain

Marcello Resti to parley with the Albanian chiefs, to visit the country, make contact with persons of influence, and bring back not only letters committing those persons but detailed accounts of the situation.

The Mantuans set off with Resti on the 14th February. On the 19th they were at Rimini and on the 20th at Fiume and here, while waiting for a tailor to make up their Oriental style garments, they had their first contacts with the Albanian rebel chiefs. One has the impression from the very beginning that whatever happened to these travellers in their encounters and conversations they met with false dealing. People winked behind their backs with an imperceptible lowering of the eyes. It was no use Dentelli's having a great coffer full of cheap rings and gold and jewelled earrings and engraved gold and silver goblets—no use his changing his name to Prospero Sogari and saying he was jeweller on a business trip to Jerusalem. There was no point in such naïve shifts which were the work of the merest dilettante compared to the refined professional lying of their companions.

Not that the Mantuans did not have an inkling that they were being tricked. For example, they sized up a certain Captain Giovanni Renesi or Resnevich for what he was, an impostor. The Albanians agreed with them, being too cunning to save someone who had committed the error of revealing himself too openly. But the Mantuans, being logical people, did not understand why they had been encouraged to set out if, in fact, the strong party which was to proclaim the Duke of Mantua king, did not exist. Even if one examines the contemporary documents, it is still not clear what these Albanians wanted from Gonzaga. Perhaps help in the shape of money, arms and men. The crown they offered was an entirely worthless title for they were reduced to a number of shifting wandering bands, forced to wrest their lives daily from the Turks with sabre in hand.

Here the Mantuans were, then, in Fiume, in an inn together with a certain Captain Marino, an exile from Ragusa and their main contact with the Albanians. There was a coming and going of strange characters to whom they gave to understand that they were agents of the King of Spain. So complicated was the conversation that by dint of trying to be prudent they ended up by being vague and saying nothing at all. Captain Giovanni Vulatconich arrived, black-avised and hairy, a theatrical figure surrounded by a troop of armed and bearded retainers. But when they got him alone, he turned out to be ready to serve whoever paid him most. Dentelli opened his jeweller's trunk for him and gave him a ring for his wife. The captain accepted and decided to go south on horseback while the Italians made the same journey by sea on their way to the Bishop of Ragusa.

They left with a favouring wind, one fresh morning when the sea had scarcely a wave, and found the bishop at Glano. He encouraged them to write letters to all his friends, to collect men and push on with the venture. Then they went to Ragusa, which was at that time a tiny independent republic, where their arrival provoked such a stir that the little senate passed a decree of banishment on them as suspicious characters. They left the town and lay low. Dentelli, who was stranded on the island of Corzolo along with Barzo, waited for his accomplices to arrange further conversations and became bored. It was here that he chanced to meet a young Slav who was both an expert in Oriental languages and a magnificent, picturesque personage to be taken back to the Duke as interpreter.

In his enthusiasm the Mantuan enlisted the young man, not knowing that he had a long story behind him. He was a slave who had fled from his Turkish master. To get his own back, the latter had pillaged a ship from Ragusa, promising to give back the booty only when he had laid hands on the fugitive. Naturally in Ragusa they wanted to lay hold on the escaped slave, and naturally the young man was wary and had taken refuge on Corzola, under the protection of the governors of the island. Dentelli was open with him but at a certain point the young man began to suspect him of trying to entrap him, bring him back to Ragusa and there hand him over to justice. In his turn he now denounced Dentelli as a suspicious person to the governor of the island and had him seized and imprisoned. Meanwhile Barzo had barely time to hide among the tall grass by the beach where, after two anxious days, he was rejoined by his companion who had been freed and brought down to the shore by gendarmes on the understanding that he left at once.

Banished from Ragusa and Corzola, surrounded by spies and suspicion, the Mantuans still kept their heads. At Glano they made contact with Count Stefano Vulatconich, a great, tall, thin man with a fair beard and blue eyes who, clasping Vincenzo's letter, kissed it, held it above his head, venerated and adored it. Now was the moment to open the case of jewels, for a distribution of gilt and silver beakers out of which everyone drank in honour of the future king, to the ground-bass of the prayers of a monk who was also present. Interest was further aroused by the distribution of rings and earrings; at last negotiations began.

Why, said Count Stefano, after a great many compliments, had Vincenzo failed them in October when the Albanians had risen according to the bargain? Slyly he pretended to deplore the Duke's non-arrival, insinuating that precisely this had made the rebellion turn out badly. When Dentelli quickly pointed out that before making such an important move, the rebels should have warned Mantua, they quickly changed the subject. The discussion came round to the present day but whenever the Mantuans talked about reaching Albania, the Count opposed it. Did they really want to be killed? he asked. They should give him the letters and he would see that they were delivered and that replies came back.

Their conversations with another chieftain had the same tenor. This was that Count Vuio who had been at Mantua. When he recalled its wonderful palace, its handsome people and the great happiness of the country, there was a gleam in his black eyes under the long hair which he had allowed to grow down to his shoulders as a vow of revenge for a brother murdered. The case of jewels grew lighter. The Mantuans had achieved nothing. It was becoming dangerous to stay on the Dalmatian coast where there was talk of nothing but of Turks who cut Christians to pieces. The frontiers of Albania were closed to them and their days passed

amid alarm and suspicion. They were always on the point of
taking flight and hiding. They had to change their appointed
meeting-places from one village to another, moving from place to
place amid a restless succession of treacherous faces. In the midst
of this desperate web, Dentelli and Barzo picked their way with
honest common sense, knowing perfectly well that it was better
for them to go with the current rather than against it. May was
in bloom when, having received letters from all the Albanian
lords and the patriarchs of Serbia, they decided to turn home with
their poor bag. All this labour and expense had been in vain as it
had been in vain to buy a vessel in Holland for the Albanian expedition—a vessel seized in the Mediterranean by the papal navy,
which suspected it of being a corsair. Iberti read the Albanian
letters, disentangled their true content from the formal ornaments
and, after listening to the envoys' reports, laid the matter before
the Duke. The decision was 'to think it over' and shortly afterwards the whole affair was duly filed in the archives.

While the Mantuan envoys were making a voyage of reconnaissance along the Dalmatian coast to prepare a kingdom for their
lord, the heir to the dynasty had been born and named Ludovico
in homage to the little King of France, Louis XIII. The direct line
of the Gonzagas seemed assured. Margherita of Savoy saw before
her a long future as princess, wife and mother. More than ever
life seemed to her a prize to be seized every morning on awaking.
She took as her due all the gracious favours and gifts which
Vincenzo gave her on condition that she stayed away from
Mantua. So, affectionately manœuvred in accordance with the
Duke's wishes, she went to rest in Goito as soon as the little prince
was born and waited to proceed to Monferrato. Meanwhile the
long, patient voyage of Leonora dei Medici was coming to an end
on the shoals of the last shore of all.

By now Leonora had reached such a pitch of equilibrium and
knowledge of mankind—her wisdom had geometrical solidity and
could almost be expressed in mathematical terms—that there only
remained the test of death for her to have experienced everything.
She had overcome the trials of ill-health in two crises, one in 1607

and another, graver one in January 1611, when she had seen her
son Francesco arrive at her bedside from Casale and realized that
she must prepare herself in earnest. How astonishing it was—how
astonishing and how ironical, to find herself ready. The moment
she had recovered, Leonora smiled and regained her Florentine
habit of curiosity about the world and things, which still gives the
old ladies in the palazzos of the Via Tornabuoni such keen eyes.

She did not mind if Vincenzo went off to his Madorno on the
lake and Adriana with him. When the singer returned Leonora
received her with detached benevolence. She had only to look at
her to recognize the old, well-known signs, to read her through
and through, to see her stripped of all veils. This relentless ability
to see through things, this state of mind which encountered no
more unknowns in the world of the feelings because they were
reduced by now to a delicate but comprehensible mechanism
of cause and effect, might have become a kind of punishment
called down by Leonora's excess of wisdom had the warmth of
the old love her husband had awoken in her as a bride not saved
her from inhuman resignation. For Vincenzo her lips and pen
still found words of love, however sober: 'Mantua is a desert and
I feel all alone for Your Highness's departure,' she wrote to him
in 1608. She believed in him only as a physical presence; but that
is one way of believing in man, one way of resisting the temptation to disassociate the masculine and feminine worlds in her own
mind—a temptation which every intelligent woman knows she
must reject to prevent the sources of charity and pity, those
twin streams which feed the roots of human life, from drying up
within her.

To the end, Leonora found a warm recompense for so much
unpleasantness in the fact that she was able to bring her children
and their father together in her thoughts—Margherita, so far
away yet always present to her mother; little Leonora with her
curly head, whom it was so amusing to deck with jewels and
flowers, as in the portrait of her by Pourbus; her beloved Francesco; the dissipated Vincenzo and Cardinal Ferdinando, in whom
his mother was continually discovering more and more clearly a

vivid personality—a rebel perhaps, only too prone to moods of exaltation and delicate torments. But not even love for her children can keep a mother from dying; even this is a good thing —or so Leonora seemed to say the day she bowed her head and accepted her sentence. There was a sharp attack of illness, a sudden worsening in her condition and Leonora died on the evening of the feast of the Madonna, on the 8th September, 1611.

Thus, after twenty-seven years of marriage, Vincenzo was alone. Certainly he suffered; yet since we know in what unexpected ways suffering can become knotted and entangled in the heart we will not be surprised if, scarcely a month after Leonora's death, Vincenzo left for her favourite resort, Madorno on Lake Garda, summoned Adriana and her family and deigned to sit at table with the whole Neapolitan tribe, drinking toasts amidst music, laughter and songs. What no one knew was that at Madorno Vincenzo kept his confessor in a remote room and that an hour a day was passed with him in conversation and religious readings. His seems a captive spirit indeed, beating at all doors— the door of love and of sensual pleasure, of religion, art and magic (the great company of alchemists was increasing daily)—almost afraid that one might be opened to him and thus preclude the others for ever. We cannot but feel that Vincenzo's smile, dawning on the verge of a solitude which he did not accept, is tortured by despair.

We believe in our body because we have one, said Vincenzo to himself. So he ordered ballets and comedies and Adriana was raised to the rank of baroness. An estate went with it—Piancerreto in Monferrato. Two months later Adriana gave birth to a girl. What if it were to be called Leonora in homage to the sainted memory of Her Ladyship? asked the singer in pathetic accents. It is not surprising to find the new baroness together with her husband at the baptism in the ducal apartments—perhaps that same room with the motto *Forse che sì, forse che no* and the emblem of the labyrinth. Vincenzo was godfather and the godmother was the Marchioness of Grana, Agnese herself.

CHAPTER THIRTEEN

Ranuccio's Revenge

THE dramatic part which Agnese is about to take in this story had been maturing for years. A woman much loved and greatly favoured, then loved less intensely but favoured still, her fortune had waned at one time so much so that, in her worst days, round about 1604, Leonora had been able to attempt a mean little vendetta on her by asking her to hand back a Madonna by Andrea del Sarto—a gift from Vincenzo perhaps—to which Agnese said she knelt every morning with an offering of prayers and sighs. Even then, however, Agnese had been able to permit herself to refuse the Duchess the picture. It was one of the few times that Leonora was seen to be out of humour—defeated once more at the very moment when she believed her adversary to be disarmed.

Still beautiful, endowed with all the powers which derived from her lively grace and her manner of speaking, distinguished as it was by bubbling warmth and life, Agnese gathered in her palace friends and courtiers, among them some of those closest to the Duke.

Agnese was an example of the picturesque in female shape. If she derived much of her wisdom from the school of Colorno and from her liberal education at the hands of the Countess of Sala, her way of passing from tears to smiles and back to tears was entirely her own, and gave a mysterious impression that her mind was a land rich with hidden humours, revealed by the play of unexpected fountains. The most surprising thing about her, however, was not so much her ability to pray, weep and smile, while

maintaining the sincerity of her emotion, as her ability to dis-
course on her prayers, tears and smiles with a depth of feeling
which sometimes paused and relaxed, sometimes rose in harmonious excitement, giving to her words the intense quality of invention. When Agnese was there everything was created anew,
feelings were fresh, passions at their moment of fullness, pain
touched its most resonant string, ambition was heroism and
rivalry emulation. Even the political advice she could give and
did give had a scintillating quality.

It was precisely this magical phosphorescent quality which had
pleased Vincenzo so much and made him constant, if unfaithful,
for many years in his love for her. Then he had moved away but
later, realizing how much he missed her, he had come back in all
friendship—to be in fact, in his chivalrous way, a devoted friend.
So when he did not see her at the court festivities, he sought her
out in her ornate palace and unconsciously asked her to help him
to think well of himself. He would present himself in bad shape,
with his nerves on edge, a compound of arid, jerky reactions and
sharp corners, knowing that when he left her again he would feel
soothed and that his bitterness would dissolve in her honeyed
balm. We do not know by what degrees Agnese agreed to accept
the role of friend but since we know that she accepted this role
and indeed gloried in it, we must presume that for her, too, the
days of love and suffering, which Vincenzo had poured out for
her, were a closed cycle. The friendship which remained flattered
her ambition, accorded with her prestige and furthered her
maternal passion by allowing her to remind Gonzaga frequently
of his sons—not only Silvio who lived at court and for whom
Vincenzo requested a place in the Council of the Knights of
Rhodes but Francesco too, the heir to the Marquisate of Grana,
who had now been promoted to the rank of favourite.

Whether or not she had had much experience of life since her
widowhood and her tumult of emotions as Vincenzo's love
declined, Agnese was certainly now living the life of a great lady
who was free but kept to herself, being both decorous and
religious. Vincenzo's sons were her friends—Francesco, Cardinal

Ferdinando, young Don Vincenzo—all of whom were tied by bands of affection to her own son. She was even considered suitable for the austere friendship of Madam her Serene Highness of Ferrara, who received her in her fortress at Sant' Orsola and talked to her in confidence as to a member of the family, knowing perfectly well, the crafty, devout old woman she was, how much power the voice of the gay marchioness still had on Vincenzo. And there was another friendship which Agnese had taken up again after a certain interval of disinclination—her friendship with her old teacher, Barbara Sanseverino, Countess of Sala.

These two experienced women—Agnese was on the point of reaching forty, and Barbara was close on sixty—could have written a compendious story full of feminine secrets. Barbara would have provided the most courageous pages—courageous to the point of madness. For the last twenty years, that is to say since he had assumed the ducal crown of Parma, Ranuccio Farnese had been a thunder-cloud in the Countess of Sala's sky. Loved only too well by two generations of Farnese dukes and used to exercising her own easy sway over men in command, the proud Countess had never understood anything of this boy locked up in his own gloomy jealousy which he nourished with mortified thoughts—a boy who used his intelligence to break things down by means of his brain's complicated alchemy. For such a person it would have been enough had Barbara, that heedless, gay and mocking woman, come near him for his flesh to creep with aversion bordering on disgust. What overwhelmed him entirely was that she continued to display so much firm friendship and support for Vincenzo Gonzaga and to nourish their relationship with secret, licentious pleasures, to which Vincenzo responded with measures such as that of 1592 exempting his dear Countess from all tribute of taxes and tolls on the lands she held in Mantuan territory.

1592. That was the time when challenges were passing between Mantua and Parma after the fire in the Gonzaga armoury—the time, too, of the mutual attempts to entrap each other, of arrested assassins, of mysterious bands riding across the frontiers. Ranuccio could imagine—and for him imagination with all its unbridled

pessimism took the place of knowledge—how the two talked of
the Farneses, with what a free satirical tone, and how laughter
and quips flowered on the Countess's full lips as they echoed the
laughter of Gonzaga's warm mouth. A cold fire pricked his pale
cheeks with red. It was a moment which brought back to him the
picture of his sister Margherita, sacrificed so long ago; then the
unsolved story of all the mortifications suffered would begin to
run through his mind.

It had been working away within him for thirty years, that
story. There had combined to render it more bitter not only
trifling challenges, displays of rivalry, slights and resentment, but
Vincenzo's whole life—the birth of his sons, his prosperity, his
wealth, the luxury of the Gonzagas, the very wisdom of his wife,
Leonora. Every time in fact that Vincenzo's state or family was
augmented the bitter wound of Ranuccio's adolescence with its
cankered lips reopened within him. Certainly the two reconciliations of 1595 and 1597 between Mantua and Parma had been in
word only. (From the documents, we could follow from year to
year the proofs of the continued enmity between Parma and
Mantua—an enmity which in the end had all the monotony of a
mania.) One might think that, by spreading thus down through
the years, this enmity might have lost its power and died away.
But if this would have been possible in Vincenzo's case because of
his tendency to forget unpleasant things and fasten only on things
of joy, thoughts of revenge and vendetta alone succeeded in
relieving Ranuccio's agitated mind.

Stumbling on one of these thoughts he had, with a tremor,
experienced a sensation of the cold, cunning joy of the serpent
when it discovers the vulnerable point in its prey. When he
thought of Vincenzo and imagined him with the Countess of
Sala, Colorno, that centre for sensual feasts between the two, must
have sprung to his mind like a dramatic vision—Colorno, the fat,
rich territory of the Sanseverinos. He had seen it clearly, the great
castellated villa, amid its vast elegant gardens in the midst of a
magnificent agricultural district not far from the Po. Then he
remembered he was a prince and called to mind certain political

concepts. Was not Colorno a gateway opening for his rivals, the Gonzagas, in the flank of the Duchy of Parma? And was it not a wise rule for a head of state to gather under his own jurisdiction territories marching with his own, which were so dangerous when in the hands of vassals who might rebel against him?

For some time now the house of Farnese had been following the policy of stifling the power of the landowners in the Duchy by all manners of vexations and by depriving them of their rights, in an attempt to concentrate as much land as possible in their own hands. Ranuccio had long since decided that Colorno must return to the Farneses and in 1593, the moment he became duke, had begun to lay a continual, creeping siege to the Countess.

For instance, a captain unexpectedly arrived in Colorno from Parma with orders from the Duke that the fortified points be handed over to him and that the populace should turn to him on questions of law and arbitration. Suddenly the lady of the place had no more powers over her liege subjects; her servants were insulted by the ducal envoys; the citizens were taken from their houses and compelled to suffer conscription. Naturally Barbara did not allow this to go unchallenged. Her first protests found Ranuccio in a cold sweat of fear, scarcely daring to breathe. Knowing that she had right on her side he was able to put himself in her place and—worse still—to admire her. What cost him the greatest effort was to overcome his sympathy with hatred and punish himself by hating her still more. Thus, with the Duke of Parma, those who were in the right were pitilessly condemned.

The skirmishes between Ranuccio and the Countess lasted twenty years. To Ranuccio it seemed that nothing should be left undone in his attempt to strike a mortal blow at his antagonist— not even the idea of putting her son, Girolamo Sanvitale, against her to claim Colorno for himself. Returning blow for blow, Barbara found support by marrying Orazio Simonetta, an honest man, a gentleman of refinement and her master of horse. (She contrived, however, as a woman and a great lady—and openly admitted it—to give herself to him as a reward.) Then Ranuccio, who could not prevent the marriage, had to give his enemy a breathing space. But while things seemed to be set towards peace, Orazio became estranged from his family through a subtle stratagem of Ranuccio's. Thus when Barbara wrote to her husband's brother, the jurist Ferrante Simonetta, to ask for certain documents necessary to prove her rights to Colorno, her brother-in-law immediately informed on her and sent her letters to Ranuccio.

Ranuccio even helped the Countess's daughter, Barbarina, in a lawsuit against her mother. (Barbarina had been unhappily married to a stingy libertine, had separated from him and on his death had married again, contrary to her mother's wishes.) In short, he tried to isolate his enemy from all her friends, kept his spies on her and stirred up protests from the peasants of Colorno, who accused Barbara of burdening them with taxes. Then he started legal proceedings against her because of the protection she had afforded to certain fugitives from Parma and finally, on the advice of his treasurer, Bartolomeo Riva, a man who struck cold-bloodedly, like a fox, he attacked her directly by denying the validity of her investiture with the fief of Colorno by Duke Ottavio. He put forward a case based on a series of legal quibbles, clutching at her failure to register the documents, referring back to an act of rebellion long ago on the part of the Sanseverinos by virtue of which, he said, they had made themselves perpetually unworthy to hold the fief. At this all the Sanvitales, including her son, who had up to now stood out against her, were united round the Countess, protesting and clamouring. The one who made most noise and uttered fiery threats of rebellion was the Countess's nephew, Gianfrancesco Sanvitale, known as the young Marquis of Sala or more simply as the young Marquis.

The young Marquis brings us back to Agnese, because this young boy, who was scarcely out of his 'teens, who called Barbara grandmother and had inherited the ardent blood of the Countess of Sala together with the sophisticated stock of the Sanvitales, was the secret lover of the Marchioness of Grana. He was an exceedingly handsome youth with a languorous, over-ripe beauty; it was as if, being ready to yield to sin, he gazed upon it with a glance that was half-astonished, half-intoxicated. If we add the sulphurous ardour of the Sanseverinos and the nervous energy of his mother's side we will have him as he was—restless, fiery, drawn irresistibly to experience of all kinds, impelled by a furious appetite and a capricious curiosity to know the nature of things, to examine their inner meaning and interpret them in his own way—which might be acute but was more often perverted. The legend about him said that at fourteen he had sold his soul to the devil and signed the pact in his own blood; but the Satanic inclinations of Gianfrancesco were considerably more complicated. Moreover, in practical matters, he was more effective than people said. This his own family knew; so did Ranuccio, who had used him in delicate affairs of state.

As for the secrets of his life, although he had been married at sixteen to a patient lady of birth, there was no form of love which did not torment him. In that he knew no reserve, no limits—it was said that more than once he had attempted his mother; but that is not credible, for the rumour comes from a slanderous source. But it was true that the young Marquis threw himself into sexual indulgence with a devouring appetite in which we may recognize the desire to cancel out the very impulse which drove him on, as if he wished to heal his soul by way of the senses. One might even ask whether vice carried to these lengths, with such concentration of energy, like a fire which purifies and releases, does not border on the heroic. But it would perhaps be too daring to carry one's investigations so far. Perhaps the boy was led to fall in love with Agnese by the tide of his destructive rage. We all know that for a woman over forty any hour of love may be her last and that beyond it there yawns the time of old age and silence. To love her is to kill her, rob her of her last, her most pathetic and most ardent breath—the very essence of her life and soul.

It would have been useless to expect Agnese to resist. Yet this lure which catches over-tender women, when youth is leaving them, with the bait of a rosy face, of a fresh complexion, of eyes to which the bright glance of a young animal gives a look of innocence, of a clean body, is a commonplace in the history of women. If their intelligence served them intelligent women would at least attempt to provide a sage ending to the tale by using the mirror of their irony. Agnese yielded. Once more Barbara had an opportunity to exercise her amorous indulgence; she revelled in her friend's torments and tempered her to her nephew's ardours, praising her, saying, 'A fairer lady has never been seen.'

In the summer of 1610 Agnese arrived in Colorno and stayed there with Barbara and her young Marquis for ten shining days, not in the least restricted by the presence of her son and her small daughter Anna. After a few days the Marquis crossed the Po and rejoined her at Viadana and upset the elegant routine she had evolved in her maturity. He threw time into disorder, claimed whole days of love and stimulated her with a burning access of passion which bordered on complete abandon. Having once begun to yield to him, Agnese could no longer keep pace with him. It was a wearing love—perhaps it was no longer even pleasant, being unequal, exciting, tormented. It had to be drained to the dregs. Agnese knew what the hours would be like afterwards— knew she would come to herself with her blood appeased and, in a dignified way, recompose the image of herself which the boy's greedy hands had ruffled but not destroyed. Then how much they talked. Agnese's generosity and intelligence consisted in this, that she measured everything and everyone not by the egotistical standards of two young lovers but with the standards of one alone—those of the young Marquis—as if she were cancelling herself out of his future life. Without understanding the preciousness and beauty of such a sacrifice, the boy abandoned himself to confidence in his lover; for he guessed that he would never find another woman who could follow him and be at one with him in everything—with her eyes, her heart, her intellect and her love.

Occasionally the Marquis would be away for a time—either in a fit of distraction or busy with family affairs such as the eternal lawsuit over Colorno or other suits the Sanvitales had elsewhere. Then he would send messages to Agnese by means of a priest—a most trusted servant of his, a certain Don Battista Gigli, a mad treasure-seeker with his pockets always stuffed with pamphlets full of formulæ, drawings and figures. The priest trotted to and fro between Parma and Mantua. Even this was not enough and Agnese sent couriers with letters, which were opened on their arrival by the boy's mother, Benedetta Pio, who was highly annoyed at this untimely love of her son's. 'She's older than me,' she said of Agnese, 'that witch, and she has charmed him away from me.' She would go to church and pray for him and was delighted if, in her letters, the Marchioness of Grana complained and rebuked her lover for not giving her more frequent news of him.

No one knew that in Parma the comings and goings of the young Marquis were carefully recorded—as were the visits of Agnese to the Countess of Sala or those of the young Marquis to Viadana. Not a movement by either of them but was noted and reported by spies. From their excessive ardour, their heedlessness and their intemperance someone was to extract a terrible death philtre.

Thus the fatal year 1611 came round. In 1610 the Conte di Fuentes, Governor of Milan, had died. He had been a great protector of Barbara and, not content with writing to Parma in her favour, had sent an envoy to say that if the Countess of Sala continued to be persecuted he would find it necessary to defend her. Immediately on his death Ranuccio unleashed his baleful desire for destruction. His treasurer, Riva, had drawn up the Duke's unfounded case for confiscating Colorno and had given it some colouring of captious truth. The proceedings were entrusted to the tribunal at Piacenza while another set of documents was sent to the influential College of Jurists at Padua for their views.

The Paduan tribunal had given Ranuccio a cruel lesson two years previously when it had declared against him in favour of a citizen of Piacenza whom Ranuccio had stripped of his belongings. (The plaintiff had won his case in vain, for Ranuccio's dagger had pursued him into the papal states and there struck him

down.) One might therefore be inclined to think these jurists
were a company of honest men. But by appealing to them
Ranuccio was tacitly asking for redress for the slight two years
before, knowing that he would not ask in vain. A number of
extremely clever agents of his had been working carefully on one
lawyer after another. So, although there was a movement within
the College in favour of Barbara, corruption carried the day and,
on the 5th May, 1611, sentence was pronounced, with thirty-
three votes to seventeen, in favour of the Duke of Parma, giving
him full rights over Colorno.

Ranuccio had won. The seventeen honest men who had
voted against him and thus gone to join the troop of ghosts who
tormented his barren sleepless nights had no power to console
Barbara, who cried that she would throw herself from the window, for she could not bear the pain of losing her Colorno, her
own lands and those of her fathers, the patrimony of her memories
and her consolation. The great Countess was gravely wounded.
At the sight, all her friends rallied to her and there was not a
gentleman or great landowner who did not feel that through her
the arm of tyranny had struck at himself. Tyranny, injustice,
oppression, were the words her friends repeated. Caught in a vice
of anguish—the thought that others hated him—Ranuccio
wondered who they were and how many. He numbered them
over, the leading gentlemen of his court—Count Pio Torelli,
Count Gianbattista Masi, Count Girolamo of Correggio, Count
Teodoro Scotti of Piacenza. They were the finest, the richest,
the noblest men in his dukedom. He seemed to hear them come
marching against him. They loomed even larger and endlessly
they repeated their indictment of him. He was overcome with
horror at the thought of being pursued by their voices and felt in
anticipation that same fit of trembling as had seized him in his
worst days when, suspecting that he had been bewitched or put
under a spell, he had filled the palace with exorcists and had
women and men whom he believed to be his enemies put to the
torture. He knew only one way of reacting—that was to think
things out coldly; but, since his logic proceeded from a false

premiss, his reason merely reinforced his error and multiplied it in a kind of lucid frenzy.

Though there was little need for them, certain obscure figures made the atmosphere round Ranuccio darker still. They were men who had grasped their lord's character, and to serve their own interests kept him in the shadows instead of casting light on his darkness—men who he knew were like himself, capable of following him in his blackest meditations. Their names were Bartolomeo Riva, his treasurer, and Filiberto Piozasco, a Piedmontese, who had begun his career in 1592 as an examiner of witches. How readily they had picked up the Duke's hints and to what extent suspicion held sway in Parma was clear from a number of terrifying events. It sufficed for a servant or agent of a noble family to make a sign to a friend who was out killing quails for a captain, seeing it, to have him imprisoned, interrogated and examined under duress. They did, it is true, eventually admit his innocence, but the wretch was banished from Parma as a criminal, while the captain got thirty crowns as a reward. Things were so out of joint that—no matter if the evidence were false or erroneous—the Duke rewarded anyone who suggested to him that there was reason to suspect another person. 'There is no doubt but that he takes flies for horses,' a contemporary said of him and a famous squib on the princes of the time shows Ranuccio shut up in a room, fencing with his shadow.

The rout of the Sanvitales had begun and although the lawsuit continued at Piacenza, and was pursued with all Barbara's energy, at the beginning of June her son, Girolamo, went to the abbey of Fonte Vivo to attempt to reach a settlement with the Duke whereby they would cede Colorno on condition that he and his mother might live there until their respective deaths. Girolamo said a few vague words of submission and entrusted himself to the mediation of Cardinal Sforza, one of the Countess's devoted admirers—one of the circle who addressed her as 'mother' and was under the sway of her splendid, voluptuous matriarchy. The Cardinal accepted the task of mediation but then, being completely immersed in his own amorous and scandalous life, he omitted to follow it up and, perhaps intentionally, let things slide. Meantime the spies were daily refurbishing their reports on the young Marquis, recounting that he could not restrain himself from bursting out against the injustices of the Farneses, that he longed to avenge himself, that he was brimming with hatred. In his subconscious Ranuccio was so convinced the other was in the right that he felt every new detail to be a sentence of death. One night, at the Abbey, he woke up as cold as ice. He had dreamt he saw the young Marquis sword in hand about to run him through. It was an omen sent by the Madonna, he was later to say as he related it to his closest followers. Naturally they—with Riva and Piozasco at their head—echoed him and bided their time. Unfortunately the madness of the Sanvitales played into their hands.

One of the young Marquis's cousins was Alfonso Sanvitale of the Fontanellato branch of the family, who almost rivalled Gianfrancesco in his temperamental instability and his mad whims. He was moreover passionately interested in magic— although no more so than many of his contemporaries, even if he turned to the witches to know who had robbed flowers from his garden and kept a flask in his bedroom containing, or so he said, a little spirit which was ready to serve anyone who guessed its name and uttered it with the power of a spell. Alfonso had for wife a good upright woman, Silvia Visdomini, who despised her husband's libertine ways and showed it. One day, in return, she was suspected by Alfonso of being in love with a gentleman from Piacenzo called Teodoro Scotti. Whatever the gentleman thought about the matter the husband took offence. He ambushed his wife and her mother and fired on them with his arquebus. The mother fell dead and the daughter wounded. Alfonso was arrested. It was the 7th June. Some days later a gentleman of the young Marquis's household, Onofrio Martani from Spoleto, an adventurer of easy ways who was not averse to brigandage, was discovered scheming to plunder a company of travellers on their way from Genoa to Venice. He was taken and cast into prison. Then the cross-examinations and the torture began. The torture was terrible. The young man from Spoleto was in an anguish of blood and pain. Knowing only too well the judicial practice of the times, he realized that they wanted a confession from him so he confessed—but what? Mere ribaldry was no use—his imagination alone did not seem to serve him sufficiently well. He was racked with pain. At last in the midst of his account of what he had been planning he dropped the words 'the affair at Lucca'. Piozasco seized upon them and, pretending to have understood 'the affair with the Duke', began to suggest revelations to the tortured man, to guide him, to co-ordinate them and make them more explicit. The wretched man understood.

From this springs the first germ of the tragic fiction which was later amplified and given a circumstantial ring with such wealth of detail. In his hatred of the Duke, who was trying to take Colorno from his family, the young Marquis was reported to have inspired a conspiracy against Ranuccio with the connivance not only of his relatives but of many of the leading gentlemen of the court and of various officers and soldiers. He was alleged to have encouraged, helped with money and otherwise incited the chief conspirator, Vincenzo Gonzaga, who was in return to have had from the plotters Piacenza with all its fortresses. The go-between between the young Marquis and the Duke of Mantua was said to have been the Marchioness of Grana. And the Countess of Sala was their accomplice.

Thus passion, friendship, joy and voluptuous pleasure lost the day at last—nor would tears alone suffice to atone for them. Blood was needed. Barbara, her relatives, her friends, the great landowners of Parma and Agnese were all in the net; Vincenzo was responsible for all, the prime mover of the conspiracy. For the former there would be death and sequestration, for Vincenzo shame and dishonour—perhaps in time, even something worse if Ranuccio reported Vincenzo's designs on Piacenza to Spain and kept hammering at the point, well knowing that the Spanish monarch boasted of his own jealous rights to the fortress. At last he could hate his old enemy, hate him aloud, have a reason for calling him a disloyal traitor, reason for casting a horrible light on the Duke of Mantua's whole life from as far back as the distant days with Margherita, who rose up in a halo of martyrdom with all trace of mortification taken from her.

Following the pattern of the hints extorted, by dint of the terrible promptings, from the young man of Spoleto, they interrogated Count Alfonso Sanvitale, who was in prison for the conjugal arquebusade. The astonished youth denied everything. At last, tortured, twisted and dislocated, he confessed in order to put an end to his suffering, agreeing to what Piozasco said and adding only—they are his own words—'a few trifles to make it more probable'. So the young Marquis was guilty? Piozasco asked inflexibly. Yes, he was, and his accomplices were Count Orazio, husband of the Countess of Sala, Barbara herself and Girolamo Sanvitale together with his wife, and so on. And everything stemmed from the Duke of Mantua, who sent money through the Marchioness of Grana? Alfonso kept on saying yes 'being more desirous to live than to die' as he later said. In short, desperate.

On the 24th June the young Marquis was arrested and with him a confidential servant of the Sanvitales, Oliviero Olivieri. Under interrogation they denied everything; the young Marquis almost believed that it was a joke. But when they were led into the presence of Alfonso and saw that poor, suffering body with its maimed limbs and the wandering gaze of a man who no longer believes in human justice the young Marquis turned pale; Olivieri half fell to the ground. They would not admit to the conspiracy; then they were swallowed up by the dark prisons of the Rocchetta prison in Parma, and for them a period of agony began.

We will not follow the trial through its pitiless developments— it was a Satanic piece of work with its succession of arrests, the cruelty of its tortures and interrogations, the way in which confessions extorted under torture were collated and sifted after the accused had been prompted, perhaps by their cell companions, in what they had to say. But perhaps this is the place to ask whether the invention of the plot was something entirely and deliberately devised and planned by Piozasco or whether, being used to examining witches—that is to say to plumbing by the light of logic the obscure kingdom of the unknowable—he did not, with his wizard's intuition, give form to what were rebellions in word only and turn into precise fact figments of heated imaginations, the only weapon of the weak when they feel themselves unjustly beaten down. We would incline to the latter hypothesis, which might give us the occult key to his character, were there not too many documents which prove his coldblooded, conscious determination to isolate and damn the accused, using any method that came to hand, removing or corrupting witnesses and lawyers, with the connivance of the treasurer, Bartolomeo Riva, and of Ranuccio himself.

Each of the accused was got at in a different way according to his temperament and character. To the weak, they promised life if they confessed and accused the others. Both Girolamo Sanvitale and Girolamo da Correggio proved extremely weak and confessed miserably under torture, gasping only for the last gift of life. The men of honour, the men of character, those who had grown up respecting themselves and their word were tortured, degraded and racked until they confessed—thus it was with Count Orazio Simonetta, Barbara's husband, with her friends, all of them great landowners, like Count Pio Torelli and Count Gianbattista Masi; but not with Count Teodoro Scotti who, although pitilessly tortured, had the moral strength to state the truth—that there was no plot, that no one had made the least move against His Highness —and repeated it at each fresh twist Piozasco ordered. His fate was to be overcome not by the assaults of his tormentors but by death at twenty-four—his only guilt that he dared to be innocent.

Two obscure servants of the Sanvitales also died under torture without confessing; another confessed—it was Oliviero Olivieri, who later wrote in a letter to Ranuccio: 'A curse be on my soul if I ever heard from Count Alfonso or from the Marchese words spoken against Your Highness.' The walls of the Rocchetta sweated blood. But so tight-sealed were they that nothing or almost nothing of what was going on leaked out to Italy. In the evening they held the executioners close within the walls—held the gaolers too and perhaps even the gaolers' gaolers. This explains why those who had remained free (the arrests followed a slow rhythm and came months apart) never thought of flight, for they were certain that they had nothing positive to reproach themselves with; nor were they sufficiently pessimistic to imagine the reality of the terrible trap which was to catch them all.

The Countess of Sala did not flee. She stayed at Colorno. When the young Marquis was arrested she warned his friend Agnese at Mantua. Then she continued to conduct the lawsuit at Piacenza with her usual vigour. She did not even move from Colorno three months later when they arrested her husband and things had begun to look black, although certainly someone— probably Agnese herself—advised her to flee. Probably Agnese, because those who watched the terrible mesh being spun at Parma, even if they knew very little about it, guessed that the toils held the arrested men in a mortal grip, and because the young Marquis wrote her long letters from prison, trusting in a gaoler whom he thought he had bribed to this end but who instead handed everything over to Piozasco. Since not all these letters are among the documents of the case we may presume that some were sent on once the judge had read them—perhaps in order to get, through Agnese's replies, even more compromising answers from the Marquis. But here Piozasco failed. The evidence at the trial is in fact all verbal; there does not exist a single letter proving in the least the existence of an agreement or plot.

But the letters the Marquis wrote from prison do exist and they show that the youth was inventing for himself a role which, while of incredible boldness, was by no means devoid of logic. We have seen how, having been caught, inculpated and confronted with his first accuser, his cousin, Count Alfonso, he confessed, sticking carefully to the line traced for him by Piozasco. Now, relying on the temporary immunity afforded him by virtue of his confession, he enjoyed a dangerous revenge by speaking out clearly and denouncing Ranuccio's injustices, his evil deeds, his faithlessness and perfidy. He roundly states—indeed he almost boasts of it—that he had conspired against the man who wished to deprive him of Colorno. And when it comes to denouncing his accomplices let them, he says, add as many people as they wish— first of all, naturally his relations and his friends among the land-owners, then Vincenzo Gonzaga and his son, Cardinal Ferdinando, and the Marchioness of Grana and the principal members of the Mantuan court, such as the Marquis Vincenzo Guerrieri and the Marquis Giulio Cesare Malaspina.

Was it true that they had thought of murdering Ranuccio on the occasion of the baptism of his firstborn son at the Abbey of Fontevivo? asked Piozasco. Certainly, the young Marquis replied —and not only the Duke but the child and his wife and the Duke's other natural son, Don Ottavio. And violate the virgins in the convent and rob the churches and take over the fortress with the ducal treasures? Yes, that was so. Was it true that he had received 1500 ducats from Mantua to cover the initial expenses and to be divided among the garrisons? Of course—but in actual fact at that time the young Marquis had not even had a bean in his pocket. So much so that when he lost some money gambling to Martiani and could not repay the trifling debt he had almost been put to scorn by the young man for behaving so grandly with so little foundation. When they asked the young Marquis who else was informed of the plot it was an invitation he could not resist. He began to speak up and accused of connivance not only Vincenzo Gonzaga but the Prince della Mirandola and the Duke of Modena who, he said, had taken part in the plot in order to snap up land and castles. Expanding his tale he brought into it the Grand Duke of Tuscany, the Duke of Savoy, the Pope and eighteen cardinals and the Viceroy of Naples.

What might appear fevered ravings were in fact the most daring part of a plan which the young Marquis himself reveals to us. Immediately after confessing to Piozasco everything the latter desired, he wrote to the Marchioness of Grana stating firmly and calmly that 'the charge on which I am in prison is false' and adding that 'not even the devil himself would have arranged

things like this'. He warned her, too, that it had all been engineered against the Duke of Mantua, for whom the most extraordinary traps had been laid. Meantime he wrote to his so-called
accomplices and fellow-prisoners: 'We must make the most
intricate general confession the world has ever seen, naming
hundreds of persons'; thus he gives us the key to his plan, which
was to speak, to speak without restraint, to swell the case with
names and unlikely lists of accomplices. Only thus would the
affair collapse and crumble suddenly under the onslaught of
ridicule, collapse like a huge dusty heap of pasteboard scenery.
Hence the young Marquis's loquacity as shown in letters, deposi-
tions, and conversations with his gaolers, one of whom, naïvely
worried, once wrote to the Duke Ranuccio to warn him that the
Marquis was really denouncing too many people and that to keep
coming back to the Pope and the cardinals seemed an imprudence
which might compromise the Duke more than the accused.

But the young Marquis had to deal with enemies who were
much more wily than he. In fact we can see Piozasco, with tight
lips, picking out of the confessions only such material as he found
useful. As for the names, he stopped short at those which interested Ranuccio. It was all very well to give Vincenzo Gonzaga,
the Duke of Modena and the Prince of Mirandola as accomplices
in crime, because Ranuccio hated them; but talk of the complicity
of the Pope and a whole company of cardinals and, above all, of
the Viceroy of Naples—which would have meant the complicity
of the King of Spain—would really have undermined everything.
So let us discard them, said Piozasco, discard them. It was a case
of going cautiously; he must set up his own mechanism from parts
of the young Marquis's making—but everything must fit properly into place. The first rule was that the evidence collected
must be confined to what the others might with some show of
verisimilitude confirm under torture and provide with a framework.

The trial lasted seven months and seemed at times to be stag-
nating; then suddenly the final blow was struck. On the 13th February 1612 guards arrived at Colorno to arrest the Countess of

Sala. They carried her away in a black coach with a single waiting-woman. Perhaps it was news which came from Mantua at this time that caused Ranuccio to strike.

We have no documents to tell us of Agnese's reactions when the young Marquis was taken off to the Rocchetta in Parma. We feel the gap in the direct evidence sorely for now the Marchioness of Grana should take over the thread of the story; for it is her problems which are about to take so tragic a turn and she alone could attempt to solve them. The trial at Parma points to her as an intermediary between the young Marquis and the Duke of Mantua. She is an essential accomplice; take her away and the chain of accusations snaps, for it was notorious that the young Marquis had no continuing relationship either with Vincenzo Gonzaga or with members of the Mantuan court—a fact which it would not have been difficult to prove if the case had been re-examined. But his relations with Agnese, who was so closely tied to Vincenzo, were proved and frequent, were extraordinary as regards both time and place and, lastly, were unexpected and unjustifiable by the light of reason. It was the easiest thing in the world to make them look like conspiracy if one chose to forget about love.

Agnese could not but shudder now that she felt the funereal breath upon her, blighting all her youthful thoughts of the past, present or future. Her old love for Vincenzo was ruined and had become a curse to the boy she loved. Her new love for the young man was ruined too and worked against Vincenzo himself who, through her, was dragged, as prime mover of the conspiracy, into the net of slanders. There was no escape for Agnese. On one side the young Marquis; on the other, Vincenzo. She was in the middle and united to them by this terrible tie. Such was the role Ranuccio imposed on her. However blameless she was, how could she, as a woman, dragged into this terrible coil, but have doubts of herself and be reduced to considering her existence a crime?

Perhaps to begin with Agnese did not believe the worst. She wrote to Barbara in great pain as she had done a month before when, following the judgment of the Paduan College of Jesuits,

Colorno had been assigned to Ranuccio—wrote placing herself at the Countess's disposal and offering the condolences of the Mantuan princes, of Vincenzo, of his sons and of Madam Her Serene Highness of Ferrara; which meant to say that they were all on Barbara's side. So in Mantua Agnese was encouraging a party which favoured Barbara and the Sanvitales, and court opinion on affairs in Parma was guided by her intelligent intuitions even before Ranuccio's machinations were made clear by the series of arrests.

When the first of these had taken place and the young Marquis had been incarcerated—one or two of his letters had perhaps arrived—she talked the matter over with the Gonzagas, particularly with Vincenzo. Being a clever woman and knowing her ex-lover only too well, she got at him not by prayers and tears, which would have moved him only fleetingly, but by using her imagination. She overcame her own fears with the cool patience of one who is used to the courtly life and aimed at the new favourite, Adriana Basile. She fêted her and showered her with gifts and encouraged her own son, Don Silvio Gonzaga, to write some extremely gallant verses for the singer. Thus once Leonora was dead, Agnese found a place in the palace, where we find her in December 1611, in Vincenzo's suite of rooms along with the Duke holding Adriana's newly-born daughter to be baptized amidst festivities and the distribution of gifts.

Our knowledge of the courtly customs of the times and of this particular period allows us to evaluate the degree of favour accorded to Agnese from this one piece of social evidence. Since it was a fashionable whim for royal and princely couples to assist at the baptism of actors' and singers' children we can easily deduce that Agnese, who played godmother to Vincenzo's godfather, filled the role of a lady in the highest favour—a sort of vice-duchess. It was her lot to play the hard game of aiding a man in his caprices, of warning and guiding him. But perhaps because her interest in Vincenzo was not absolute, perhaps because her emotional impulses were centred on another man, she did not succeed in keeping Gonzaga firmly under her influence and attached to her person. Nor did she succeed in healing the spot where he suffered in his loneliness.

For Vincenzo apparently felt vulnerable to Ranuccio's sorcery which made him the protagonist of a drama of which he was ignorant. Now he began to totter indeed. His mind and senses were still served by Agnese's tactful friendship, by Adriana's sensual dalliance, by other women, by the festivities and the poetry and the music, by his great palace full of treasures—things to be caressed with a glance, with the hands or through the ear, all pretexts for the sensations to flare up more rapidly. But Leonora was gone and there was no longer her dominant presence, the constant thought of her. Given his stolid male egoism *vis-à-vis* women, Vincenzo perhaps felt the lack of his wife as a weakness on her part, as if she had left him when he had need of her aid. So, like so many widowers in his case, out of love of Leonora, Vincenzo could reach no other conclusion than that he must marry again.

I shall avoid the opportunity of sinning, he murmured to his confessor, with a sincerity which became falsified the moment it was translated into words—the same adulterated sincerity as prompted him when he said that he wanted to change his mode of life. He would say it, perhaps, as he left a party, a concert or at the end of a day of *fêtes galantes* at Madorno, where the confessor patiently followed him about at the tail of the turbulent crowd of Neapolitans with Adriana at their head. Besides, how could I live without a woman with this blood of mine which cannot endure mortification? said Vincenzo. In him delight in displaying his sensuality was almost a way of rendering thanks for existence—a direct and certain mode of communication with life. Once he had discovered the exultation to be found in the thought of marriage he would not relinquish it. And in order to give it point he began to look around and seek out a new bride.

He fantasticated, for instance, over the Princess of Mondragone, a young Neapolitan relative of his, both languid and proud. With her dowry, which would be high (400,000 gold crowns), he would acquire an investment for his future children and leave intact his Mantuan possessions for Leonora's. The more he thought of it, the more the idea of a new wife seemed to Vincenzo to be the candid, gleaming promise of a future which would reconcile his sensual impulses and his desire for spiritual renewal. He sent for Chieppio and told him to begin to examine marriage plans which they would study together.

At once the whole family coalition was up in arms against him. His children, as soon as they heard of their father's plan, all turned against him in irritation and concern, fearing to find in the new bride and her probable offspring rivals who might impoverish and threaten Leonora's brood. Francesco, the heir, was particularly annoyed, and was certainly egged on by the intolerant Margherita of Savoy. Being too young to understand the drama of Vincenzo's life, they already considered that this man of fifty was violating other people's rights by permitting himself so many liberties and they barely tolerated his capricious ardours out of respect for his rank. But that he should actually wish to rob his children of the roles of suitor and bridegroom and create a new situation in court with a new duchess who might be ambitious and itching to rule, who might perhaps even rule her husband, made not only Francesco and his wife shudder but Cardinal Ferdinando and even young Don Vincenzo as well.

Madam Her Serene Highness of Ferrara agreed with them. She still had the old sway over her brother and having, since her sister-in-law's death, resumed a direct influence on court and government affairs, she feared the rise of a new female star. Quickly she organized a system of defence. All the priests were on her side, so, from the Bishop of Mantua to Vincenzo's confessor, they busied themselves to restrain the Duke from his matrimonial follies. Vincenzo resisted with gentle obstinacy and took refuge behind a vague defensive smile. He knew that his children were hostile to him but he did not know the exact words with which Francesco had threatened a family schism. 'We will see a tragedy in this house,' said the young man, thus showing how the gentleness of the meek can be corrupted and become venomous anger, brutal resentment. Two people planned to derive great advantages from Vincenzo's marriage schemes. Of one we can be certain from the documents—it was the minister Chieppio; to the other the documents barely refer but we seem to feel her secret, compelling influence. It was the Marchioness of Grana.

It was some time between the end of 1611 and the beginning of 1612. Among the names of the candidates for matrimony we find a name appearing which we have become used to reading with a feeling of tender compassion—that of Margherita Farnese. Finding it in the documents one can hardly believe one's eyes, yet it is no mere fantasy that Vincenzo should have thought of her as his betrothed after so many years; on the contrary it was a project which had its own good grounds, which was to be studied in all its details, one in pursuit of which important steps were taken. It was impossible and could never be, said the members of Vincenzo's family; his confessors no longer knew what to think. But if Chieppio, who was not a man for dreams, clung to this project, fathered it and brought it into the open, we must believe that it implied the existence of a clear-cut and practical plan. Exactly what the minister was aiming at is the real mystery and since the documents do not help us more than half-way we must attempt an explanation by hypothesis.

At the Mantuan court they had some idea of what part in hatching the conspiracy had been attributed to Vincenzo by the prisoners in the Rocchetta at Parma—so much so that Vincenzo himself sent word to the Pope that he was ready, at all times and in any honourable way, to testify not only that he had no complicity in it but that he was completely ignorant of it. Perhaps this was Agnese's moment. But how, without evidence, can one risk the hypothesis that the daring idea of the marriage between Vincenzo and Margherita Farnese came from her mind and was suggested by her hope of saving the young Marquis from the scaffold in Parma?

It is quite clear that had Vincenzo, who was considered the prime mover in the conspiracy, married Margherita and thus miraculously healed the thirty-year-old wound the accusation against him, which was the basis of the trial mounted by Piozasco, Riva and Ranuccio Farnese, would have collapsed and the prison gates would have opened to release the gentlemen in Parma, including the young Marquis. Was this Agnese's line of thought? Did she have sufficient intelligence to reach these conclusions and to translate them with her affectionate and subtle eloquence into advice? Did she suffer all the cruelty of the delays, of the slowness of the hours spent in preparing her plan, of her shrinking hopes, of agony masked with smiles?

There is no mention in the documents of any of this romantic but hypothetical story and perhaps no one will ever bring it to light, for it is buried with Agnese. So we must not hope to tell the tale. But it is different in Chieppio's case. A Venetian source tells us that Vincenzo's children—particularly Francesco—cursed the minister for his obstinacy in wishing to conclude the marriage between the Duke and Margherita. Certainly Vincenzo, who had no lover he wished to save in Parma and was not a prey to senti-ment, must have had strong reasons for insisting on a plan so hazardous in conception. Events in the Rocchetta were enough to give food for thought to even the most matter-of-fact and logical minds; Chieppio knew the circles round Ranuccio too well not to realize that the accusation of conspiracy levelled at Vincenzo might gravely damage Mantua and even bring war in its train, should the King of Spain be convinced that Vincenzo was harbouring projects for expansion and the conquest of territory within Italy.

Like everyone else, and perhaps better than anyone else, Chieppio understood that Ranuccio's hatred for the house of Gonzaga pro-ceeded from Vincenzo's divorce of Margherita. So it must have seemed to him an excellent idea to solve everything by marriage —even by such an extraordinary marriage. Indeed it was on the strangeness of the case that Chieppio based his proof of how well he had spun his plans. He understood the hostility of Vincenzo's children and perhaps even found it reasonable; he was subtle enough to calculate that the consummation of the marriage—if impossible so many years before—could now not even be attempted. Thus Leonora's children would have no rivals and affairs at court would not become complicated as might happen if Vincenzo had a different bride. By a strange chance the very nature of this virginal marriage, which would smooth out for ever the quarrel with Parma, bring in Margherita's great dowry and satisfy Vincenzo's vague desire for matrimony, might become the guarantee for a general pacification.

How precisely Vincenzo imagined he was going to save his soul with a marriage which would have remained a betrothal we do not know, but he became enamoured of the idea. Already Chieppio was making cautious moves and had mentioned the scheme, not directly yet, but in secret, through friends—first to Ranuccio at Parma and then, since he did not show himself hostile, to someone who brought back a web of memories, that Cardinal Federico Borromeo, nephew of San Carlo, of whom Manzoni writes in *The Betrothed*. Apparently Cardinal Federico replied that if Rome assented, he would join what Carlo had put asunder. The first thing was to discuss the matter in the Vatican, and proceed covertly with the affair which must be treated with reserve so that proper negotiations might begin later on a firm basis.

The few documents which exist, although they suffice to confirm the facts, do not give us particulars and do not speak of Margherita. No one tells us how the news struck the cloistered nun, who had been immured for thirty years in the silence of the convent. Did Ranuccio tell her something of the extraordinary proposal? Was she terrified at the thought of returning among men now that she was accustomed to her physically unruffled life among women, to the transfer of her passion for spectacles and festivities to the stage provided by religion? We might ask how the image of a man could enter a world so constituted and not tear it apart. Perhaps Margherita Farnese felt stunned and shocked —provided always that the thought of Vincenzo Gonzaga had renewed its power to disturb her by awakening the old cruel desire. Perhaps for some time she showed in her white face the pallor of a woman profaned. We would prefer to think that she knew nothing of it, that she did not feel the shame of the tardy bridal posies brought to her forty-five years' virginity. Let us hope that this time at least, this last time, she was spared.

As for Vincenzo, he rediscovered to his surprise, when thinking of Margherita Farnese, the idea that he might recapture his youth. So he assented to Chieppio's plan and allowed Agnese to hope that the young Marquis might be saved, and perhaps was even glad to be able to link his plan to the fortunes of the Countess of Sala to whom once again he would be of service. But he was unaware that the time was drawing near when he would no longer be able to do anything for anyone nor anyone for him.

Already the fabric of his days was wearing thin with the delicacy of old linen, growing more precious with age. And there came back to him, purified somehow, the qualities which belonged to a good prince and a loving master. His generosity, which up to now had been impulsive and ill-directed, focused on the common people, becoming civic charity. The time even came when he felt it inadequate to have chosen a secret almoner and entrusted to him the work of assisting the poor.

One evening on the 2nd February, 1612, he called his almoner and his confessor, requiring them to bring the register of poor families in Mantua and had them go over their grey stories, page by page. Tears shone in his blue eyes to think that so many human beings should be denied the joy of all that is abundant and good. Help them, he told the almoner, help all of them so that they may be continually relieved of their sufferings, but let them not know from whom the help comes, he added. Thus he cancelled out his personal vanity with the thought of how they would live in comfort, free even from the burden of gratitude.

It was late when the two friars left the ducal suite with calm in their hearts and walked away beneath the ceiling where the maze was figured. They were accompanied by the rhythm of that phrase *forse che sì, forse che no*, scanned out by the gilt letters over their heads. The night and the high fever which fell upon Vincenzo raised him to heights of warm tenderness which grew pale along with the dawn. Then seeing the distress of those around him, he sent for his sister Margherita.

Madam her Serene Highness of Ferrara arrived in haste from her neat observatory at Sant'Orsola and brought to the sick man's pillow her vast, reassuring, pedagogic shadow. For a fortnight she remained at her post, giving instructions to the little body of attendants amid priests and friars who surrounded the bed where Vincenzo was attempting once more to discover himself. The fever came and went. In his quiet moments he asked them to talk to him on consoling texts from the Gospels to which he listened with a deep desire to consent. He made his will, said he wanted to revise it, made confession and prayed. But he knew that even this was not enough for he realized only too well that the discreet friar who exhorted him to repent desired from him proof of his true contrition. In the end with a sigh he asked what he must do.

The friar trembled and, feeling himself unable to discharge the task alone, went off to consult the Bishop of Mantua. For a whole day and night, the two sat weighing and discussing Vincenzo's sins and the steps to be taken, until at last they reduced his spiritual problems to three heads which we naturally do not know for they are secrets of the confessional.

We only know that Vincenzo lay and listened and said he accepted them but then when it came to carrying them out, he had doubts and found the conditions hard, so that he tried to avoid them as something he found painful. Undoubtedly it was a question of making a break with the past, of sending away certain women, such as Adriana and perhaps also Agnese. Vincenzo grew tender at the thought of past pleasures and felt so affectionately disposed that he could not resolve to renounce them. He passed them in review, savouring their sweetness, and even now when he was vanquished he loved them secretly.

The day came when he felt he had succeeded in overcoming them and with clasped hands he struck a bargain with God for his recovery and swore that, if he got better, he would do as much good as he had done bad till now. Then by a single order he nullified all his religious and meditative gains. Let them bring his jewel cases at once, he said. They were brought. One by one, Vincenzo fingered their contents, feeling substances and materials take shape as with loving fingers he traced the noble outline of a medal, unravelled the tepid pearly knots of a many-stringed necklace or placed the jewel in the middle of his palm with his fingers stretched out round it like a monstrance. Nothing reveals to us so well as this gesture of his hands—an evocation descending through the finger tips as if to establish a tactile relationship between the remote essence of the object and human sensitivity—to what depths Vincenzo was still anchored and to what extent only the senses gave him certainty even after so many confessions, prayers and attempts at liberation.

No one helped him and religion hardly at all, although he clung desperately to this shred of mercy. So be it. Since to the last, he could find no absolution, a more difficult destiny awaited him—a humble but entirely human coming-to-terms with life and death. He had abandoned his soul to his confessor and now commended it to him once more, placing it in his hands for he felt it no longer belonged to him. In the loneliness of his body, his life was finishing; he followed with calm tenderness the total extinction of his blood.

February went on, the month of sad days which once had been transfigured in Mantua by garlands, masks, silks, lace, by the gold and silver of carnival in an artificial, palpitating springtime. Vincenzo would no more know the impulse of energy a man feels when he enters a festive hall for a ball, concert or play after a day of exhausting physical exercise at the hunt, in the lists, swimming or on horseback—that impulse which makes the joints more supple, causes the web of nerves to glow, renders the play of the muscles more fluid and sends the gay river boiling in the veins. All this was now lost—the way a plume nods over the velvet with supple, luxuriant grace, the way a jewel dangling from a necklace beats on a man's breast and gives off flashes of light, the way a lace ruff closes round a woman's face and isolates it from her body, the way poetry, painting and music prepare the way for that full climax. Vincenzo only now began to realize that there was no more prospect of exciting plans and unlimited adventures.

We must say farewell to Margherita whose wedding-day is postponed to some day not in this world. The doors of the convent closed upon her and there remained only for her to die after another thirty years. Vincenzo had been in bed for ten days. The news of his illness was known and had reached Ranuccio Farnese who brooded over it, relishing each succeeding confirmation of Vincenzo's doom. The idea of the tardy marriage with his sister may perhaps have disarmed his rancour for a time and even have perplexed him because it required him to change the terms of his own spiritual equations. But the promise that Vincenzo would soon die restored him to himself with all his dark pleasures and long-pondered plans. He was the very man to feel an access of vitality now that he almost sucked the breath of his sinking enemy and prepared to accuse him, to cast a shadow on his memory, weigh upon him and tear him to pieces. Revenge of this kind, which Ranuccio had awaited for years, was at one with his necrophilic ways and gave him a kind of diabolical intoxication. So the young Marquis was lost. Agnese would be able to do nothing for him except bewail in Vincenzo's death all her lost loves. She was to grow old, worn by remorse that she had unconsciously brought the extreme sentence down on the head of a heedless youth.

The Countess of Sala was lost, too. It was of no avail, except to make her condemnation more absolute, that she combined in almost heroic quantities human and womanly courage. She had to atone and would atone for each daring action, each sign of independence, all her powers of inventing joy and making it linger. It was no chance that only now, when it was certain that the Duke of Mantua was dying, was she arrested at Colorno and brought to be interrogated by Piozasco, a process during which Vincenzo would be presented to her as the great culprit, the instigator of all the crimes and the man responsible for the conspiracy. Under the hail of infamous questions from the Piedmontese judge, Barbara would be brought to curse and renounce Vincenzo. Would that he had died ten years ago, she said in an access of despair when they had given her the Duke's guilt as absolutely certain and more than proved. But not even her denial of the friend of her youth and her maturity, her dear pupil, her sensual 'son', was to help Barbara, nor did it help any of the others.

They were all split now and on the way towards the solitude of the end. Vincenzo would never know how Barbara was taken out to die on the scaffold in the main square at Parma one mild day in May. He would not know the story of the terrible execution on a scaffold as high as the houses so that the condemned were visible only from afar and already reduced to phantoms. He would not know how the Countess's head fell, nor the atrociously indecent gesture of the executioner who could not resist lifting the dress on the headless body so that all could see how wretchedly beautiful those limbs were which had been so proudly vaunted. In her funeral train, they all fell one by one—her honest husband Orazia Simonetta, her son Girolamo Sanvitale, her nephew the young Marquis, astonished and incredulous at such a tragic jest. Her friends were beheaded—Count Pio Torelli and Count Gianbattista Masi. Girolamo di Correggio was to die later in prison of poison. Onofrio Martani and Oliviero Olivieri were hanged on the gallows.

Nor would Vincenzo know how, once the blood had been shed, a Jesuit rose up, tall and black on the scaffold, to exhort the shuddering spectators, now that they had seen the punishment meted out to the rebels, to have faith in the clemency of the Duke who was so careful of his people, that same people as, paralysed with horror, was to feel the full impact of his tyranny and high-handedness. Not only would they not dare for years to speak of the conspiracy or name the conspirators; they would abase themselves to the point, as did the citizens of Piacenza, of asking permission to raise a statue of Ranuccio in the main square, as an ex voto from the citizens, for the Duke's narrow escape from peril.

But even if Vincenzo was not to feel the presentiment of so much blood spilt in his name, he was not to end in peace. On the 13th February, while the sinister black coach was transporting the Countess of Sala on her journey from Colorno to Parma, his fever waned and left him with a languid sensation of exhaustion. Then he realized that he must see his children and take leave of them, handing over to the youth of his heirs as much as may be consigned to others of our human message. He had them called and lay thoughtfully looking at them and then smiled, first and foremost at Francesco.

Free for the moment from the sharp goadings of his wife, whom he had left to govern Monferrato, Francesco perhaps showed more clearly than usual that intense, puzzled expression which contemporaries describe for us and which Rubens has handed down in a little portrait where the young Gonzaga turns to look out at life as if taken unawares by a summons. Taken unawares; that is the phrase which would fit Francesco Gonzaga for the brief space that he was to survive his father's death—a bare ten months during which his only vigorous action would be to threaten Ranuccio Farnese that he would march on Parma if Ranuccio did not withdraw the accusation of conspiracy publicly made against Vincenzo. In this he would be egged on by his sense of honour but even more by the voice of his father-in-law, Carlo Emanuele I, who was intoxicated at the thought of finding some new *casus belli* and dreamt of such 'gallant exploits' (the words are his), as raids on Piacenza and Borgo San Donnino.

In the end Ranuccio withdrew his accusations against Vincenzo but, faithful to his serpentine ways, did so with a mixture of reservation and assurance. But it seems that Francesco's vitality waned after his father's death. Before the end of 1612 and between September and December of that year, Francesco was to see first the death of his youngest daughter, then immediately after, that of his beloved half-brother, Don Silvio Gonzaga, son of the Marchioness of Grana and, a little later, that of the young heir to the dynasty, Ludovico, whose birth had been so greatly celebrated. Finally, he would die himself at twenty-six of smallpox, leaving Margherita of Savoy, racked and rebellious at her fate, alone with her surviving daughter, Maria.

Then it would be Cardinal Ferdinando's hour. We shall not see the young Cardinal with his long, delicate, sensual face at the bedside of his dying father. Certainly Vincenzo must have been pleased to think of him as he was, a favourite nephew at the court of Maria dei Medici, Queen of France. From the Grand Duke Ferdinando dei Medici, his uncle, Ferdinando Gonzaga had inherited, along with his name and certain physical resemblances, the destiny of having to leave the purple, which he would pass to his brother Vincenzo, and assume power. But from his father he had the burdensome heredity of his blood, which he extenuated and weakened by the exercise of meditation and sentimental sophistries. His best fate would have been to marry his sister-in-law, as Margherita of Savoy instinctively felt. Very shortly after she was widowed she would try to gain the ascendancy over Ferdinando in order to remain duchess in her own right, and almost succeeded, thanks to the fervour with which she pressed her proposal. But then, defeated and isolated by the implacable campaign waged by her aunt, Madam her Serene Highness of Ferrara, at the head of a party of nuns and nationalist friars, she would be forced back to Piedmont, leaving her only remaining daughter to be educated at Sant'Orsola under her old rival. Had she stayed a little longer, she would have seen Ferdinando's love shift to a fifteen-year-old damsel of her court. Meanwhile Carlo Emanuele I, on the pretext of safeguarding his daughter's interests, finally invaded Monferrato and plunged it into bloody war which first of all Chieppio and later that no less excellent minister, Alessandro Striggi, would contain by dint of diplomatic appeals, manœuvring ably between France and Spain. Ferdinando would show himself capable of taking part in this exhausting game and would be intelligent and quick to see the possibilities of the situation, making use of the ties of blood, of law and of good advice. He would succeed in winning back Monferrato, although greatly ravaged. But he was the first of his dynasty who, feeling and accepting his own weakness, renounced all plans for territorial expansion between the old mass of the Spanish monarchy and the robust new growth of the French kingdom. He was, if you like, too clever to resume his father's ideas of grandeur. But we must also conclude that he was considerably less generous. His very instincts were weaker and although he was content with the handiwork of his minister, which left him free to enjoy his brief span of life amidst poetry and music, spectacles and love, those bright flames which cast a red glow on Vincenzo di Gonzaga's days were never lit in him.

He liked to make his reason keep step with his heart and perhaps even with his desires. If his heart strayed, he followed it, for he wished intoxication, but there was in him a cold quality inherited from the Medicis—curiosity, which restrained and congealed any attempt at adventure. He had loved the beautiful Adriana Basile and abandoned her—alas, how many sacrifices I have made in vain for these Gonzagas, the singer was to groan bitterly when Ferdinando left her letters unanswered—and would fall in love with a damsel at the court of Margherita of Savoy—a girl from Monferrato called Camilla Faà. He would marry her secretly and have a son by her and take pleasure in the warm secrecy of this story of love. But under the hail of dynastic wrath unleashed by his aunt, Madam Her Serene Highness, he would be forced to repress himself, to have the woman he loved shut up in a convent, abandoned and without hope, while he agreed to deny the validity of marriage. Then, remembering his wise mother, he would marry a Medici, a relative of his called Caterina who was very different from Leonora, being a vivid, discontented woman, imperious, fiery and sterile. Ferdinando was to die, barely forty years old, saddened by such political events as the harrying of Monferrata and the siege laid to it by foreign powers, worn down by remorse over Camilla, by the sadness of a house without heirs, by a presentiment that the dynasty was ending and by the knowledge of his brother Vincenzo's twisted morality.

Vincenzo, the youngest of Leonora's sons, was at his father's bedside. Seeing him in the grace of his eighteen years with his airy curls and bright blue Hapsburg eyes, it was impossible not to think well of him, as did even the wily Venetian ambassador, Marosini, who mistook the boy's bravado for signs of ardour. How could it be foreseen that, having assumed the purple, he would try to get rid of it without dignity, so that the Pope would

with right be so incensed as to forbid the cardinal's hat forever to
the House of Gonzaga—and that he would do so without attempting to cover up decently the scandal of his marriage with a widow,
a very beautiful lady, Isabella di Novellara, the mother of many
children and eighteen years older than the bridegroom. How
could it be foreseen that he would attempt to break the marriage
off, accusing his wife of having bewitched him, while he courted
his young niece, Maria Gonzaga? Vincenzo II's life would be a
series of troubled days, of shifts and stratagems. In him there
remained nothing of his father's enthusiasms, or his brother
Ferdinando's literary bouts of melancholy; neither political
passions, nor the remotest sense of defeat and withdrawal. Worn
out by illness, sapped by sensuality which lacked abandon and by
the spiritual vices of *accidia* and indifference, full of whims for
parrots and monkeys, ornaments and extravagant luxuries, he
would soon fall victim to an early death. But first his hand would
sign away the glorious art treasures of the Gonzagas to Charles I
of England for a pittance, condemning to exile the Mantegnas,
the Raphaels, Titians, Tintorettos and Rubens, which had belonged to Francesco and Isabella, to Federico and to Vincenzo I,
pictures for which they had accumulated debts, paid pensions,
granted fiefs and created apartments and galleries.

There among her brothers was the thirteen-year-old Leonora,
Vincenzo's youngest daughter, who filled her father with tenderness as he looked at her and seemed to him very small and
defenceless. Defenceless she was, like most women, and although
she was destined for an Imperial crown and would marry Ferdin-
and II of Hapsburg with a sumptuous dowry, the splendour of the
title did not avail to spare her bewilderment and desolation. She
alone of Vincenzo's children would live to see the marriage of her
niece, Maria, to Carlo Gonzaga of the French line of the family,
a descendant of Ludovico of Nevers, brother and rival of Guglielmo the Hunchback. She alone would know the wrath of the
Spanish and Austrian Hapsburgs over this marriage which
brought French influence—the influence of the France of Riche-
lieu—so deeply into Italian affairs. She would see the war of

succession, the new invasion of Monferrato by the unbridled troops of Carlo Emanuele I and the descent of the Imperial armies from Germany, the war against Mantua and the city ravaged by plague and hunger. She alone would hear, word by word, the terrible story of the capture and sack of Mantua by the Imperial lances when the wonderful palace was abandoned to obscene hands with all its gold and silver plate, its jewels, its statues and pictures, its miraculous crystals, its onyx and lapis lazuli and malachite, its velvet, lace and silk hangings, its wardrobes which had clothed so many ladies and princesses, so many pompous singers and actresses from the court theatre. And she would have to add the terrible story of its citizens, ill-treated and tortured, of denuded churches, of burnt houses, of loot and murder. All this she would have to suffer, having begged her Imperial husband in vain, on her knees, to keep the house of the Gonzagas from ruin.

Barely eighteen years after Vincenzo's death the end came; for the French branch of the family, grafted through Maria Gonzaga with the Mantuan, although it was replanted on the ruins of 1630 and flourished for almost a century in Mantua, has little weight in history. It was a period of withdrawal and mere decoration, lived by people who tried to maintain their rank rather than direct the government, to the accompaniment of blatant decay caused by internal corrosion, both physical and moral, which in vain roused them from time to time to attempt some reaction. With Vincenzo all ideas of expansion and glory for the House of Gonzaga fell away. It is true that he had been lost in a maze of error because he had answered the continual distraction of too many extraneous appeals. It is true that his policy had been uncertain and that his means had been inadequate for his dreams. It is perhaps even true that with his unbounded prodigality he had begun the economic decline of his house. But he must be allowed the merit for lighting certain generous fires which would have brought him glory a century before when things were less hard and fast; and he deserves, for it is his, the limited but concrete glory of a benign, though sometimes untidy, government. The people loved this prince. Perhaps it is more important than is generally thought that with him the Mantuans felt themselves less subjects than citizens, and that many people lived under his rule safe even from the terrors of the Inquisition. Perhaps this respect for others helped him at last to attain self-respect and freedom.

Having blessed his children, he dismissed them—it turned out to be a simple act. Although all need for human assistance had been stripped away, he did not, however, refuse it altogether, and gently he parted from Carlo de Rossi, his old companion in the Hungarian wars, and from Madam Her Serene Highness, who sailed slowly round him like a great mourning barque on a calm sea of prayers. From his unconscious memory of his ancestors, who had been sure of their vigorous inner laws, Vincenzo drew the strength to ask on the evening of 18th February, 1612, how much life he had left. When his confessor broke it to him that, unless God performed a miracle, that night was his last, he let his eyelids fall in resignation. He did not struggle, as his father had done at the time, against accepting death, because before he could wonder whether his time was ripe he felt it in the loosening of his limbs as they became remote from him and in the broken flow of his blood. 'I feel the rigour of death,' he said quietly and listened to his own words. He asked to confess himself once more and felt in his sins now absolved the warmth and gusto of life. He, too, breathed a hope that he might continue to exist in some other place at some other time, where there must be a reply to all our questions. As he sank into the dark current, he sought for a word and spoke the name of Jesus.

INDEX

Acosta, 152
Acquapendente, 39
Agnese, *see* Argotta
Alba, Bishop of, *see* Zibramonti, Aurelio
Albert, Archduke, 245
Albizzi, Giulia, 81, 83, 86–7, 92–3
Aldobrandini, Gian Francesco, 166, 168, 182, 185, 191
Alençon, Anne of, 7
Alessandro of Correggio, Count, 146
Alexander VI, Pope, 154
Allegories, 95, 179, 233, 241–3
Amadei, 162
Ambrosia, Alessandro dell', 124
Amedio, Don (brother of Carlo Emanuele I), 214
Amorevoli, Academy of the, 18
Andreasi, Antonio, 174
Andreini, Isabella, 169–70
Andreini, Virginia ('Florinda'), 231, 240, 243
Angelo, Father Piero, 47, 58–9
Anna, Signora, 30–1
Antinori, Bernardino, 93
Aquaviva, Claudio, 152–3, 220
Arco, Livia d', 16
Argotta, Agnese de, Marchioness of Grana, 130–9, 153, 156–7, 162–3, 178–9, 197, 203, 243, 270–3, 276–9, 283–4, 286–7, 289–91, 293–4, 296–7, 299, 301
Ariosto, 35, 51, 76, 109
Armellino, 116
Asinello, Fabio, 105
Avila, Bishop of, 164

Bardellini, Antonio, 105
Baroni, Muzio, 253, 255–6, 258
Barzo, Laurenzo, 264–8
Basile, Adriana, 252–9, 264, 269–70, 290–1, 297, 303
Basile, Gianbattista, 257–8, 260
Basta, Giorgo, 173
Bathory, Sigismond, 160
Batory, Stefan, 176
Bellarmino, Cardinal Roberto, 135
Bendidio, Lucrezia, 16
Bertani, Giambattista, 2

Boccalini, Traiano, 232
Bonati, Cellario, 251
Borgau, Marquis of, 173–5
Borgia, Alexander, *see* Alexander VI
Borgia, Lucrezia, 16
Borromeo, Carlo, Cardinal Archbishop of Milan, 50–61, 69, 71, 142, 295
Borromeo, Ersilia Farnese, 60
Borromeo, Cardinal Federico, 295
Boschetti, Alfonso, 126
Boschetti, Isabella, 97, 133, 304
Brandolino, Abbot, 219

Caccini, 240
Caccini, Cecchina, 93, 252
Caccini, Giulio, 93, 259
Camprezzi, Camillo, 5
Canissa, Siege of, 187 ff.
Canossa, Count of, 199
Canossa, Tomasso, 224–5
Capello, Oliviero, 3–4
Cappello, Annibale, 62
Cappello, Bianca, 26, 72, 75, 78, 82, 87, 89–90, 92–6
Cappello, Vittorio, 82
Carafa, Don Luigi, Prince of Stigliano, 253, 255
Carbonelli, Father Gregorio, 255, 259
Cario, Giacomo, 157
Carretto, Agnese del, *see* Argotta
Carretto, Aleramo del, 136–7
Carretto, Francesco del, 131
Carretto, Prospero del, 131, 156
Casale, 3–4, 117, 132–3, 207–8
Casalmaggiore, Marquis of, *see* Vasto, Marquis del
Castiglione, Count Buldassare, 134
Castiglione, Marquis of, *see* Gonzaga, Rudolfo
Castro, Pedro de, 48–9
Caterina (daughter of Philip II, wife of Carlo Emanuele I of Savoy), 211–12
Cattaneo, Claudia, 226–7, 234, 243
Cattaneo, Count, 111
Cattaneo, Valeriano, 64
Cavriani, Cesare, 39–40, 45, 60
Cecchini, Pier Maria, 214

Ceruti, Antonio, 2
Cesi, Cardinal, 72–4
Charles I of England, 304
Charles V, 1, 3, 25, 34, 58, 69, 247
Chiabrera, Gabriello, 234
Chieppio, Annibale, 155, 186–7, 196, 207, 216–17, 219, 221–5, 228–9, 231, 242, 244, 247, 262, 264, 292–6, 302
Chiesi, 4
Clement VIII, Pope, 152, 161–2, 173, 177, 207
Colorno, 18–19, 21–3, 30–3, 43, 68, 130–2, 271, 274–6, 278–81, 283, 286–8, 290, 299–300
Condé, Prince of, 211
Cornaro, Alvise, 62–4
Correggio, Count Girolamo da, 280, 285, 300
Cosimo I, see Medici, Cosimo dei
Crichton, James, 62–6, 68, 107
Crichton, Lord Robert, 62
Critonio, see Crichton, James
Council of Ten, 196, 220
Council of Trent, 1, 5

Denmark, King of, 9
Dentelli, Ippolita, 264–8
Dianti, Laura, 73, 177
Dona, Leonardo (Doge of Venice), 220
Donati, Marcello, 12–13, 27–8, 37–8, 55, 57, 61, 66–7, 78–82, 84–6, 90, 92–4, 103, 118, 123, 153, 186
Doria, Monsignor, 166

Elizabeth of Valois, see Valois
Ephraim Pasha, 185
Este, Alfonso I d', 73, 177
Este, Alfonso II d', 13–14, 16, 19, 25, 40–1, 54, 73, 80, 100, 109, 114, 123–5, 152–3, 155, 161, 175, 177, 183
Este, Don Alfonso d', 73, 76–7
Este, Don Alfonso d' (husband of Isabella of Savoy), 216, 234, 248
Este, Don Cesare d', 73, 75, 177
Este, Cardinal Ercole d', 7
Este, Cardinal Ippolito d', 76
Este, Isabella d', 1
Este, Lucrezia d', Duchess of Urbino, 16
Este, Cardinal Luigi d', 16
Este, Marfisa d', 16, 77
Este, Duchess Margherita d', see Gonzaga, Margherita
Estrées, Gabrielle d', 180

Faà, Camilla, 302–3
Facconi, Paolo, 226, 252–3
Fallaguerra, Gianantonio, 101
Fano, Andrea da, 55, 57
Fantocci, Alfonso, 124

Farnese, Alessandro (later Duke of Parma), 19, 25, 34–5, 48–9, 58, 69, 140, 145, 147–8, 172
Farnese, Cardinal Alessandro, 44, 50, 179
Farnese, Giulia, 154
Farnese, Margherita (wife of Vincenzo Gonzaga), 25, 27, 34–40, 42–51, 53, 55–60, 68–72, 80, 94, 145, 151, 154, 172, 274, 284, 293–6, 299
Farnese, Margherita (Margherita of Austria, Duchess of Parma), 34, 69
Farnese, Maria (Maria of Portugal), 25, 35
Farnese, Cardinal Odoardo, 35, 150–1
Farnese, Ottavio, Duke of Parma, 18–19, 36, 38–9, 44, 47–9, 52–3, 58–9, 71, 140, 145, 276
Farnese, Don Ottavio, 287
Farnese, Pope Paolo III, 25
Farnese, Pier Luigi, 25
Farnese, Ranuccio, 35, 45–7, 55, 71, 140, 145–56, 165, 171–2, 177, 235, 262, 273–7, 279–91, 294–5, 299–301
Farnese, Vittoria, Dowager Duchess of Urbino, 47
Ferdinand I, Emperor, 1, 9
Ferdinand II, Emperor, 304–5
Ferdinand of Austria, Archduke, 24, 26, 72, 165, 185, 234
Ferrara, 13–16, 20, 43–4, 54, 76–7
Ferrara, Dukes of, see Este
Fideli, The, 198, 231
Flavia, Countess, 232
Florence, 87, 94–6
'Florinda', 231, 240, 243
Follino, Frederico, 181, 193, 230–1
France and the Gonzagas, 7, 22, 42, 71, 80, 85, 103, 119–20, 141, 180, 246–7, 262, 302, 304
Francesca, Signora, 126
Frederick of Hapsburg, Archduke, see Hapsburg
Fuentes, Conte di (Spanish Governor of Milan), see Spain and the Gonzagas
Fulvia, Signora, 126

Gagliano, Marco di, 227
Gagliardi, Father, 222
Gentile, Ottavio, 254–9
Gigli, Don Battista, 279
Giovanna of Austria, see Medici, Giovanna dei
Goito, 2, 64, 110, 198, 268
Gondi, Signora, 219
Gonzaga, Anna Caterina, 9
Gonzaga, Anna Caterina (Archduchess of Hapsburg), 108, 159, 164, 181
Gonzaga, Carlo, 82, 85–6
Gonzaga, Carlo (of Nevers), 246–7, 304
Gonzaga, Cesare, 174

Gonzaga, Count Claudio, 32
Gonzaga, Claudio, 172
Gonzaga, Cardinal Ercole, 1, 25
Gonzaga, Fabio, 138, 184
Gonzaga, Marchioness Felicità, 126, 156-7
Gonzaga, Federico, 2
Gonzaga, Ferdinando Teodoro (later Cardinal) (son of Vincenzo Gonzaga), 103, 126, 169, 217, 233-4, 238, 254, 258-60, 269-70, 272-3, 287, 292, 301-4
Gonzaga, Ferrante, 25
Gonzaga, Francesca (daughter of Vincenzo Gonzaga), 156-7
Gonzaga, Francesca, 203
Gonzaga, Duke Francesco, 7, 304
Gonzaga, Francesco (son of Vincenzo Gonzaga), 102, 126, 169, 181, 202, 207-8, 210, 214-17, 228-30, 232-3, 235-7, 242-3, 248-9, 263, 269, 272, 292, 294, 301
Gonzaga, Frederico, 97, 304
Gonzaga, Frederico, 174
Gonzaga, Guglielmo, Duke of Mantua:
  character, 1-2, 4-9, 41, 157-8, 184, 202
  and the revolt at Casale, 3-4, 117
  quarrels with the Inquisition, 5-6
  as a ruler, 7, 101-2, 117-18, 124, 142, 206
  marriage, 8-9
  relationship with his son, 8, 10-13, 20-4, 27-8, 31-2, 54, 60-1, 67-8, 100-101, 103-4, 107, 111
  and Vincenzo Gonzaga's marriage to Margherita Farnese, 24-6, 37, 39-44, 46-55, 57-8, 71
  in love, 44
  and James Crichton, 62-4, 66-7, 107
  and Vincenzo's marriage to Leonora dei Medici, 26, 72-5, 78, 81-2, 85, 87-8, 95, 97-8
  zeal for protocol, 91-2
  illness, 101, 104, 107-8, 110
  death, 110-12, 306
Gonzaga, Guglielmo (son of Vincenzo Gonzaga), 126
Gonzaga, Guido, 116
Gonzaga, Isabella, Princess of Stigliano, 255
Gonzaga, Duchess Leonora (of Austria) (mother of Vincenzo Gonzaga), 1, 9-11, 13-15, 22-4, 42, 91, 93, 98, 103, 111, 114, 125, 136-7, 142, 153, 155, 159, 176, 201-2
Gonzaga, Leonora (daughter of Vincenzo Gonzaga), 270, 290
Gonzaga, Leonora Anna Maria (daughter of Vincenzo Gonzaga), 178, 249, 269, 304-5
Gonzaga, Ludovico, Duke of Nevers, 7, 22, 42, 48, 71, 103, 120, 304
Gonzaga, Ludovico (grandson of Vincenzo Gonzaga), 268, 301

Gonzaga, Marquis Ludovico, 217
Gonzaga, San Luigi, 142-3, 154, 170-1
Gonzaga, Margherita (later Duchess of Ferrara), 9, 13-14, 16, 25, 30, 41, 44, 68, 77, 114, 125, 155, 157-8, 177, 183-4, 206, 208-10, 219, 221-2, 229, 237-8, 249, 273, 290, 292, 297, 302-3, 306
Gonzaga, Margherita (daughter of Vincenzo Gonzaga), 126, 176, 218, 245, 269
Gonzaga, Maria (daughter of Francesco Gonzaga), 248-9, 262, 301, 304-5
Gonzaga, Orazio, 170
Gonzaga, Rudolfo (Marquis of Castiglione), 142, 154, 170-1
Gonzaga, Cardinal Scipione, 116, 136
Gonzaga, Silvio, 157, 178, 243, 272-3, 278, 290, 301
Gonzaga, Vincenzo, Duke of Mantua:
  birth and baptism, 1-2
  popularity, 8, 232, 305-6
  relationship with his father, 8-12, 21, 23-4, 60-1, 98-101, 104, 157
  character, 8, 10-11, 36-7, 100-101, 107-8, 111-12, 124-7, 132-3, 142-3, 157-9, 163-4, 180, 192, 197-9, 202-5, 216, 233, 236, 239, 244, 248, 260-1, 263-4, 270, 291, 296, 298, 302-3, 306
  relationship with his mother, 11-12, 23
  tutors, 12-13
  youthful exploits, 11, 14-15, 20, 22, 61
  friendship with Tasso, 14-15, 108-10
  friendship with Barbara, Countess of Sala, 19-21, 32, 68-9, 197, 273-4, 296, 299-300
  affair with Hippolita Torelli, 19-21, 27-33
  marriage to Margherita Farnese, 24-7, 32, 36-9, 41-5, 47, 51, 53-4, 56, 58-60, 71-2
  as a ruler, 26, 101, 108, 118-19, 123, 132-3, 141, 143, 170-2, 177-8, 181, 184, 200, 207, 216, 222-5, 261-3, 305
  letters, 21, 27-32, 102, 139, 141, 165
  relations with women, 43-4, 201, 203-5, 226-30, 243, 245, 249-50, 252, 291, 297
  and Ranuccio Farnese, 46, 140, 145-56, 165, 171-2, 273-4, 283-4, 287-9, 291, 294-5, 299, 301
  and James Crichton, 64-9, 101
  marriage to Leonora dei Medici, 24, 72-8, 80-2, 84-9, 92, 94-100, 102, 123, 127-9, 229, 237, 270
  children, 92, 102-4, 126, 131, 156-7, 169, 178, 181, 201, 203, 218, 228, 269-70
  military ambitions, 102-3, 120, 141, 143, 160, 163, 176, 179, 182, 197, 216-7, 224

Gonzaga, Vincenzo—*continued*
  rival of Ruggero de Trofeis, 105–8
  coronation, 112–7
  and Alfonso d'Este, Duke of Ferrara, 123–5, 152
  affair with Agnese de Argotta (Marchioness of Grana), 130–9, 142–3, 153, 156–7, 162, 197, 203, 270–3, 289–91, 294, 297
  Catholicism, 142–3, 163, 192, 221, 245–6, 270, 297–8, 306
  travels (*see also* Crusades), 179, 217–9, 245
  crusades, 160 ff., 172 ff., 181 ff., 217–8, 239, 241
  intrigues for throne of Poland, 175–6
  faith in alchemists, 182, 190–1, 218, 221, 249, 270
  and Carlo Emanuele I of Savoy, 207 ff., 235–6, 238, 247, 263
  founds Order of the Redeemer, 239–40
  intrigues for Imperial throne, 242, 246–7
  as a grandfather, 248
  and the *gusano*, 249–52
  illnesses, 251–2, 296–303
  and Adriana Basile, 252–60, 269–70, 290–1, 297
  and Albania, 247–8, 264–8
  contemplates a third marriage, 291–6
  death, 305–6
Gonzaga, Don Vincenzo (son of Vincenzo Gonzaga), 243, 269, 273, 292, 302–4
Grana, Marchioness of, *see* Argotta, Agnese de
Gregory XIII, Pope, 47, 50
Gregory XIV, Pope, 137
Grimaldi, Giulia, 158
Gualtieri, Cristoforo, 223–5
Guarini, Anna, 16
Guarini, Battista, 18, 134, 136, 178, 231, 242
Guerrieri, Barbara, 126
Guerrieri, Felicità, 203, 229
Guerrieri, Scipione, 22
Guerrieri, Tullio, 156
Guerrieri, Marquis Vincenzo, 229, 250, 287
Guglielmo, Duke, *see* Gonzaga, Guglielmo
Gusano, 249–52

Hannam Pasha, 187–8, 193
Hapsburg, Archduchess Anna Caterina of, *see* Gonzaga, Anna Caterina
Hapsburg, Archduke Frederick of, 113
Hapsburg, Giovanna, *see* Medici, Giovanna dei
Hapsburg, Leonora (wife of Guglielmo Gonzaga), *see* Gonzaga, Leonora
Henry II, 147

Henry III, 103, 120
Henry IV, 91, 103, 147, 161, 180, 198, 211, 219–21, 231, 245–7, 261–2
Hippolita, *see* Torelli

Iberti, Annibale, 207, 229, 247, 264, 268
Inquisition, The, 5–6, 14, 306
Ippolita, 258, 260
'Isabella, Little', 30, 32
Isabella of Spain (daughter of Philip II), 147, 165, 245

Jesuits, expulsion from Venice, 220–1
Jesuits, re-admitted to Mantua, 1
John of Prininstein, Don, 174

Kepler, 165

Langosco, Baldassare, 65
Langosco, Countess, 48–50
Lanzoni, Ippolito, 61, 64–8
Lavinia, Signora, 30–2
Leonora of Austria, *see* Gonzaga, Leonora
Leonora dei Medici, *see* Medici, Leonora dei
Lerma, Duke of, 200, 206
Lesdiguères, High Constable of France, 262
Lichtenstein, Charles of, 195
Ligorio, Pirro, 76
Lomasso, Alessandro, 105–6
Lorraine, Christine of, 158
Lorraine, Dukes of, 80, 85, 103, 218
Louis XIII, 218, 268
Loyola, St. Ignatius, 152

Malespina, Marquis Giulio Cesare, 287
Malvezzi, Count Camillo, 107
Manfredi, Muzio, 125–6
Manfredi, Nunzio, 18
Mantua, 1–2, 5, 8, 15, 31, 62–6, 71, 97–8, 105–6, 109, 114–7, 133–5, 162–3, 178, 221, 238, 305
Mantua, dukes of, *see* Gonzaga
Marcobruno, Evangelista, 250–2, 264
Margherita of Austria, Duchess of Parma, *see* Farnese, Margherita
Margherita of Austria, Queen of Spain, 178–9
Maria of Portugal, *see* Farnese, Maria
Marino, Captain, 265
Marino, Gianbattista, 134, 232, 235
Marmirolo, Palazzo, 64, 152
Martani, Onofrio, 282–4, 300
Martinelli, Caterinuccia, 226–8, 231, 252
Martinelli, Tristano, 214, 245
Martinengo, Count Camillo, 214
Masi, Count Gianbattista, 280, 285, 300
Mathias of Austria, Archduke, 166–7, 175, 180, 191, 234, 242, 246–7

Maura Lucenia, Sister, *see* Farnese, Margherita
Maximilian II, Emperor, 3
Maximilian of Austria, Archduke, 165–6, 173, 185, 188
Medici, Anna dei, 25, 79, 81, 85
Medici, Antonio dei, 104, 122
Medici, Don Antonio dei, 167–8
Medici, Bianca dei (Grand Duchess of Tuscany), *see* Capello, Bianca
Medici, Caterina dei, 303
Medici, Catherine dei, 79, 147
Medici, Cosimo dei (Cosimo I), 25, 74, 91, 185
Medici, Cardinal Ferdinando dei (later Grand Duke of Tuscany), 91, 94, 96–8, 104, 120–3, 125, 128, 151–3, 158, 161, 180–1, 185, 200, 221, 230, 259, 287, 302
Medici, Francesco dei, Grand Duke of Tuscany, 24, 26, 72, 74–81, 83, 87, 89–90, 92–6, 100–101, 104, 113–4, 120–3, 127
Medici, Giovanna dei (Giovanna of Austria), 24, 26, 42, 90, 123, 127
Medici, Giovanni dei, 96
Medici, Don Giovanni dei, 167–8, 181, 185, 187, 191
Medici, Leonora dei (wife of Vincenzo Gonzaga), 24, 26, 42, 72, 79–81, 85, 87–91, 93–100, 104, 114, 117, 121, 123, 126–30, 135–7, 151, 153–7, 161, 163–4, 169–70, 178, 180–5, 196–8, 201–3, 207, 218–9, 228–30, 233, 237–8, 242, 248–9, 252, 254, 256–7, 259–61, 268–71, 274, 290–2, 295, 303
Medici, Leonora dei (Leonora of Toledo), 93
Medici, Maria dei (later Queen of France), 79, 91, 123, 128, 180, 198, 202, 211, 218, 225, 231, 245. 263, 302
Medici, Don Piero dei, 93, 104
Medici, Virginia dei, 73, 91
Medici, don Virginio dei, 167
Milan, Spanish Governor of, *see* Spain and the Gonzagas
Millini, Cardinal, 242
Mirandola, Prince della, 287–8
Mishowsky, Sigmund, 176
Modena, Duke of, 287–8
Mondragone, Princess of, 291–2
Montalta, Cardinal, 258, 260
Monteverdi, Claudio, 40, 94, 162, 166, 225–8, 231, 233, 240, 243, 260
Montmorency, Charlotte de, 245
Morosini, Francesco, 229
Morti, Antea, 143

Naples, Vicereine of, 254–6
Nassau, Maurice of, 179

Nemours, Duke of, 213
Nevers, Charles de, 179
Nevers, Duke of, *see* Gonzaga, Ludovico
Nola, Bishop of, 131
Novellara, Isabella di, 304

Olivieri, Oliviero, 284–5, 300
Olivo, Luigi, 53–4, 66
Orange, Duke of, 179
Orfeo, 225–6, 231
Orfeo, Colonel, 187
Orizia, Signora, 126, 138
Osimo, Bishop of, 31–2, 38, 44
Ostiglia, Bishop of, 124

Paleologa, Margherita, 2
Paleologi, Rule of, 3
Paleologo, Flaminio, 4–6
Panizza, 164–5
Pantara, Ruggero, 144–50
Paolo III, Pope, 25
Parma, 31–2, 34, 36–7, 39, 46–9, 54–7, 60, 71
Parma, Bishop of, 140
Parma, Dukes of, *see* Farnese
Pastor Fido, 134–6, 178–9
Paul III, Pope, 148, 154
Paul V, Pope, 207, 216–7, 220, 223–4, 246
Peperara, Laura, 16
Peri, Iacopo, 180, 225
Petrarch, 35
Petrozzani, Tullio, 132, 164, 207, 229
Philip II of Spain, 22, 34–5, 103, 118–20, 141, 145, 147, 165, 177, 211
Philip III, 176, 178, 200, 206, 210–11
Piacenza, 35
Piozasco, Filiberto, 281–8, 294, 299
Pius II, Pope, 217
Pius V, Pope, 3, 5
Poland, the Gonzagas and, 175–6
Pomponazzi, Aurelio, 12–13, 21–2, 118
Possevino, Antonio, 153
Pourbus, 199, 203, 269
Prininstein, Don John of, 174

Quadruple Alliance (Estes, Farneses, Gonzagas and House of Savoy), 25

Ragusa, Bishop of, 266
Ranuccio, *see* Farnese
Ravaillac, 262
Reggio, 61
Renée of France, 175
Renesi, Captain Giovanni, 265
Resnevich, *see* Renesi
Resti, Captain Marcello, 264–5
Revere, 46
Rinuccini, Ottavio, 180, 231
Riva, Bartolomeo, 276, 279, 281–2, 285, 294

INDEX

Rivara, Count di, 174
Ro, Count Alessandro da, 213–4
Romano, Giulio, 97, 199
Rossi, Carlo de, 162, 166, 306
Rossi, Signora de, 219
Rossi, Ercole, 174
Roswurn, Colonel Hermann Christoph, 191, 194, 196
Rousillon, Marguerite de, 209
Rubens, Peter Paul, 182, 199–203, 206, 218, 222, 301
Rudolf, Emperor, 91, 113, 160–1, 165–6, 170–1, 173, 176, 181, 194, 196, 211, 215, 217, 242, 246–7

Sala, Marquis of, see Sanvitale, Gianfrancesco
Sala, Countess of, 16–21, 23, 29–32, 35–6, 39, 68–9, 77, 130–2, 134, 139–40, 197, 271, 273–6, 278–81, 283–6, 288–90, 296, 299–300
Saluzzo, Marquisate of, 3
Sangiorgio, Count Teodoro, 11
Sanseverino Sanvitale, Barbara, see Sala, Countess of
Sanvitale, Count, 17, 139–40
Sanvitale, Alfonso, 282, 284–6
Sanvitale, Barbarina, 276
Sanvitale, Benedetta Pio, 279
Sanvitale, Gianfrancesco, 276–8, 282–4, 286–90, 293–4, 296, 299–300
Sanvitale, Girolamo, 18, 140, 275–6, 281, 284–5, 300
Saraceni, Canon, 219
Sarpi, Paolo, 216, 220, 222
Savorgnan, Germanico, 133, 207
Savoy, Carlo Emanuele I, Duke of, 119, 123, 133, 175, 207–16, 221–2, 234–8, 247–9, 262–4, 301–2, 305
Savoy, Emanuele Filiberto, Duke of, 3
Savoy, Prince Emanuele Filiberto of, 236, 238, 243–4
Savoy, Filippo Emanuele of, 210
Savoy, Isabella of, 210, 213–6, 234, 248
Savoy, Margherita of, 207–11, 213–7, 229–30, 232–40, 242, 248–9, 261, 263, 268, 292, 301–3
Savoy, Prince Vittorio Amadeo of, 236, 238, 243–4, 263
Scandiane, 16
Scotti, Teodoro, 282
Scotti, Count Teodoro, 280, 285
Serguidi, Antonio, 79, 89
Sforza, Cardinal, 138, 281–2
Sforza, Paolo, 166
Simonetta, Ferrante, 276
Simonetta, Count Orazio, 140, 275–6, 284–6, 300

Sixtus V, Pope, 103, 122
Sogari, Prospero, see Dentelli, Ippolita
Spadari, Cesare, 176
Spain and the Gonzagas, 2, 22, 80, 118–20, 132, 140–1, 171, 179, 196–7, 200, 206–7, 215–6, 222–3, 234, 250, 260, 262–3, 279, 283, 294, 302
Spinelli, Donna Emilia, 254
Statera, Father, 222
Stigliano, Prince of, 154
Stigliano, Prince of, see Carafa, Don Luigi
Striggi, Alessandro, Count, 191, 225–6, 236, 302
Strozzi, Giambattista the Younger, 95

Tassis, Donna Mariana de, 211
Tasso, Bernardo, 110
Tasso, Torquato, 14–16, 18, 30, 108–10, 125, 134
Te, Palazzo del, 64, 97, 133–5, 137, 190, 221, 237, 244, 249
Thiene, Count Giulio of Vincenza, 16
Tintoretto, 64
Toledo, Leonora of, see Medici, Leonora dei
Torelli, Countess Hippolita, 19–21, 24, 27–33, 36, 38, 43, 61, 68, 131
Torelli, Count Pio, 280, 285, 300
Trent, Council of, 1, 5
Trofeis, Ruggero de, 105–6, 108
Tullio, Father, 32
Tuscany, Grand Dukes of, see Medici

Urbino, Dowager Duchess of, see Farnese, Vittorio
Urbino, Duchess of, see d'Este, Lucrezia

Valeriano, Father, 208–9
Valois, Elizabeth of, 147
Valois, Margot de, 180
Vasto de Calmaggiore, Marquis del, 145–150, 152–5, 181
Venice, 82–6, 99
Venice, Excommunication of, 219–21
Verri, Cavaliere, 101
Viadana, 21–2
Vincenzo Gonzaga, Duke of Mantua, see Gonzaga, Vincenzo
Vinta, Belisario, 78–88, 91–2, 98–9, 122, 151, 180, 230
Visdomani, Ginevra, 55
Visdomini, Silvia, 282
Vuio, Count, 264, 267
Vulatconich, Captain Giovanni, 266

Zibramonti, Aurelio, 50, 55, 61, 68, 72–3